Character Recognition

edited by
Minoru Mori

Character Recognition

Edited by Minoru Mori

Republished by InTech

Janeza Trdine 9, 51000 Rijeka, Croatia

Publishing Process Manager Iva Lipovic

Technical Editor Goran Bajac

Cover Designer Martina Sirotic

Additional hard copies can be obtained from orders@intechopen.com

Character Recognition, Edited by Minoru Mori
p. cm.
ISBN 978-953-307-105-3

For EU product safety concerns:
IN TECH d.o.o., Prolaz Marije Krucifikse Kozulić 3, 51000 Rijeka, Croatia, info@intechopen.com or visit our website at intechopen.com.

Meet the editor

Dr. Minoru Mori received the B.E. and Ph.D. degrees in electrical engineering from Tokyo Institute of Technology in 1993 and 2008, respectively. In 1993, he joined Nippon Telegraph and Telephone (NTT). He was engaged in developing character recognition and Image processing systems. He was an assistant manager in Broadband Business Development Division of NTT-East Corp. from 2003 to 2006 and a manager in NTT Advanced Technology Corp. from 2006 to 2007. Since 2007, he has been an senior research scientist in NTT Communication Science Laboratories. He was also an assistant professor of IREIIMS of Tokyo Women's Medical University from 2008 to 2010. His interests include document analysis, pattern recognition, and image processing. He is a senior member of IEICE.

Contents

Preface

Character Recognition is a topic that has been most actively researched and it has yielded practical applications in the pattern recognition field. Studies in this area have provided a lot of useful methods and knowledge, and have greatly influenced the progress of other areas in both theory and practice.

Recognition in constrained or controlled conditions such as machine-printed characters and clear handwriting has basically been achieved, and many commercial products are available. However, many of the tasks needed to create truly practical systems remain outstanding. The keys to the breakthrough in character recognition include unconstrained handwriting recognition, modern or ancient unique font recognition, multi-lingual OCR, character detection from complex backgrounds like natural scenes, and the discrimination of characters from non-characters.

An interesting trend is the rapid shift away from paper as the sole medium of interest. Whereas paper documents were previously the only recognition target, various new media such as video and natural scene images have recently started to attract attention because of the growth of the Internet/WWW and the rapid adoption of low-priced digital cameras/videos. Character input systems suitable for these new media and recognition techniques for the human-computer interface have been also studied.

This book aims to bring together selected recent advances, applications, and new ideas in character recognition. It covers various methods such as image processing, feature extraction, classification, hybrid approach, evaluation, new applications, and the human-computer interface.

Chapter 1 reviews several pre-processing techniques that are crucial for enhancing recognition efficiency, and discusses the suitability for feature extraction in character recognition. Chapter 2 presents a comprehensive system for the recognition of text in video: it provides summaries of the techniques used in each stage and some use cases. Chapter 3 provides a category-dependent feature extraction method that adaptively compensates the influence of both degradation and deformation in the recognition of text in video. Chapter 4 introduces a hybrid approach, a combination of Fuzzy logic for syntactical analysis and the Hidden Markov Model as a statistical model for handwritten character recognition. Chapter 5 describes problems in the recognition of Bengali as one of the languages with no efficient OCR system and the current status of its research. Chapter 6 provides a method of evaluating handwriting quality: this attempt leads to an increase in the accuracy of handwriting recognition. Chapter 7 presents a video-based character input system that uses an on-line character recognition technique and demonstrates the feasibility of the proposed system.

Chapter 8 proposes the use of sympathetic skin response as a character input device for physically challenged people and discusses the problems encountered in the real world. Chapter 9 also addresses a communication system for deaf-blind people. This system uses finger Braille to recognize and output characters.

The editor would like to thank the many authors for their contributions.

September 2010

Editor

Minoru Mori
NTT Corporation
NTT Communication Science Laboratories
Japan

1

Preprocessing Techniques in Character Recognition

Yasser Alginahi
Taibah University
Kingdom of Saudi Arabia

1. Introduction

The advancements in pattern recognition has accelerated recently due to the many emerging applications which are not only challenging, but also computationally more demanding, such evident in Optical Character Recognition (OCR), Document Classification, Computer Vision, Data Mining, Shape Recognition, and Biometric Authentication, for instance. The area of OCR is becoming an integral part of document scanners, and is used in many applications such as postal processing, script recognition, banking, security (i.e. passport authentication) and language identification. The research in this area has been ongoing for over half a century and the outcomes have been astounding with successful recognition rates for printed characters exceeding 99%, with significant improvements in performance for handwritten cursive character recognition where recognition rates have exceeded the 90% mark. Nowadays, many organizations are depending on OCR systems to eliminate the human interactions for better performance and efficiency.

The field of pattern recognition is a multidisciplinary field which forms the foundation of other fields, as for instance, Image Processing, Machine Vision, and Artificial Intelligence. Therefore, OCR cannot be applied without the help of Image Processing and/or Artificial Intelligence. Any OCR system goes through numerous phases including: data acquisition, preprocessing, feature extraction, classification and post-processing where the most crucial aspect is the preprocessing which is necessary to modify the data either to correct deficiencies in the data acquisition process due to limitations of the capturing device sensor, or to prepare the data for subsequent activities later in the description or classification stage. Data preprocessing describes any type of processing performed on raw data to prepare it for another processing procedure. Hence, preprocessing is the preliminary step which transforms the data into a format that will be more easily and effectively processed. Therefore, the main task in preprocessing the captured data is to decrease the variation that causes a reduction in the recognition rate and increases the complexities, as for example, preprocessing of the input raw stroke of characters is crucial for the success of efficient character recognition systems. Thus, preprocessing is an essential stage prior to feature extraction since it controls the suitability of the results for the successive stages. The stages in a pattern recognition system are in a pipeline fashion meaning that each stage depends on the success of the previous stage in order to produce optimal/valid results. However, it is evident that the most appropriate feature vectors for the classification stage will only be produced with the facilitation from the preprocessing stage. The main objective of the preprocessing stage is to normalize and remove variations that would otherwise complicate the classification and reduce the recognition rate.

2. Factors affecting character recognition quality

There are a number of factors that affect the accuracy of text recognized through OCR. These factors include: scanner quality, scan resolution, type of printed documents (laser printer or photocopied), paper quality, fonts used in the text, linguistic complexities, and dictionary used. *"Foxing"* and *"text show through"* found in old paper documents, watermarks and non-uniform illumination are examples of problems that affect the accuracy of OCR compared to a clean text on a white background. For example, Fig.1 (a) shows a grey-level document image with poor illumination and Fig.1 (b) shows a mixed content document image with complex background. Other factors include features of printing such as uniformity, text alignment and arrangement on the page, graphics and picture content (Tanner, 2004).

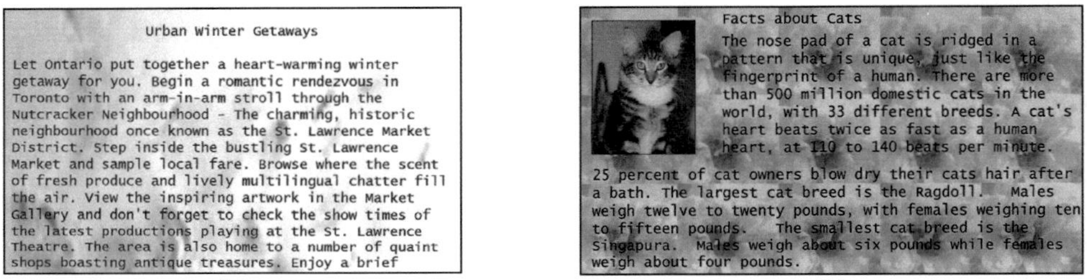

Urban Winter Getaways

Let Ontario put together a heart-warming winter getaway for you. Begin a romantic rendezvous in Toronto with an arm-in-arm stroll through the Nutcracker Neighbourhood - The charming, historic neighbourhood once known as the St. Lawrence Market District. Step inside the bustling St. Lawrence Market and sample local fare. Browse where the scent of fresh produce and lively multilingual chatter fill the air. View the inspiring artwork in the Market Gallery and don't forget to check the show times of the latest productions playing at the St. Lawrence Theatre. The area is also home to a number of quaint shops boasting antique treasures. Enjoy a brief

Facts about Cats

The nose pad of a cat is ridged in a pattern that is unique, just like the fingerprint of a human. There are more than 500 million domestic cats in the world, with 33 different breeds. A cat's heart beats twice as fast as a human heart, at 110 to 140 beats per minute.

25 percent of cat owners blow dry their cats hair after a bath. The largest cat breed is the Ragdoll. Males weigh twelve to twenty pounds, with females weighing ten to fifteen pounds. The smallest cat breed is the Singapura. Males weigh about six pounds while females weigh about four pounds.

(a) (b)

Fig. 1. Examples of document images with non-uniform/complex backgrounds

3. Importance of preprocessing in character recognition

The importance of the preprocessing stage of a character recognition system lies in its ability to remedy some of the problems that may occur due to some of the factors presented in section 2 above. Thus, the use of preprocessing techniques may enhance a document image preparing it for the next stage in a character recognition system. In order to achieve higher recognition rates, it is essential to have an effective preprocessing stage, therefore; using effective preprocessing algorithms makes the OCR system more robust mainly through accurate image enhancement, noise removal, image thresholding, skew detection/correction, page segmentation, character segmentation, character normalization and morphological techniques.

4. Preprocessing techniques

Preprocessing techniques are needed on colour, grey-level or binary document images containing text and/or graphics. In character recognition systems most of the applications use grey or binary images since processing colour images is computationally high. Such images may also contain non-uniform background and/or watermarks making it difficult to extract the document text from the image without performing some kind of preprocessing, therefore; the desired result from preprocessing is a binary image containing text only. Thus, to achieve this, several steps are needed, first, some image enhancement techniques to remove noise or correct the contrast in the image, second, thresholding to remove the background containing any scenes, watermarks and/or noise, third, page segmentation to separate graphics from text, fourth, character segmentation to separate characters from each other and, finally, morphological processing to enhance the characters in cases where thresholding and/or other preprocessing techniques eroded parts of the characters or added pixels to them. The above techniques present few of those which may be used in character recognition systems and in some applications; few or some of these techniques or others may be used at different stages of the OCR system. The rest of the chapter will present some of the techniques used during the preprocessing stage of a character recognition system.

4.1 Image enhancement techniques

Image enhancement improves the quality of images for human perception by removing noise, reducing blurring, increasing contrast and providing more detail. This section will provide some of the techniques used in image enhancement.

4.1.1 Spatial image filtering operations

In image processing, filters are mainly used to suppress either the high frequencies in the image, *i.e.* smoothing the image, or the low frequencies, *i.e.* enhancing or detecting edges in the image. Image restoration and enhancement techniques are described in both the spatial domain and frequency domain, i.e. Fourier transforms. However, Fourier transforms require substantial computations, and in some cases are not worth the effort. Multiplication in the frequency domain corresponds to convolution in the time and the spatial domain. Using a small convolution mask, such as 3x3, and convolving this mask over an image is much easier and faster than performing Fourier transforms and multiplication; therefore, only spatial filtering techniques will be presented in this chapter.

Images captured often may be influenced by noise; however, the resulting images may not provide desired images for analysis. In addition, in images with acceptable quality, certain regions may need to be emphasized or highlighted. Spatial processing is classified into point processing and mask processing. Point processing involves the transformation of individual pixels independently of other pixels in the image. These simple operations are typically used to correct for defects in image acquisition hardware, for example to compensate for under/over exposed images. On the other hand, in mask processing, the pixel with its neighbourhood of pixels in a square or circle mask are involved in generating the pixel at (x, y) coordinates in the enhanced image.

4.1.1.1 Point processing

Point processing modifies the values of the pixels in the original image to create the values of the corresponding pixels in the enhanced image this is expressed in equation (1).

$$O(x,y) = T[I(x,y)] \tag{1}$$

Where, $I(x, y)$ is the original (input) image, $O(x, y)$ is the enhanced image and T describes the transformation between the two images. Some of the point processing techniques include: contrast stretching, global thresholding, histogram equalisation, log transformations and power law transformations. Some mask processing techniques include averaging filters, sharpening filters, local thresholding… etc.

4.1.1.1.1 Contrast stretching

The level of contrast in an image may vary due to poor illumination or improper setting in the acquisition sensor device. Therefore, there is a need to manipulate the contrast of an image in order to compensate for difficulties in image acquisition. The idea is to modify the dynamic range of the grey-levels in the image. A technique that could work in this case is called linear mapping, equation (2), to stretch the pixel values of a low-contrast image or high-contrast image by extending the dynamic range across the whole image spectrum from $0 - (L\text{-}1)$.

$$O(x,y) = O_1 + \left(\frac{O_2 - O_1}{I_2 - I_1} \right) \left[I(x,y) - I_1 \right] \tag{2}$$

where O_1 corresponds to 0 and O_2 corresponds to the number of desired levels which is ($L\text{-}1 = 255$). I_1 and I_2 provide the minimum and maximum values of the input grey-level range. The simplest form of processing is to adjust the brightness of an image by adding a bias value, b, to all the pixel values of an image; where $b > 0$ would increase the brightness of an image and $b < 0$ would darken the image. Also, a gain factor, a, may be used instead of a bias, where the product of a with the input pixel values modify the brightness of the output image. Values of $0 < a < 1$ will produce a darker image and values of $a > 1$ will produce a brighter image. Combining both bias and gain produces equation (3).

$$O(x, y) = a * I(x, y) + b \tag{3}$$

In this case, we need to specify both the gain and bias values, but in practicality it may be difficult to do so; therefore, the solution would be to map the input image range (I_1, I_2) to the output image range (O_1, O_2) where O_1 corresponds to 0 and O_2 corresponds to the number of desired levels, hence linear mapping defined in equation (2).

4.1.1.1.2 Global image thresholding

Image thresholding is the process of separating the information (objects) of an image from its background, hence, thresholding is usually applied to grey-level or colour document scanned images. Thresholding can be categorised into two main categories: global and local. Global thresholding methods choose one threshold value for the entire document image, which is often based on the estimation of the background level from the intensity histogram of the image; hence, it is considered a point processing operation. On the other hand, local adaptive thresholding uses different values for each pixel according to the local area information. There are hundreds of thresholding algorithms which have been published in the literature and presenting all methods would need several books, therefore, the purpose here is to present some of the well-known methods.

Global thresholding methods are used to automatically reduce a grey-level image to a binary image. The images applied to such methods are assumed to have two classes of pixels (foreground and background). The purpose of a global thresholding method is to automatically specify a threshold value, *T*, where the pixel values below it are considered foreground and the values above are background. A simple method would be to choose the mean or median value of all the pixels in the input image, the mean or median will work well as the threshold, however, this will generally not be the case especially if the pixels are not uniformly distributed in an image. A more sophisticated approach might be to create a histogram of the image pixel intensities and use the valley point (minimum) as the threshold. The histogram approach assumes that there is some average value for the background and object pixels, but that the actual pixel values have some variation around these average values. However, this may be computationally expensive, and image histograms may not have clearly defined valley points, often making the selection of an accurate threshold difficult. One method that is relatively simple and does not require much specific knowledge of the image is the iterative method (Gonzalez, et al., 2004) which is explained below.

The iterative procedure is

Step 1: Select an initial threshold value (*T*), randomly or according to any other method desired such as the mean or median value of the pixels in the image.

Step 2: Segment the image, using *T*, into object and background pixels. R_1 (background region) consists of pixels with intensity values $\geq T$ and R_2 (objects region) consists of pixels with intensity $< T$.

Step 3: Calculate the average of each region, μ_1 and μ_2 for regions R_1 and R_2, respectively.

Step 4: Compute the new threshold value *T* as given in equation (4).

$$T=1/2(\mu_1 + \mu_2) \quad (4)$$

Step 5: Repeat the steps from 2 – 4 using the new *T* until the new threshold matches the one before it.

In the literature, many thresholding methods have been published, for example, Sahoo et al. compared the performance of more than 20 global thresholding algorithms using uniformly or shape measures. The comparison showed that Otsu class separability method gave best performance (Sahoo et al., 1988; Otsu, 1979). On the other hand, in an evaluation for change detection by Rosin & Ioannidis concluded that the Otsu algorithm performed very poorly compared to other global methods (Rosin & Ioannidis, 2003, Otsu, 1979). The OCR goal-directed evaluation study by Trier and Jain examined four global techniques showing that the Otsu method outperformed the other methods investigated in the study (Trier & Jain, 1995). In addition, Fischer compared 15 global methods and confirmed that the Otsu method is preferred in document image processing (Fischer, 2000). The Otsu method is one of the widely used techniques used to convert a grey-level image into a binary image then calculates the optimum threshold separating those two classes so that their combined spread (intra-class variance) is minimal.

The Otsu method searches for the threshold that minimises the intra-class variance, defined in equation (5) as a weighted sum of variances of the two classes (Otsu, 1979).

$$\sigma_{\omega}^2(t) = \omega_1(t)\sigma_1^2(t) + \omega_2(t)\sigma_2^2(t) \quad (5)$$

weights ω_i are the probabilities of the two classes separated by a threshold t and σ_i^2 is the variance of these classes. Otsu shows that minimising the intra-class variance is the same as maximising inter-class variance, equation (6):

$$\sigma_b^2(t) = \sigma^2 - \sigma_\omega^2(t) = \omega_1(t)\omega_2(t)[\mu_1(t) - \mu_2(t)]^2 \qquad (6)$$

this is expressed in terms of class probabilities ω_i and class means μ_i which in turn can be updated iteratively.

The algorithm steps are:

- Compute the histogram and probabilities of each intensity level
- Initialize $\omega_i(0)$ and $\mu_i(0)$
- Step through all threshold values $t = 1$ .... to maximum intensity.
  - Update $\omega_i(0)$ and $\mu_i(0)$
  - Compute the maximum $\sigma_b^2(t)$, which corresponds to the desired threshold.

4.1.1.1.3 Histogram processing

Histogram processing is used in image enhancement and can be useful in image compression and segmentation processing. A histogram simply plots the frequency at which each grey-level occurs from 0 (black) to 255 (white). Scanned or captured images may have a limited range of colours, or are lacking contrast (details). Enhancing the image by histogram processing can allow for improved detail, but can also aid other machine vision operations, such as segmentation. Thus, histogram processing should be the initial step in preprocessing. Histogram equalisation and histogram specification (matching) are two methods widely used to modify the histogram of an image to produce a much better image.

4.1.1.1.3.1 Histogram equalisation

Histogram equalisation is considered a global technique. It stretches the histogram across the entire spectrum of pixels (0 – 255). It increases the contrast of images for the finality of human inspection and can be applied to normalize illumination variations in image understanding problems. This process is quite simple and for each brightness level j in the original image, the new pixel level value (k) is calculated as given in equation (7).

$$k = \sum_{i=0}^{j} N_i / T \qquad (7)$$

where the sum counts the number of pixels in the image (by integrating the histogram) with brightness equal to or less than j, and T is the total number of pixels (Russ, 2007). In addition, histogram equalisation is one of the operations that can be applied to obtain new images based on histogram specification or modification.

4.1.1.1.3.2 Histogram specification (Matching)

Histogram matching is a method in image processing of colour adjustment of two images using their image histograms.

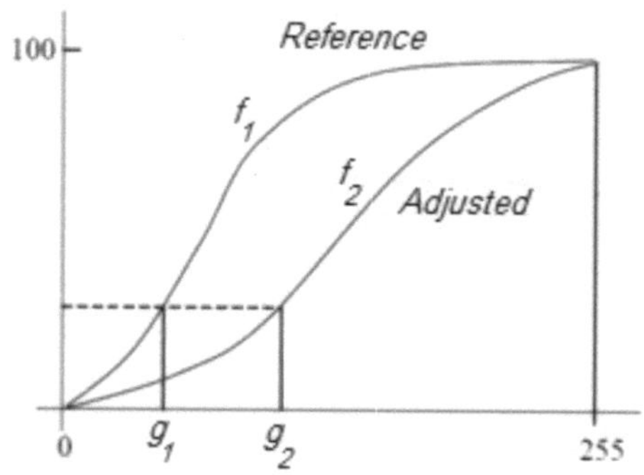

Fig. 2. Cumulative distributive functions for reference and adjusted images.

Histogram modification is the matching of the cumulative function f_2 of the image to be adjusted to the Cumulative Distribution Function (CDF) of the reference image f_1. Histogram modification is done by first computing the histograms of both images then the CDFs of both the reference (f_1) and to be adjusted (f_2) images are calculated. This output of the histogram matching is obtained by matching the closest CDF f_2 to the reference image CDF f_1. Then for each grey-level g_1 the grey-level g_2 is calculated for which $f_1(g_1) = f_2(g_2)$ as shown in Fig. 2, and this is the result of histogram matching function $M(g_1) = g_2$ (Horn & Woodham, 1979).

4.1.1.1.4 Log transformations

The general form of the log transformation is equation (8).

$$s = c \log (1 + r) \tag{8}$$

where c is a constant and it is assumed that $r \geq 0$. This transformation maps a narrow range of low grey-level values in the input image into a wider range of output levels and vice versa (Gonzalez et al., 2004).

4.1.1.1.5 Power law transformation

Power-law transformations have the general form shown in equation (9).

$$s = c(r + \varepsilon)^{\gamma} \tag{9}$$

where c and γ are positive constants and ε is an offset which is usually ignored since it is due to display calibration. Therefore; $s = c \cdot r^{\gamma}$, where values of $0 < \gamma < 1$ map a narrow range of dark input values into a wider range of output values, with the opposite being true for values of γ greater than 1. This shows that the power-law transformations are much more versatile in such application than the log transformation. However, the log function has the important characteristic that it compresses the dynamic range of images with large variations in pixel values. Due to the variety of devices used for image capture, printing, and display respond according to the power law exponent, gamma, (γ), this factor needs to be corrected, thus power-law response phenomena or gamma correction which is given by $s = c \cdot r^{1/\gamma}$ (Gonzalez et al., 2004).

4.1.1.2 Mask processing

In mask processing, a pixel value is computed from the pixel value in the original image and the values of pixels in its vicinity. It is a more costly operation than simple point processing, but more powerful. The application of a mask to an input image produces an output image of the same size as the input.

4.1.1.2.1 Smoothing (Low-pass) filters

Average or mean filter is a simple, intuitive and easy to implement method of *smoothing* images, *i.e.* reducing the amount of intensity variation between one pixel and the next. It is often used to reduce noise in images. In general, the mean filter acts as a low-pass frequency filter and, therefore, reduces the spatial intensity derivatives present in the image. The idea of mean filtering is simply to replace each pixel value in an image with the mean (`average') value of its neighbours, including itself. This has the effect of eliminating pixel values which are unrepresentative of their surroundings. Mean filtering is usually thought of as a convolution filter. Like other convolutions it is based around a kernel, which represents the shape and size of the neighbourhood to be sampled when calculating the mean. Often a 3×3 square kernel/mask is used, as shown in Fig. 3, although larger masks can be used (*e.g.* 5×5, 7x7, 9x9 ...) for more severe smoothing. Note that, a small kernel can be applied more than once in order to produce a similar, but not identical, effect as a single pass with a larger kernel. Also, the elements of the mask must be positive and hence the size of the mask determines the degree of smoothing. Therefore, the larger the window size used a blurring effect is produced causing small objects to merge with the background of the image (Nixon & Aguado, 2008).

	1	1	1
1/9 x	1	1	1
	1	1	1

Average filter

	1	2	1
1/16 x	2	4	2
	1	2	1

Average Weighted filter

Fig. 3. 3×3 averaging kernels used in average filter.

The center coefficient of the mask is very important and other pixels are inversely weighted as a function of their distance from the center of the mask. The basic strategy behind weighting the center point the highest and then reducing the value of the coefficients as a function of increasing distance from the origin is simply an attempt to reduce blurring in the smoothing process.

4.1.1.2.2 Sharpening (High-pass) filter

A sharpening filter is used to emphasize the fine details of an image (i.e., provides the opposite effect of smoothing). The points of high contrast can be detected by computing intensity differences in local image regions. The weights of the mask are both positive and negative. When the mask is over an area of constant or slowly varying grey-level, the result of convolution will be close to zero. When grey-level is varying rapidly within the neighbourhood, the result of convolution will be a large number. Typically, such points form the border between different objects or scene parts (i.e. edge). An example of a sharpening filter is the Laplacian filter which is defined in equation (10) below.

$$\nabla^2 f = [f(x+1,y) + f(x-1,y) + f(x,y+1) + f(x,y-1)] - 4f(x,y) \tag{10}$$

This implementation can be applied at all points (*x,y*) in an image by convolving the image with the following spatial mask Fig. 4(a) with an alternative definition of the digital second derivatives which takes into account the diagonal elements and can be implemented by the mask in Fig. 4(b).

0	1	0
1	-4	1
0	1	0

(a)

1	1	1
1	-8	1
1	1	1

(b)

Fig. 4. 3x3 Laplacian filter masks

The Laplacian filter is a derivative operator which sharpens the image, but drives constant areas to zero; therefore, adding the original image back restores the grey-level tonality, equation (11).

$$g(x,y) = f(x,y) + c[\nabla^2 f(x,y)] \tag{11}$$

Where, *f(x,y)* is the input image, *g(x,y)* is the output image and *c* is 1 if the centre coefficient of the mask is positive, or -1 if it is negative (Gonzales and Woods, 2002).

4.1.1.2.3 Median filter

A commonly used non-linear operator is the median, a special type of low-pass filter. The median filter takes an area of an image (3x3, 5x5, 7x7, etc.), sorts out all the pixel values in that area, and replaces the center pixel with the median value. The median filter does not require convolution. (If the neighbourhood under consideration contains an even number of pixels, the average of the two middle pixel values is used.) Fig. 5 illustrates an example of how the median filter is calculated. The median filter is effective for removing impulse noise such as "salt and pepper noise" which is random occurrences of black and white pixels.

123	127	150	120	100
119	115	134	121	120
111	120	122	125	180
111	119	145	100	200
110	120	120	130	150

(a)

		121		

(b)

Fig. 5. (a) Input image (b) Filtered image using median filter showing only the centre pixel.

The sorted pixel values of the shaded area are: (100, 115, 119, 120, 121, 122, 125, 134 and 145), providing a median value of 121 in the output image.

4.1.1.2.4 Maximum filter

The maximum filter is defined as the maximum of all pixels within a local region of an image. The maximum filter is typically applied to an image to remove negative outlier noise. For the example in Fig. 5 the center pixel will take the maximum value 145.

4.1.1.2.5 Minimum filter

The minimum filter enhances dark values in the image; therefore, the darkest pixel then becomes the new pixel value at the centre of the window. For the example in Fig. 5 the centre pixel will be replaced by the minimum value of 100.

4.1.1.2.6 Range filter

The range filter is defined as the difference between the maximum and minimum pixel values within the neighbourhood of a pixel. For the example in Fig. 5 the centre pixel will be replaced by 45.

4.1.1.2 Local thresholding

Local thresholding techniques are used with document images having non-uniform background illumination or complex backgrounds, such as watermarks found in security documents if the global thresholding methods fail to separate the foreground from the background. This is due to the fact that the histogram of such images provides more than two peaks making it difficult for a global thresholding technique to separate the objects from the background, thus; local thresholding methods are the solution. The local thresholding techniques developed in the literature are mainly for specific applications and most of the time they do not perform well in different applications. The results could be over thresholding or under thresholding depending on the contrast and illumination. From the literature, several surveys have compared different thresholding techniques. The work of Trier and Jain evaluated the performance of 11 well-established locally adaptive binarisation methods (Trier & Jain, 1995). These techniques were compared using a criterion based on the ability of an OCR module to recognize handwritten numerals from hydrographical images. In this evaluation, the Niblack's method, (Niblack, 1986), appears to be the best. This observation was applied for a specific application on certain hydro-graphic images using an OCR system. However, as concluded by the authors, if different sets of images used with different feature extraction methods and classifiers, then this observation may not be accurate and another method could outperform the Niblack's method (Trier & Jain, 1995). The Niblack's method calculates the threshold by shifting a window across the image, and use local mean, μ, and standard deviation, σ, for each center pixel in the window. The threshold value for a pixel within fixed neighbourhood is a linear function of the mean and standard deviation of the neighbourhood pixels, with a constant gradient of $T(x, y)$, which is highly tunable, to separate objects well. Then the threshold is equation (12).

$$T(x, y) = \mu\ (x, y) + k\ \sigma\ (x, y) \quad (12)$$

The size of the neighbourhood should be small enough to serve local details, but at the same time large enough to suppress noise. The value of k is used to adjust how much of the total print object boundary is taken as a part of the given object. There have been several methods which introduced modifications to the Niblack's method, such as the work of Zhang and Tan who proposed an improved version of the Niblack's algorithm (Zhang and Tan, 2001). In addition, too many other thresholding methods based on different properties of the image were also developed. For example, the local thresholding method developed by Alginahi, uses the MLP-NN to classify pixels as background or foreground using statistical texture features to characterize the set of neighbourhood values of pixels related to its moments and measures of properties such as smoothness, uniformity and variability (Alginahi, 2004, 2008). In this work, five features were extracted from a window size 3x3 these are the centre pixel value of the window, mean, standard variation, skewness and entropy. These features were extracted from each pixel and its neighbourhood in the image and then passed into a MLP-NN to classify pixels into background (white) and foreground (black). The MLP-NN thresholding method proved to provide excellent results in thresholding documents with bad illumination, containing complex background and/or non-uniform background, such as those found in security documents. The MLP-NN thresholding method is a non-application specific and can work with any application provided that sufficient training is carried out.

4.2 Noise removal

The advancements in technology produced image acquisition devices with better improvements. While modern technology has made it possible to reduce the noise levels associated with various electro-optical devices to almost negligible levels, there are still some noise sources which cannot be eliminated. Images acquired through modern sensors may be contaminated by a variety of noise sources. By noise we refer to stochastic variations as opposed to deterministic distortions, such as shading or lack of focus. There are different types of noise that are related to the electronic capturing devices or the light source used such types of noise are photon, thermal, On-Chip electronic and quantisation. Most of the noise may be eliminated by the capturing sensors or the CCD cameras.

Document analysis systems benefit from the reduction of noise in the preprocessing stage this can provide a substantial improvement in the reliability and robustness of the feature extraction and recognition stages of the OCR system. A common manifestation of noise in binary images takes the form of isolated pixels, salt-and-pepper noise or speckle noise, thus; the processing of removing this type of noise is called filling, where each isolated pixel salt-and-pepper "island" is filled in by the surrounding "sea" (O'Gorman, et al., 2008). In grey-level images or median filters and low-pass filters such as average or Gaussian blur filters proved to eliminate isolated pixel noise. Gaussian blur and average filters are a better choice to provide smooth texture to the image. On the other hand, periodic noise which manifests itself as impulse-like bursts which often are visible in the Fourier spectrum can be filtered using notch filtering. The transfer function of a Butterworth notch filter of order *n*, $H(u,v)$, is given by equation (13).

$$H(u,v) = \frac{1}{1+\left[\frac{D_0^2}{D_1(u,v)D_2(u,v)}\right]^n} \tag{13}$$

Where

$$D_1(u,v) = [(u - M/2 - u_0)^2 + (v - N/2 - v_0)^2]^{1/2} \tag{14}$$

And

$$D_2(u,v) = [(u - M/2 + u_0)^2 + (v - N/2 + v_0)^2]^{1/2} \tag{15}$$

where (μ_0, υ_0) and by symmetry ($-\mu_0$, $-\upsilon_0$) are the locations of the notches and D is their radius, equations 14 - 15. The filter is specified with respect to the centre of the frequency rectangle. (Gonzalez et al., 2004).

4.3 Skew detection/correction

Due to the possibility of rotation of the input image and the sensitivity of many document image analysis methods to rotation of the image, document skew should be corrected. Skew detection techniques can be roughly classified into the following groups: analysis of projection profile, Hough transform, connected components, clustering, and Correlation between lines techniques. The survey by Hull and Taylor, investigated twenty-five different methods for document image skew detection. The methods include approaches based on Hough Transform analysis, projection profile, feature point distribution and orientation-sensitive feature analysis. The survey concluded that most of the techniques reported a range of up to 0.1 degrees accuracy, evidencing a strong need for further work in this area to help show the strengths and weaknesses of individual algorithms (Hull & Taylor, 1998). In addition, there are new techniques emerging for specific applications such as the method of Al-Shatnawi and Omar which is based on the center of gravity for dealing with Arabic document images (Al-Shatnawi & Omar, 2009). Therefore, the choice of using a skew detection/correction technique depends on the application and the type of images used.

4.4 Page segmentation

After image enhancement, noise removal and/or skew detection/correction, the next step in mixed content images or composite images is to perform page segmentation in order to separate text from halftone images, lines, and graphs. The result of interest should be an image with only text; therefore, document/page segmentation. Document segmentation can be classified into three broad categories: top-down, bottom-up and hybrid techniques. The top-down methods recursively segment large regions in a document into smaller sub-regions. The segmentation stops when some criterion is met and the ranges obtained at that stage constitute the final segmentation results. On the other hand, the bottom-up methods start by grouping pixels of interest and merging them into larger blocks or connected components, such as characters which are then clustered into words, lines or blocks of text. The hybrid methods are the combination of both top-down and bottom-up strategies.

The Run-Length Smearing Algorithm (RLSA) is one of the most widely used top-down algorithms. It is used on binary images (setting 1 for white pixels and 0 for black pixels), by linking together the neighbouring black pixels that are within a certain threshold. This method is applied row-by-row and column-by-column, then both results are combined in a logical OR operation and finally a smoothing threshold is used to produce the final segmentation result. From the RLSA results, black blocks of text lines and images are produced. Finally a statistical classifier is used to classify these blocks (Wahl et al., 1982).

An example of bottom-up algorithm is the recursive X-Y method, which is also known as the projection profile cuts, it assumes documents are presented in a form of a tree of nested rectangular blocks (Nagy & Stoddard, 1986). Although the recursive X-Y cuts could decompose a document image into a set of rectangular blocks no details were given on how to define cuts. On the other hand, an example of a hybrid method is the segmentation approach of Kruatrachue and Suthaphan which consists of two steps, a top down block extraction method followed by a bottom-up multi-column block detection and segmentation method (Kruatrachue & Suthaphan, 2001). The segmentation is based on blocks of columns extracted by a modified edge following algorithm, which uses a window of 32 x 32 pixel so that a paragraph can be extracted instead of a character.

The above are only a few examples and hundreds of methods developed for document layout segmentation. To ensure the performance of most of these algorithms, a skew detection and correction algorithm is required in the preprocessing stage. In literature, the surveys in (Mao et al., 2003) and (Tang et al., 1996) provide detailed explanation on document analysis and layout representation algorithms. Most of the techniques explained are time consuming and are not effective for processing documents with high geometrical complexity. Specifically, the top-down approach can process only simple documents, which have specific format or contain some a priori information about the document. It fails to process the documents that have complicated geometric structures. The research in this area concentrates on binary images and grey images with uniform backgrounds. The images used were mainly scanned from technical journals and magazines that usually have specific formats. Document segmentation on grey-level images with complex or non-uniform backgrounds have not been widely investigated due to the complications in thresholding these images. Therefore, techniques are mainly geared to specific applications with specific formats and they tend to fail when specific parameters do not match. Alginahi, et al. used a local MLP-NN threshold to threshold images with uniform background and applied the RLSA with modified parameters to segment a mixed content document image into text, lines, halftone images and graphics (Alginahi et al., 2005,2008).

4.5 Character segmentation

Character segmentation is considered one of the main steps in preprocessing especially in cursive scripts such as Arabic, Urdu and other scripts where characters are connected together. Therefore, there are many techniques developed for character segmentation and most of them are script specific and may not work with other scripts. Even in printed handwritten documents, character segmentation is required due to touching of characters when written by hand. For example, printed Latin characters are easy to segment using horizontal and vertical histogram profiles; however, smaller fonts and those containing serifs may introduce touching which will need further processing to solve the touching problem.

4.6 Image size normalization

The result from the character segmentation stage provides isolated characters which are ready to be passed into the feature extraction stage; therefore, the isolated characters are normalized into a specific size, decided empirically or experimentally depending on the application and the feature extraction or classification techniques used, then features are extracted from all characters with the same size in order to provide data uniformity.

4.7 Morphological processing

Segmentation results may cause some pixels to be removed producing holes to some parts of the images; this could be seen from characters having some holes in them where some of the pixels were removed during thresholding. Larger holes can cause characters to break into two or more parts/objects. On the other hand, the opposite can also be true, as segmentation can join separate objects making it more difficult to separate characters; these solid objects resemble blobs and are hard to interpret. The solution to these problems is Morphological Filtering. Useful techniques include erosion and dilation, opening and closing, outlining, and thinning and skeletonisation. These techniques work on binary images only. (Phillips, 2000)

4.7.1 Erosion and dilation

Dilation and Erosion are morphological operations which increase or decrease objects in size and can be very useful during the preprocessing stage. Erosion makes an object smaller by removing or eroding away the pixels on its edges; however, dilation makes an object larger by adding pixels around its edges. There are two general techniques for erosion and dilation these are: the threshold and masking techniques. The threshold technique looks at the neighbours of a pixel and changes its state if the number of differing neighbour pixels exceeds a threshold. Basically, if the number of zero pixels in the neighbourhood of a pixel exceeds a threshold parameter then the pixel is set to zero. Fig. 6 shows the result of eroding the rectangle using a threshold value of three (Russ, 2007).

0	0	0	0	0	0	0	0
0	0	0	0	0	0	0	0
0	0	255	255	255	255	0	0
0	0	255	255	255	255	0	0
0	0	255	255	255	255	0	0
0	0	255	255	255	255	0	0
0	0	0	0	0	0	0	0
0	0	0	0	0	0	0	0

(a)

0	0	0	0	0	0	0	0
0	0	0	0	0	0	0	0
0	0	0	255	255	0	0	0
0	0	255	255	255	255	0	0
0	0	255	255	255	255	0	0
0	0	0	255	255	0	0	0
0	0	0	0	0	0	0	0
0	0	0	0	0	0	0	0

(b)

Fig. 6. The result of eroding a rectangle using a threshold of 3.

The dilation process does the opposite of erosion. It counts the value of pixels next to a zero pixel, if the count exceeds the threshold parameter, then the zero pixel is set to the value of the pixel. The dilation in Fig. 7 uses a threshold value of two.

(a)

0	0	0	0	0	0	0	0
0	0	0	0	0	0	0	0
0	0	255	255	255	255	0	0
0	0	255	255	255	255	0	0
0	0	255	255	255	255	0	0
0	0	255	255	255	255	0	0
0	0	0	0	0	0	0	0
0	0	0	0	0	0	0	0

(b)

0	0	0	0	0	0	0	0
0	0	0	255	255	0	0	0
0	0	255	255	255	255	0	0
0	255	255	255	255	255	255	0
0	255	255	255	255	255	255	0
0	0	255	255	255	255	0	0
0	0	0	255	255	0	0	0
0	0	0	0	0	0	0	0

Fig. 7. The result of dilating (a) is given in (b) using a threshold of 2.

The masking technique uses an *nxn* (3x3, 5x5, etc.) array of 1s and 0s on top of an input image and erodes or dilates the input. Using masks, the direction of erosion or dilation can be controlled. Square masks are more widely used such sizes are 3x3, 5x5, 7x7... etc. with other sizes could be used (Myler & Weeks, 1993, Phillips, 2000). Masks of sizes 3x3 in different directions are shown below:

vertical mask	horizontal mask	horizontal and vertical masks	
0 1 0	0 0 0	0 1 0	1 1 1
0 1 0	1 1 1	1 1 1	1 1 1
0 1 0	0 0 0	0 1 0	1 1 1

Fig 8. below shows the result of dilation using the horizontal mask.

(a)

0	0	0	0	0	0	0	0
0	0	0	0	0	0	0	0
0	0	255	255	255	255	0	0
0	0	255	255	255	255	0	0
0	0	255	255	255	255	0	0
0	0	255	255	255	255	0	0
0	0	0	0	0	0	0	0
0	0	0	0	0	0	0	0

(b)

0	0	0	0	0	0	0	0
0	0	0	0	0	0	0	0
0	255	255	255	255	255	255	0
0	255	255	255	255	255	255	0
0	255	255	255	255	255	255	0
0	255	255	255	255	255	255	0
0	0	0	0	0	0	0	0
0	0	0	0	0	0	0	0

Fig. 8. The result of dilating (a) using the horizontal mask is shown in (b)

Mask erosion is the opposite of dilation. It applies an *nxn* mask on the image so that the center of the array is on top of a zero. If any of the 1s coefficients in the mask overlap a white pixel (255) in the image then it is set to zero. Vertical mask erosion removes the top and bottom rows from an object, horizontal mask removes the left and right columns and the horizontal and vertical masks remove pixels from all edges.

To conclude, dilation causes objects to grow in size as it will exchange every pixel value with the maximum value within an *nxn* window size around the pixel. The process may be repeated to create larger effects. However, erosion works the same way except that it will cause objects to decrease because each pixel value is exchanged with the minimum value within an *nxn* window size around the pixel (Phillips, 2000).

4.7.2 Opening and closing

Opening and closing are morphological operators that are derived from the fundamental operations of erosion and dilation, and are normally applied to binary images. The basic effect of an opening is somewhat like erosion in that it tends to remove some of the foreground pixels from the edges of regions of foreground pixels. However, it is less destructive than erosion in general. Closing is similar in some ways to dilation in that it tends to enlarge the boundaries of foreground regions in an image, but it is less destructive of the original boundary shape.

Opening spaces objects that are too close together, detaches objects that are touching and should not be, and enlarges holes inside objects. Fig. 9 shows two objects joined by a thread; opening was used to remove this thread and separate the two objects, thus, by eroding the object twice the thread is erased. In this case, dilation would enlarge the two objects back to their original size, but does not re-create the thread (Phillips, 2000).

0	0	0	0	0	0	0	0
0	255	255	0	0	255	255	0
0	255	255	0	0	255	255	0
0	255	255	255	255	255	255	0
0	255	255	0	0	255	255	0
0	255	255	0	0	255	255	0
0	255	255	0	0	255	255	0
0	0	0	0	0	0	0	0

(a)

0	0	0	0	0	0	0	0
0	255	255	0	0	255	255	0
0	255	255	0	0	255	255	0
0	255	255	0	0	255	255	0
0	255	255	0	0	255	255	0
0	255	255	0	0	255	255	0
0	255	255	0	0	255	255	0
0	0	0	0	0	0	0	0

(b)

Fig. 9. The result of opening two objects joined by a thread

Opening can also enlarge a desired hole in an object; it involves one or more erosions followed by a dilation process. Closing joins broken objects and fills in unwanted holes in objects, Fig. 10 shows two objects that should be joined to make a line and Fig. 11 shows how closing fills a hole in an object.

0	0	0	0	0	0	0	0
0	0	0	0	0	0	0	0
0	255	255	255	0	255	255	0
0	255	255	255	0	255	255	0
0	0	0	0	0	0	0	0
0	0	0	0	0	0	0	0

(a)

0	0	0	0	0	0	0	0
0	0	0	0	0	0	0	0
0	255	255	255	255	255	255	0
0	255	255	255	255	255	255	0
0	0	0	0	0	0	0	0
0	0	0	0	0	0	0	0

(b)

Fig. 10. The result of closing unwanted holes in objects to form a line.

0	0	0	0	0	0	0
0	255	255	255	255	255	0
0	255	255	255	255	255	0
0	255	255	0	255	255	0
0	255	255	0	255	255	0
0	255	255	255	255	255	0
0	255	255	255	255	255	0
0	0	0	0	0	0	0

(a)

0	0	0	0	0	0	0
0	255	255	255	255	255	0
0	255	255	255	255	255	0
0	255	255	255	255	255	0
0	255	255	255	255	255	0
0	255	255	255	255	255	0
0	255	255	255	255	255	0
0	0	0	0	0	0	0

(b)

Fig. 11. The result of closing unwanted holes in objects.

The opening and closing operators work well, but sometimes produce undesired results where closing may merge objects which should not be merged and opening may enlarge holes and cause an object to break. The answer is special opening and closing that avoid such problems, for further information the reader is referred to (Phillips, 2000; Russ, 2007; Gonzalez et al., 2004).

4.7.3 Outlining

Outlining is a type of edge detection; it only works for binary images, but produces better results than regular edge detectors. Outlining binary images is quick and easy with erosion and dilation. To outline the interior of an object, erode the object and subtract the eroded image from the original, for example Fig. 12. To outline the exterior of an object, dilate the object and subtract the original image from the dilated image, for example Fig. 13. Exterior outlining is easiest to understand where dilating an object makes it one layer of pixels larger and subtracting the input from this dilated larger object yields the outline.

255	255	255	255	255	255	255	255
255	255	255	255	255	255	255	255
255	255	0	0	0	0	255	255
255	255	0	0	0	0	255	255
255	255	0	0	0	0	255	255
255	255	0	0	0	0	255	255
255	255	255	255	255	255	255	255
255	255	255	255	255	255	255	255

(a)

0	0	0	0	0	0	0	0
0	255	255	255	255	255	255	0
0	255	0	0	0	0	255	0
0	255	0	0	0	0	255	0
0	255	0	0	0	0	255	0
0	255	0	0	0	0	255	0
0	255	255	255	255	255	255	0
0	0	0	0	0	0	0	0

(b)

Fig. 12. The result of showing the interior outline of an image.

0	0	0	0	0	0	0	0
0	0	0	0	0	0	0	0
0	0	255	255	255	255	0	0
0	0	255	255	255	255	0	0
0	0	255	255	255	255	0	0
0	0	255	255	255	255	0	0
0	0	0	0	0	0	0	0
0	0	0	0	0	0	0	0

(a)

0	0	0	0	0	0	0	0
0	255	255	255	255	255	255	0
0	255	0	0	0	0	255	0
0	255	0	0	0	0	255	0
0	255	0	0	0	0	255	0
0	255	0	0	0	0	255	0
0	255	255	255	255	255	255	0
0	0	0	0	0	0	0	0

(b)

Fig. 13. The result of showing the exterior outline of an image.

4.7.4 Thinning and skeletonisation

Skeletonisation is a process for reducing foreground regions in a binary image to a skeletal remnant that largely preserves the extent and connectivity of the original region while removing most of the original foreground pixels. It is clear to imagine that the skeleton is as the loci of centres of bi-tangent circles that fit entirely within the foreground region being considered, this can be illustrated using the rectangular shape in Fig. 14.

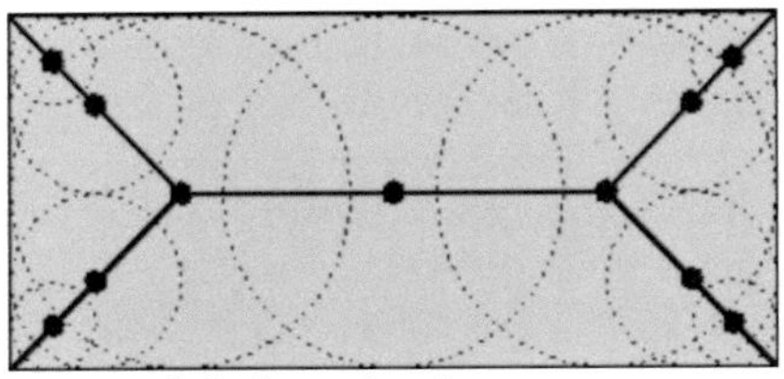

Fig. 14. Illustration of the concept of skeletonisation

There are two basic techniques for producing the skeleton of an object: basic thinning and medial axis transforms. Thinning is a morphological operation that is used to remove selected foreground pixels from binary images, somewhat like erosion or opening. Thinning is a data reduction process that erodes an object until it is one-pixel wide, producing a skeleton of the object making it easier to recognize objects such as characters. Fig. 15 shows how thinning the character E produces the skinny shape of the character. Thinning is normally only applied to binary images, and produces another binary image as output. Thinning erodes an object over and over again (without breaking it) until it is one-pixel wide. On the other hand, the medial axis transform finds the points in an object that form lines down its center (Davies, 2005).

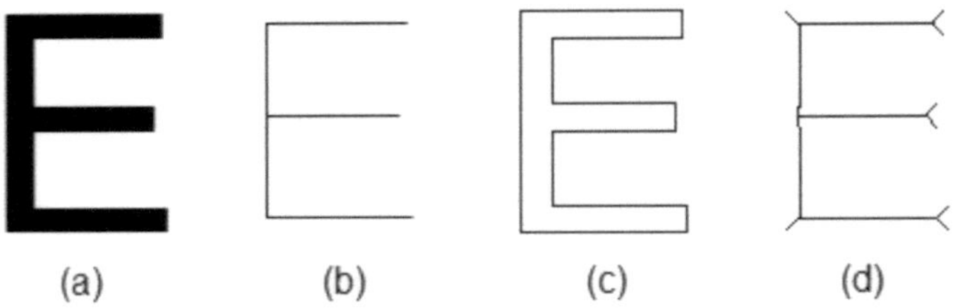

Fig. 15. (a) Original Image (b) Medial Axis Transform (c) Outline (d) Thinning

The medial axis transform is similar to measuring the Euclidean distance of any pixel in an object to the edge of the object, hence, it consists of all points in an object that are minimally distant to more than one edge of the object (Russ, 2007).

5. Conclusion

In this chapter, preprocessing techniques used in document images as an initial step in character recognition systems were presented. Future research aims at new applications such as online character recognition used in mobile devices, extraction of text from video images, extraction of information from security documents and processing of historical documents. The objective of such research is to guarantee the accuracy and security of information extraction in real time applications. Even though many methods and techniques have been developed for preprocessing there are still problems that are not solved completely and more investigations need to be carried out in order to provide solutions. Most of preprocessing techniques are application-specific and not all preprocessing techniques have to be applied to all applications. Each application may require different preprocessing techniques depending on the different factors that may affect the quality of its images, such as those introduced during the image acquisition stage. Image manipulation/enhancement techniques do not need to be performed on an entire image since not all parts of an image is affected by noise or contrast variations; therefore, enhancement of a portion of the original image maybe more useful in many situations. This is obvious when an image contains different objects which may differ in their brightness or darkness from the other parts of the image; thereby, when portions of an image can be selected, either manually or automatically according to their brightness such processing can be used to bring out local detail. In conclusion preprocessing is considered a crucial stage in most automatic document image analysis systems and without it the success of such systems is not guaranteed.

6. References

Alginahi, Y.; Sid-Ahmed, M. & Ahmadi, M. (2004). Local Thresholding of Composite Documents Using Multi-Layer Perceptron Neural Network, *Proceedings of the 47th IEEE International Midwest Symposium on Circuits and Systems*, pp. I-209 - I-212, ISBN: 0-7803-8346-X, Hiroshima, Japan, July 2004, IEEE.

Alginahi, Fekri & Sid-Ahmed. (2005). A Neural Based Page Segmentation System, *Journal of Circuits, Systems and Computers*, Vol. 14, No. 1, pp. 109 - 122.

Alginahi, Y. M. (2008). Thresholding and Character Recognition in Security Documents with Watermarked Background, Digital Image Computing: Techniques and Applications, DICTA 2008, Canberra, Australia, December 1-3.

Al-Shatnawi, A. & Omar, K. (2009). Skew Detection and Correction Technique for Arabic Document Images Based on Centre of Gravity, *Journal of Computer Science* 5 (5), May 2009, pp. 363-368, ISSN 1549-3636.

Davies, E. (2005). *Machine Vision – Theory Algorithms Practicalities,* Third Edition, Morgan Kaufmann Publishers, ISBN 13: 978-0-12-206093-9, ISBN-10: 0-12-206093-8, San Francisco, CA, USA.

Fischer, S., (2000). *Digital Image Processing: Skewing and Thresholding,* Master of Science thesis, University of New South Wales, Sydney, Australia.

Gonzalez, R.; Woods, R. & Eddins, S. (2004). *Digital Image Processing using MATLAB*, Pearson Education Inc., ISBN 0-13-008519-7, Upper Saddle River, NJ, USA.

Horn, B.K.P. & R.J. Woodham (1979). Destriping LANDSAT MSS Images using Histogram Modification, *Computer Graphics and Image Processing,* Vol. 10, No. 1, May 1979, pp. 69–83.

Hull, J. J. & Taylor, S.L. (1998). Document Image Skew Detection Survey and Annotated Bibliography, *Document Analysis Systems II, Eds.,* World Scientific, pp. 40-64.

Kruatrachue, B. & Suthaphan, P. (2001). A Fast and Efficient Method for Document Segmentation for OCR, TENCON, *Proceedings of IEEE region 10 Int. Conf. On Electrical and Electronic Technology,* Vol. 1, pp. 381-383.

Mao, S., Rosenfeld, A. and Kanungo, T. (2003). Document Structure Analysis Algorithms: A Literature Survey, *Proceedings of SPIE Electronic Imaging,* pp. 197-207.

Myler, H. R. & Weeks, A. R. (1993). *Computer Imaging Recipes in C,* Prentice Hall Publishing, Englewood Cliffs, New Jersey.

Nagy, S. & Stoddard, S. (1986). Document Analysis with an Expert System, *Pattern Recognition in Practice II,* pp. 149-155.

Niblack, W. (1986). *An Introduction to Digital Image Processing,* Prentice Hall, ISBN-10 0134806743, ISBN-13 : 978-0134806747, Englewood Cliffs, NJ. USA, pp. 115-116.

Nixon, N. & Aguado A. (2008). *Feature Extraction & Image Processing,* second edition, ISBN 978-0-12-372538-7, Elsevier Ltd., London, UK.

O'Gorman, L.; Sammon, M. & Seul, M. (2008). *Practical Algorithms For Image Analysis,* Cambridge University Press, ISBN 978-0=521-88411-2, New York, NY, USA.

Otsu, N. (1979). A Threshold Selection Method From Grey-level Histograms, *IEEE Transactions On systems, Man and Cybernetics,* SMC-9, pp. 62-66.

Phillips, D. (2000). *Image Processing in C.* Electronic Edition 1.0, 1st Edition was published by R & D Publications, ISBN 0-13-104548-2, Lawrence, Kansas, USA.

Rosin, P. & Ioannidis, E. (2003). Evaluation of Global Image Thresholding for Change Detection, *Pattern Recognition Letters,* Vol. 24, pp. 2345-2356.

Russ, J. (2007). *The Image Processing Handbook,* Fifth Edition, CRC Press, Boca Raton, FL, USA.

Sahoo, P.; Soltani, S. & Wong, A. (1988). A Survey of Thresholding Techniques, *Computer Vision Graphics Image Processing,* Vol. 41, pp. 233-260.

Tang, Y. Y., Lee, S.W & Suen, C. Y. (1996) Automatic Document Processing: A Survey, *Pattern Recognition,* Vol. 29, No. 12, pp. 1931-1952.

Tanner, S. (2004). Deciding whether Optical Character Recognition is Feasible, King's Digital Consultancy Services, http://www.odl.ox.ac.uk/papers/OCRFeasibility_final.pdf

Trier, O. & Jain, A. (1995). Goal-Directed Evaluation of Binarization Methods, *IEEE Trans. On Pattern Recognition and Machine Intelligence,* Vol. 17, No. 12, pp. 1191-1201.

Wahl, F. Wong, K. & Casey, R. (1982). Block Segmentation and Text Extraction in Mixed Text/Image Documents, *Computer Vision, Graphics and Image Processing,* Vol. 20, pp. 375-390.

Zhang Z. & Tan, C. (2001). Restoration of Images Scanned from Thick Bound Documents, *Proceedings of the International Conference On Image Processing,* Vol. 1, pp. 1074-1077.

2

Recognition of Characters from Streaming Videos

Tanushyam Chattopadhyay,
Arpan Pal and Aniruddha Sinha
Innovation Lab, Kolkata,
Tata Consultancy Services Ltd.
India

1. Introduction

Over the past few years, Video has become one of the prime source for recreation, be it Television or Internet. Television brings a whole lot of professionally produced video content (International or local, sports or educational, news or entertainment) to the home for the masses. Similarly, Internet hosts a whole lot of video content uploaded by other users. Understanding the context of the video automatically can open up avenue for a lot of value-added applications. Now, what do we mean by understanding the context? Video context is usually associated with audio, image, graph, text etc. that are embedded within the Video - these are the information that help us understand the content of the video. Video texts can provide a lot of contextual information on the video clips.

In general, there are two types of texts embedded inside video namely, scene texts and artificial texts. Scene texts appear naturally in scenes shot by the cameras. Artificial texts are separately added to video frames (normally in Production Studios) to supplement the visual and audio contents (Lienhart, 1996). Since artificial text is purposefully added, it is usually more structured and closely related to context than a scene text.

The text data in video frames contain useful information for automatic annotation, indexing and summarization of the visual information. Extraction of the text information involves the following processes -

1. Detection of Text Region
2. Localization of Text Region from the detected region
3. Tracking of Text from Localized Region
4. Extraction of Tracked Text
5. Enhancement of the Extracted Text
6. Recognition of the text from the Enhanced Input
7. Post-processing (language dependant) of Recognized Text

This is elaborated in Fig. 1.

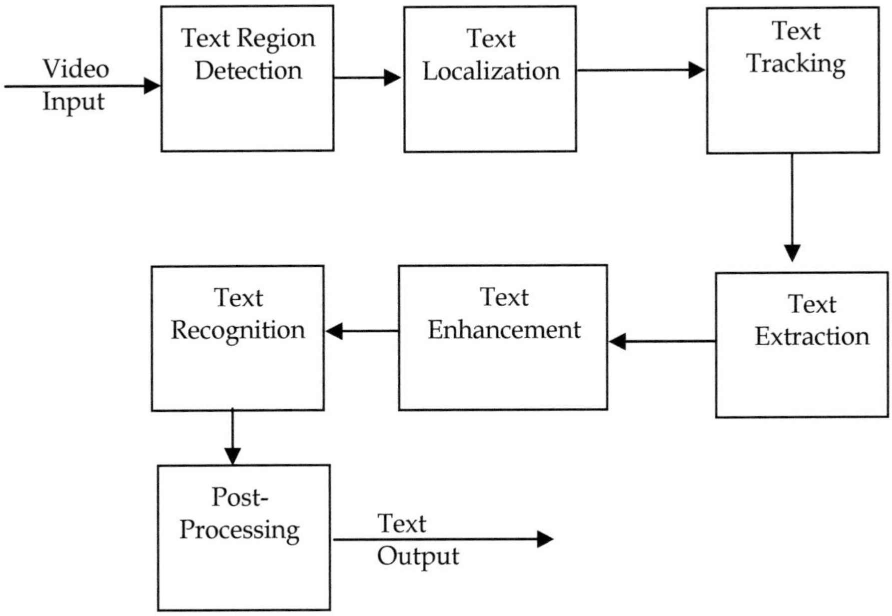

Fig. 1. Flow Diagram of the Character Recognition Process

There are several challenges in the Text Information Extraction from live videos (as compared to standard OCR problem of scanned documents) –

1. Very Low text resolution often affects the reliability of the available Optical Character Recognition (OCR)
2. Text is often embedded on complex background so text separation from background is a difficult task.
3. Text has varying size and font style
4. Text may have touching characters
5. Video has changing contrast and brightness
6. Quality of the Video Signal can vary depending upon the source (Source can be stored media, video broadcast over satellite or cable, video downloaded or streamed from internet etc.)
7. Real-time requirement for extracting text on-the-fly as the Video plays
8. Moving text in the video in form of Tickers (stock, weather, breaking news etc.) poses a challenging Text Tracking problem

To address these challenges, one needs good and robust pre-processing techniques for enhancing the text before passing to standard OCR. Even after good amount of pre-processing, there is no OCR which can give 100% accurate results in the presence of uncontrolled environment. Hence there is a need for post-processing of the OCR output which is then corrected using the help of dictionary, language model and natural language processing in the presence of the extracted context.

Section 2 talks about the Text Localization problem. It first outlines the different formats of the video that can be available as inputs. It then discusses about three different techniques for text localizing -

- Pixel Domain Processing
- Compressed Domain Processing
- Hybrid processing in both domain

Section 3 talks about the Text Tracking problem. Once the candidate text regions are localized, the very next activity should be confirming them as text regions. It can be done by utilizing the fact that text regions would usually be slowly changing compared to video. Two techniques of text tracking are discussed -

- Motion-vector based processing in the compressed domain
- Block Matching method

Section 4 discusses about Video Screen Layout Segmentation problem. Once the text regions are identified, the layout of the video screen is marked. The video background / foreground analysis is done to identify scene texts and artificial texts so that these are marked as separate text segments.

Section 5 talks about Text Pre-processing techniques in the context of video. It mainly talks about three techniques -

- Text Enhancement
- Binarization
- Touching Character Segmentation

Section 6 describes the main Optical Character Recognition techniques. In addition to describing the OCR theory, it also introduces two popular Open-source OCR technologies available - GOCR (GNU Optical Character Recognition) and Tesseract OCR, and gives a comparative analysis of the two.

Section 7 discusses about the Text Post-processing techniques. In particular, it covers three areas -

- Natural Language Processing (NLP) based Spelling Correction
- Dictionary based Spelling Correction
- Language Model based Word Correction

Finally section 8 lists a few applications from real-life that can use Video OCR technique to create compelling use cases for the end user.

2. Text Localization from the video

The format of the video which is the input for the proposed recognition system may be different for different source of origin. The input video may come from a Direct To Home (DTH) service or in form of Radio Frequency (RF) cable. In case DTH, the input video is in MPEG or any other compressed digital video format and on the other hand in case of RF cable feed video, the input is an analog video signal. In the second case initially the video is digitized for further processing. The Text Information Extraction (TIE) module localizes the candidate text regions from the video. The state of the art shows that the approaches for TIE can be classified broadly in two sets of solution: (i) Using pixel domain information when the input video is in raw format and (ii) Using the compressed domain information when the input video is in compressed format. We shall give a brief overview of both type of approaches as the input to the system can also be either raw or compressed depending on the service provider namely RF cable or DTH respectively. A comprehensive survey on TIE is described in the paper (Jung 2004) where all different techniques in the literature between 1994 and 2004 have been discussed. So we shall discuss about the work between 2005 and 2010.

2.1 Using the pixel domain video information

The (Jung, 2004) paper classifies the pixel domain TIE in two classes namely (i) Region based (RB) and (ii) Texture based (TB) approach. TB approach can be classified into two classes namely (i) Connected component based (CC) and (ii) Edge based (EB) approach. But most of the recent works are based on texture based approach or edge based approach. It is also observed that the authors prefer to use different features followed by a classifier to localize text regions. A comprehensive survey on the recent work is presented below.

TB approach: In (Lee 2007) 12 wavelet based features are given as input to some classifier to recognize TIE. In (Shivakumara, 2009) a gradient difference based texture is used to localize the graphics and scene text from the video. Moreover they have applied a novel zero crossing technique that outperforms the projection profile based technique to identify the bounding boxes. In (Shivakumara, ICDAR 2009) authors have used wavelet transform, statistical features and central moments for detection of both graphics and scene text. They have used projection profile and heuristics to reduce the false positives. In (Emmanouilidis, 2009) structure elements are used to localize texts from binarized printed documents. (Y. Jun, 2009) have used local binary patterns to extract text features followed by a polynomial neural network (PNN) for classification. (J. Zhong, 2009) have used a sliding window over the frame to extract hybrid features followed by a SVM classifier to localize text regions. They have used morphological operations and vote mechanism to reduce false positives.

EB approaches: (Ngo, 2005) proposed an approach based on background complexities. They presented an iterative method to remove non textual regions based on edge densities. (M. Anthimopoulos, 2008) have used edge based features with minimum computational complexity to localize the text regions so that there is no false negative. They have used SVM to minimize the false positives in turn. (P. Shivakumara et.al., ICME 2009), (P. Shivakumara, IAPR 2008), (P. Shivakumara, ICPR 2008) have used edge based features and heuristic based filters to localize text regions and applied some geometry based heuristics to reduce the false positives.

Combined feature based approach: (Y. Song, 2009) have used degree of texture rough-detail to localize the candidate text regions and subsequently used Sobel edge operator to minimize the false positives. (S. Yuting, 2008) have used both texture and edge based approach to localize the candidate text regions and then they have applied SVM to segregate background from foreground.

2.2 Using the Compressed domain video information

Though there has been a lot of work done on pixel domain TIE, there is only a little amount of work can be found on TIE when the input is a compressed video. (Gargi et.al., 1999) and (Lim et.al., 2000) use DCT coefficients of I frames and number of Macroblocks (MB) decoded as Intra in a P or B frame for TIE. (Zhong et. al., 1999) uses the horizontal and vertical DCT texture to localize TIE and refine the candidate text regions respectively. (Qian and Liu,

2006) use DCT texture of compressed video to detect TIE. They have considered diagonal edges to handle the Asian Languages like Chinese, Japanese which are not taken care in other papers. They have also used Foreground (FG) background (BG) integrated video text segmentation method to make it robust even in case of complex BG. (Zhong et. al., 2000) also used horizontal and vertical energy computed from the DCT coefficients of MPEG stream for TIE. They have used Morphological operations in post processing. (Xu et al., 2009) used DCT texture followed by a 3x3 median filter in spatial domain for TIE. They have also used some heuristic that the text must reside for at least 2 sec to remove the false positives.
Now the state of the art clearly reveals that a huge amount of research is going on to detect text regions from a streamed video. But the problem with the existing solutions is that they are not considering H.264 as an input video format which is coming to market as a future generation video Codec. Moreover the compressed domain features are more or less based on the texture property of the video. They didn't consider the edge based features that gives good result in pixel domain. Over and above the accuracy of compressed domain approaches are not as accurate as those obtained from pixel domain approach. But the novelty of the compress domain TIE is that they are computationally very efficient. So we have proposed an approach where the text regions are initially localized using compressed domain features of H.264 video and then they are further processed in pixel domain to remove the false positive. As the compressed domain TIE eliminates a huge part of the video at very beginning of the processing, the complexity of the proposed system is also within acceptable range. We are describing the method in brief below.

2.3 Text Localization using Hybrid Approach

2.3.1 Localization of the text region

The input to the proposed system is video. Now the video format may be different for different scenarios. In this paper we have considered all those cases.
In the first case, we assume that the input is coming from DTH and thus the video is in MPEG format. So in this case we have used the text localization module based on the work described by Jain et al.
In the second case we assume that the input is coming from RF cable. In that case we use an AD converter and use the raw video data as input.
In case of PVR enabled boxes where the video can be stored in H.264 format; one H.264 encoder converts the raw input video into compressed H.264 format.
Our proposed methodology is based on the following assumptions derived from observations.

- Text regions have a high contrast
- Texts are aligned horizontally
- Texts have a strong vertical edge with background
- Texts of Breaking news persists in the video for at least 1-2 seconds

Our proposed method is based on the following two features which can be directly obtained from compressed domain H.264 stream during decoding it.

2.3.2 DC component of transformed Luma coefficient based features

In H.264 4x4 Integer transformation is used which is different from the 8x8 DCT transformation of MPEG series video codec.

DC components of the integer transformed luma coefficients is a representative of the original video at a lower resolution. In H.264, unlike previous video codecs, 4x4 block size is used. So it gives the iconic representation of the video more precisely.
The pseudo code of the algorithm in the proposed method is given below:

- Get the Luma DC value (dc_l) for each 4x4 sub block from decoder
- Compute the first order difference ($\partial_x(dc_l)$ and $\partial_y(dc_l)$) of dc_l with neighbouring sub blocks in x and y direction.
- From observation it is found that the difference is very high for a high contrast region. Obtain such $\partial_x(dc_l)$ and $\partial_y(dc_l)$ for different sub-blocks (not including the test sequences)
- Run K-Means algorithm (with K = 2) on them and find the centroid (τ_{dc}) for the high valued cluster.
- If $\partial_x(dc_l)$ or $\partial_y(dc_l)$ is greater than the experimentally obtained threshold value (τ_{dc}) mark that MB as a candidate text in this frame and store this MB number in an array (a_l)

2.3.3 De-blocking filter based feature

Based on our observations on different TV shows containing texts, it is found that the texts are displayed with high contrast difference from the background. As a consequence the texts results in a strong edge at the boundaries of text and background. But in this approach an additional time complexity is required for detecting edges. One of the new features of H.264 which was not there in any previous video CODEC is deblocking (DB) filter. We have used the edge information extracted from the decoder during the process of decoding without computing the edges explicitly.
A conditional filtering is applied to all 4x4 luma block edges of a picture, except for edges at the boundary of the picture and any edges for which the DB filter is disabled by disable_deblocking_filter_idc, as specified in the slice header. This filtering process is performed on a macroblock after the picture construction process prior to DB filter process for the entire decoded picture, with all macroblocks in a picture processed in order of increasing macroblock indices. For each macroblock and each component, vertical edges are filtered first. The process starts with the edge on the left-hand side of the macroblock proceeding through the edges towards the right-hand side of the macroblock in their geometrical order. Then horizontal edges are filtered, starting with the edge on the top of the macroblock proceeding through the edges towards the bottom of the macroblock in their geometrical order.
The pseudo code for selecting candidate frames using this feature is given below:

- Get the strength of DB filter for each MB
- If it is a strong vertical edge Mark that MB as a candidate one

2.3.4 Identifying the Text regions

The pseudo code for removing the non textual part is as bellow:

- For each candidate MB, identify the X and Y coordinate top left position for each MB (c_x and c_y)
- Find the frequency (f_r) of candidate MB in each row.
- Remove all MBs from a_l If f_r <2
- Check for continuity of MBs in each row: For this check the column number (c_x) for candidate MBs in a row.
- If $c_x(i+1) - c_x(i) > 2$ unmark the MB from a_l Where $c_x(i)$ is the column number for i^{th} candidate MB in a particular row
- To ensure that time domain filtering we store one frame into buffer and display the ith frame while decoding the $(i-1)^{th}$ frame.
- Unmark all candidate MBs in i^{th} frame if there is no candidate MB in adjacent $(i-1)^{th}$ frame and $(i+1)^{th}$ frame.
- Finally all marked candidates MBs are decided as Text content in the video.

2.3.5 Morphological closing

Because of the video quality, in V_{cont} the text components are not getting disjoint. Moreover the non textual regions are also coming as noises. So a morphological closing operation is applied on V_{cont} to get a video frame V_{morph}

$$V_{morph} = Dilate(Erode(V_{cont}))$$

In this application we have used a rectangular structural element with dimension of 3x5.

2.3.6 Confirmation of the Text regions using shape feature

This is the method to remove the non textual regions from the video frame based on the observation that text characters are adjacent. The pseudo code for removing the non textual part is as below:

- Run connected component analysis for all $P_c \in V_{morph}$ to split the candidate pixels into n number of components (c_i) where P_c is a pixel in V_{morph}
- Find the area for each c_i
- Remove the components with area smaller or greater than two experimentally obtained threshold values.
- Remove all components for which compactness

  $compactness > 1.0 \; or \; compactness < 0.2$ where

  $$compactness = PixelCount / Area$$

- Find the mode for x and y coordinate of top left and bottom right coordinate (tl_x, tl_y, br_x, br_y) for all remaining components
- Find the threshold (τ) for removing non textual components as
- $\tau = \text{mod}\, e(median(pos_i) - pos_i)$

  Mark all c_i for which $median(pos_i) - pos_i < \tau$ to get a video frame containing only candidate text regions (V_{cand})

2.3.7 Confirmation of the Text regions using Temporal Consistency

This portion of the proposed method is based on the observation that texts of Breaking news persists in the video for at least 1-2 seconds. V_{cand} sometimes contains some noises coming because of some high contrast regions in the video frame satisfying all the shape constraints. But these noises usually come for some isolated frames only. In a typical video sequence with 30 FPS one frame gets displayed for 33 millisecond. So, we ruled out those candidate frames to finally obtain a video frame containing only text regions V_{text}.

2.3.8 Decision making process

The image received in .264 format is decoded by H.264 Decoder and is processed to obtain the localized text. This is done using compressed domain features. The text after getting compressed undergoes text localization processing.

The first step involves computation of vertical and horizontal energy of the sub block based on the assumption that the blocks with text have high energy levels. After we get the information about the sub block, we check which rows contain high vertical and horizontal energy which indicate the presence of text. The regions with lower energy are marked as black after they are checked using a threshold value based on the analysis of the different energy levels in a row. Then we plot a histogram to show the energy levels in a row. With the help of histogram we determine the two major peaks of energy levels. If the graph is not smooth enough we perform mean filtering and obtain the two major peaks. The mid value of the peaks is taken as threshold and the values of the pixel above threshold is set as white and the values below the threshold is set as black. This step is called binarization. Thus we obtain a localized text with shows the regions where the text is located. The image obtained also contains some false positives i.e. noise along with the text detected. Hence, we go for some morphological operations and filtering which enhance the image and give better localization with less false positives. The image obtained is further processed to represent the text regions as white rectangular blocks so as to mark the presence of text.

3. Text Tracking

Once the candidate text regions are localized, the very next activity should be confirming them as text regions. One way to achieve this in a video is using the temporal consistency of text regions. It is observed that if any text region exists in the video, it usually persists for some consecutive frames. Thus there is a need for tracking module that can track the motion of the text.

The text tracking algorithms described in the literature can be classified into two classes based on the type of input video. In case compressed video file as input, Motion Vector (MV) of the compressed video is used to track textual region (TTR). On the other hand if the video comes as a raw file, the authors have suggested different techniques for motion estimation (ME). Some common ME techniques are Minimum Mean Absolute Difference (MMAD) or Sum of Squared Difference (SSD). But the problem with SSD based ME is that they assume only translational motion of text and thus they are not Affine Transformation Invariant in nature. In this section we shall describe each type of TTR algorithms very briefly.

MV based approach: MV of the compressed MPEG video file is used for TTR in the works by (Antani et. al., 1999), (Gllavata et al., 2004) and (Gargi et al., 1999). Here is a brief overview of the approach described by (Gllavata et al., 2004).

They have used normalized motion vector which is derived by dividing the actual motion vector (both x and y component) by the frame distance. Frame distance is the difference between current and reference frame. The tracking is done only if the frame is a frame of type B or P. The new position is computed by adding the mode motion vector of the block where the text resides. Applying motion vectors for text tracking is difficult due to noise factors and the problem of identifying which motion vectors probably describe the text motion and which the background motion.

Block matching methods: Two major block matching techniques are MMAD and SSD.

MMAD: In this method for each block in the current frame the following operations are performed:

- Compute the absolute value of difference (AD) between pixels values of current frame and the reference frame.
- Compute the average of the AD and let it be denoted as MAD
- Compute MAD for all neighbouring blocks within the search window
- Find the minimum of all the MAD and that block with minimum MAD is marked as the candidate matching location
- The euclidian distance in X and Y direction are derived as the distance between them

4. Video Screen Layout Segmentation

Once the candidate text regions are localized, and tracked, the false positives are mostly removed and the candidate text regions are obtained. But within streamed video texts are usually inscribed in different areas. For example in the video frame shown in Fig. 2, eight different regions (R1-R8) can be found containg text information. Now for text in R1 and R5 represents some Breaking news, R2 is a text within a graphics, R3 and R4 gives information about the reporter and reporting venue, R7 gives the details of breaking news, R6 gives the channel logo and text and R8 gives the ticker news.

Now the video page layout segmentation module plays an important role for getting better performance in term of time complexity and as well as for recognition accuracy. For example R5, R6 and R7 are very contiguous text lines and so they are given as a single entry for OCR. Now In R5 text color (FG) is black and background color (BG) is yellow. On the other hand in R7 FG is yellow and BG is black. So the binarization module discards either of the FG as BG when given to OCR. Moreover R6 does not contain any relevant information showing in R5 or R7. So there arises a need for good Video Page Layout segmentation module.

Document page layout segmentation is a very common problem for Document Image Analysis. But the text document layouts are much simple than those of actual videos.

Fig. 2. Presence of text in different segments

We have used a version of XY tree cut method for document page layout segmentation which is based on quantized color space.

5. Text Recognition

5.1 Pre-processing

Once the ROI is defined manually we can directly give this ROI to the recognition module of some OCR engine. But it is found that a lot of blurring and artifacts in the ROI reduces the recognition rate of the OCR. We have used two different algorithms to condition the image before giving it to the input of the OCR.

Interpolating the image to higher resolution and applying Low pass Filter (LPF):

In this method we have done the following steps:

- Apply six tap FIR filter with filter coefficients (1, -5, 20, 20, -5,1) to zoom the ROI two times in height and width
- Apply simple interpolation technique to zoom it further two times in height and width
- Apply DCT on the higher resolution image
- Apply Butter Worth Low Pass Filter to discard the high frequency components
- Apply Inverse DCT to reconstruct the image in higher resolution
- ICA based approach can also produce very good result.

5.2 Binarization

The output of the preprocessed model is then binarized using an adaptive thresholding algorithm. There are several ways to achieve binarization so that the foreground and the background can be separated. However, as both the characters present in the relevant text region as well as the background are not of a fixed gray level value, adaptive thresholding is used in this approach for binarization. To obtain the threshold image, Otsu's method is used in this solution.

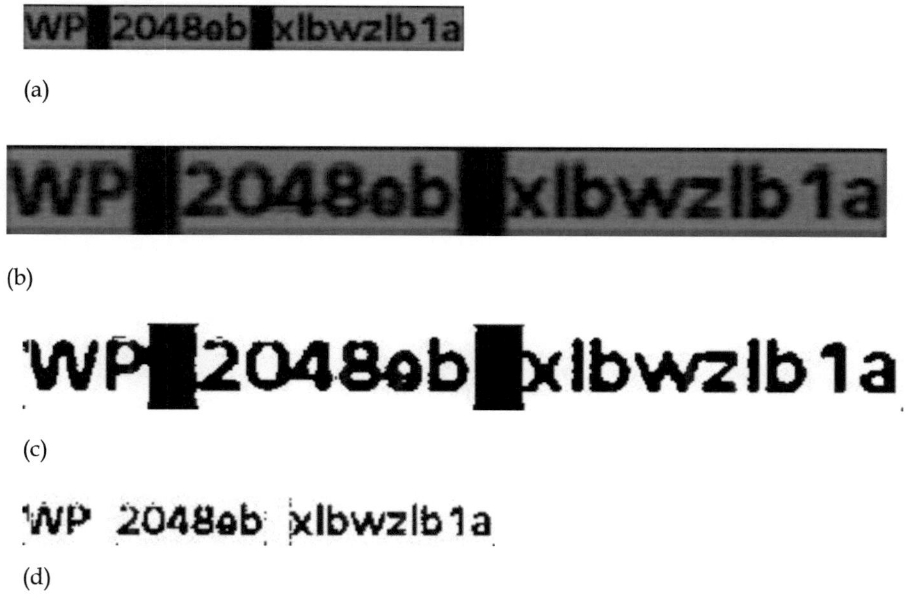

Fig. 3. (a) Original Video (b) After Preprocessing (c) After Binarization (d) After Touching Character segmentation and rescaling

5.3 Touching Character Segmentation

Once the binarized image is obtained very frequently it is observed that the image consists of a number of touching characters. These touching characters degrade the accuracy rate of the OCR. Hence the Touching Character segmentation is required to improve the performance of the OCR. Here is the pseudo code for the same

- Find the width of each character. It is assumed that each connected component with a significant width is a character. Let the character width for the ith component be WC_i
- Find average character width $\mu_{WC} = \frac{1}{n}\sum_{i=1}^{n} WC_i$ where n is the number of character in the ROI
- Find the Standard Deviation of Character Width (σ_{WC}) as $\sigma_{WC} = STDEV(WC_i)$

- Define the threshold of Character Length (T_{WC}) as $T_{WC} = \mu_{WC} + 3\sigma_{WC}$
- If $WC_i > T_{WC}$ mark the ith character as candidate touching character
- The number of touches in i^{th} candidate component is computed as $n_i = \left\lceil \frac{WC_i}{T_{WC}} \right\rceil + 1$
- Divide WC_i in n_i equally spaced segments

Results of each of the above steps are depicted in Fig. 3.

6. Optical Character Recognition

The pre-processed output is fed to standard OCR engines for recognizing the characters. In a video frame there can be texts with different font sizes, different styles, varying intensities with complex background. The adverse effects due to these are taken care in the previous section by pre-processing, where the binarized output is used for the subsequence character recognition operations.

A standard OCR engine consists of the following three stages:

a. Segmentation and creation of bounding box and normalization
b. Feature extraction
c. Classification

A set of training and test data is used to build an OCR. Initially these data is scaled to normalize the size and create a bounding box around each character. The images of the normalized characters are processed to generate characteristics vectors of features that are further used to classify the characters. Some of the basics features used in the OCR analysis are compactness, anisometry, zero crossing etc.

The standard OCR systems are usually used as black-box and don't allow the user for tuning or re-training which leads to a drastic reduction in performance, especially whenever the input to the OCR is not a regular scanned document.

A couple of examples of public domain OCRs are GOCR and Tesseract. These are primarily meant for recognizing texts from the scanned documents. We compare the performance of these OCR engines with and without the pre-processing algorithms. Fig. 4 (a)-(j) shows different images where the text ROI are extracted using text localization and video layout segmentation. These images are then binarized and fed to OCR engines to extract the texts.

A comparison of the accuracy of the extracted texts is shown in Table 1, where it is seen that Tesseract clearly outperforms GOCR. For the image (b), GOCR fails to recognize a single character, whereas Tesseract is able to recognize two words ("SMS" and "56633") correctly. Similar is the case for the image (j) where none of the characters are recognized by GOCR and all the words are recognized by Tesseract.

Further improvement of recognized text is achieved by using the proposed pre-processing algorithms. Table 1 clearly demonstrates the marked improvement of using the pre-processing for the GOCR engine. However, the Tesseract performs much better compared to GOCR, hence we hereby analyze the improvement results obtained with the Tesseract. For image (a), the name "Reema Sen" is recognized correctly after the pre-processing, whereas the names "Govinda" and "Rajpal" failed by one character each. In case of image (b), there is no improvement in the recognized words but it doesn't degrade the performance in recognizing the key information ("SMS" and "56633"). The preposition "to" in image (c) is recognized correctly. In case of small words, the pre-processing clearly improves the performance due to the filtering algorithm in the pre-processing.

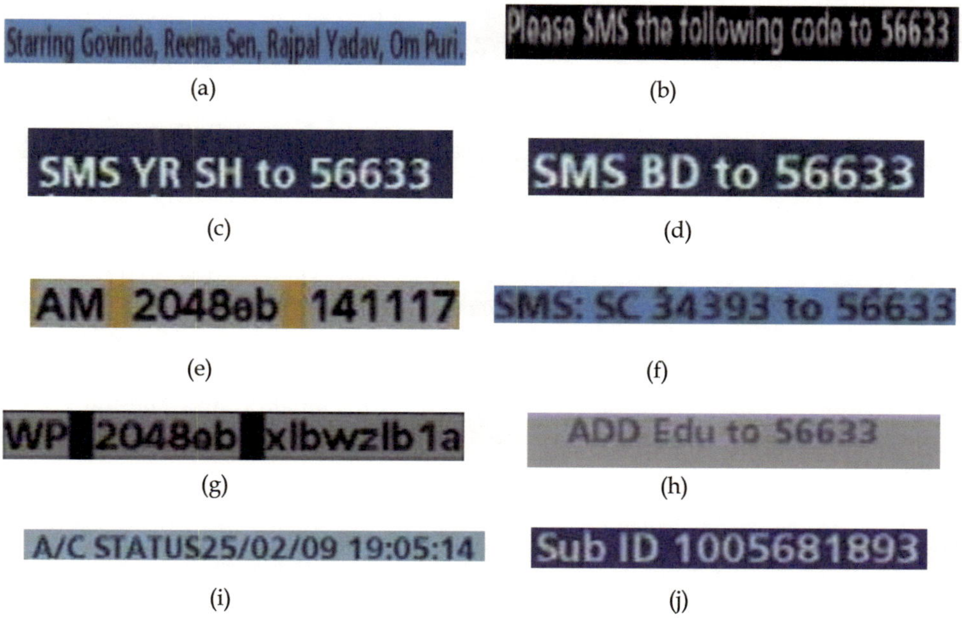

Fig. 4. (a) – (j) Represents different images under consideration.

Image	Output of GOCR	Output of Tesseract	After Applying Proposed Pre-processing Algorithms	
			GOCR	Tesseract
(a)	Sta_ring Govind_. Reem_ _n. RajpaI Yadav. Om Puri.	Starring Guvinda, Rcema Sen, Raipal Yadav, Om Puri.	Starring Govind_. Reem_ _n. RajpaI Yadav. Om Puri.	Starring Guvinda. Reema Sen, Raipal Yadav. Om Puri.
(b)	_____ ___ ___ _________ _____ __ __	Pluww SMS thu fnlluwmg (adn In 56633	___ SMS th_ follcmng cod_ to S__	Planta SMS tha Iullmmng mda tn 56633
(c)	SmS YR SH to	SMS YR SH in 56633	SmS YR SH to _____	SMS YR SH to 56533
(d)	_m_ BD to _____	SMS BD to 56633	SMS BD to S____	SMS BD to 56633
(e)	AM t___o_,_b _q____	AM 2048eb 141117	AM tOa_gb _q____	AM 2048eb 141117

(f)	_M_= _ _A___ to Sd___	SMS: SC 34393 tn 56533	_M_= _ _A___ to Sd___	SMS: SC34393 tn 56633
(g)	_W _' _b _ Ib_lb _a	W6.} 048abl;lbwzIb1a	___ _Y_b yIbw_Ib_a	WP 2048ab Mlbwzlb 1 a
(h)	ADD Ed_J to S____	ADD Eau to $6633	ADD Ed_J to S____	ADD Edu to 56633
(i)	AIC STAIUSIS/OUO_ t_;OS;t_	AIC STATUS25/02/09 1 9:05:1 4	mlC S_ATUSIS/OUO_ t_;OS=tA	A/C STATUS 25/02/09 1 9:05:14
(j)	_ ________'__	Sub ID 1005681893	WbID_OOS_B_B__	Sub ID 1005681893

Table 1. Output of the different OCR engines before and after applying the image pre-processing algorithms

It can be seen from Table 1 that even after the improvement due to pre-processing algorithms, we don't achieve complete recognition of the texts. Thus there is a need for context based post-processing of the OCR output. The output of image (a) can be corrected by using a context based dictionary database of proper nouns, whereas the output of image (b) can be only be corrected using certain high level information and Natural Language Processing (NLP). The preposition error in image (f) can be corrected using Language Models (LM).

7. Text Post-Processing

The output of commercially available OCRs is pretty acceptable for neatly scanned document images with nearly 300 dots per inch resolution. However, in case of streamed videos, the video quality is comparatively very poor; as a consequence the accuracy of OCR is also not very good as seen in Table 1. Hence there is a need for some post processing module like language module based approach, NLP based approach or dictionary based approach to rectify the errors and increase the recognition accuracy. There has been a considerable amount of research done on correcting the words automatically in the output of OCR. A good survey of the research in this area is provided by (Kukich, 1992).

7.1 NLP Based Spelling Correction

Natural language processing is a computer based approach in analyzing and representing texts using a range of computational techniques for achieving human-like language processing. The goals of NLP are primarily to

a. Parse and paraphrase a text
b. Translate to another language
c. Respond to the queries about the text contents
d. Infer from texts

However, the tools of NLP can be used to perform the spelling and word correction using the knowledge of different levels of a language which are also used by humans to gain understanding (Liddy, 2003). The capability of NLP systems too depend on the utilization of the following levels of language:

a. Phonology - This is a study which deals with the inventory and interactions of sounds (Phonetics) in a specific language. This forms the basis for further work in morphology, syntax, discourse etc.
b. Morphology - This deals with the study of formation and structure of words in a language.
c. Lexical - This refers to classes of things or to concepts in a language.
d. Syntactic - This provides the principles and rules for constructing sentences in languages.
e. Semantic - This is a study of meaning in a language.
f. Discourse - This deals with the study of deriving meaning from the connections of multiple sentences.
g. Pragmatic - This is a study which deals with how context contributes to meaning in a language.

Most of the NLPs use the lower levels of processing as these are thoroughly researched and implemented; lower levels deal with smaller units of analysis e.g., morphemes, words and sentences. Some of the major applications of NLP are information retrieval, information extraction, question-answering, summarization and machine translation and dialogue systems. The word level error correction capability of NLP is a powerful tool to improve the accuracy of text extraction compared to a standalone OCR. This can be used to correct articles, prepositions and verbs.

(Pal et al., 2000) proposed OCR error correction in morphologically rich Indian language, where they have shown 84% word correction for a single character error.

(Chodorow et al., 2007) presented a work on detecting errors in preposition for non-native English speakers. They have proposed maximum entropy (ME) model to estimate the probability of prepositions in their local context to detect the errors due to "incorrect selection". The ME combined with Bayesian classifiers improves the precision to 0.88.

Generative probabilistic OCR model is proposed by (Kolak et al., 2003) which is implemented using a weighted finite state model (FSM) framework of AT&T FSM Toolkit. The reduction in word error rate is 70% over the English-on-French for a standard OCR with an overall accuracy of 97%.

(Taghva and Stofsky, 2001) presents the selection of candidate words by using multiple knowledge sources for spelling correction. They proposed a system which has three parts namely, a two level word generator for incorrect words, a confusion generator for longest common subsequence and confusion of words, finally a user interface that allows the user to review the candidate corrections and change accordingly.

Thus we see that NLP plays a very important role in improving the word recognition rate which helps for better understanding of the sentences.

7.2 Dictionary Based Spelling Correction

Spelling correction using dictionary is the most widely used post-processing module for OCR. The most popular commercially available software for the spelling correction in OCR is Abby's Finereader. The video OCR for digital news archives proposed by (Sato et al., 1998) matches the OCR output with the words from the dictionary. A distance measure based on correlation is used to calculate the similarity of the word in OCR output with the dictionary database. They have used two types of dictionary, namely, Oxford Dictionary for general words and database for noun words to accommodate names of people, organization

or places. It is shown that after the dictionary based spelling correction the word recognition rate increased to 65.2% from 48.3%.
(Hauptmann et al., 2002) has demonstrated an increase in accuracy of Information retrieval from broadcast video by using n-gram analysis and dictionary spelling correction on the output of the OCR. The MS word is used to perform the spelling correction. The n-gram post-processing improved the word recognition accuracy by 100% compared to the basic video OCR output.
Sometimes, the post-processing algorithms and the actual OCR are integrated to allow information exchange between the two. (Hanson et al., 1976) reported 2% word error rate and 1% reject rate without using any dictionary.
By using an augmented dictionary and ignoring punctuation, (Sinha and Prasada, 1988) achieved 97% of word recognition with a Viterbi type algorithm.
In the context of text recognition, certain possible way of partitioning a dictionary is proposed by (Sinha, 1990). The word-length, word-envelop and character combination is used for the basis of partitioning the dictionary.
Wherever possible, it is always recommended building a context based dictionary which improves the word recognition rates further compared to a normal dictionary.

7.3 Language Model Based Word Correction

The spelling checkers often used in correcting texts are mostly based on non-word errors. The words which are outside the valid list of words in a particular language are treated as erroneous words. However, there are several types of spelling errors, where the words being part of the language are incorrectly used in the current context. These require recognizing the context and creating a model for the same. *Confusibles* is a class of error, where the words belong to a particular language but are incorrectly used in their local context. Most of the research is done for confusables due to homophony (by, bye or center, centre) and similar spellings (abjure, adjure or founder, flounder). The context sensitive spelling errors are tackled by using a specially trained machine learning classifier for a specific confusable set. Word prediction based on the knowledge of a language is an alternative approach to solve the confusable errors. Language modeling can be used to solve the errors by selecting the best alternative from the confusable sets. Probabilities are assigned to sequences of words in a language model to predict the most likely word in a given context.
Language models used as generic classifiers to build a system that can be generic for all set confusable disambiguation is presented by (Stehouwer et al., 2009).
(Srihari et al., 1983) treats OCR as a black box and performs n-grams analysis on word and/or character level along with character confusion probabilities. They report up to 87% error correction on artificial data while relying on a lexicon for correction.
Several knowledge sources are specific to a particular language can be used to aid the test extraction. (Bansal and Sinha, 2000) proposed integrating several knowledge sources for Devanagari script (for Hindi which is official language of India) in hierarchical manner.
The time dependent language model (TDLM) based on weighted mixture of long-term news scripts and latest scripts as training data is used to improve the correctness of extraction of text information from the broadcast video by (Kobayashi et al., 1998).

Given all the above tools to improve the accuracy of OCR output, one is still far away from achieving 100% accuracy in recognizing the texts especially for the videos generated or captured in an un-controlled environment.

8. Some Real-Life Uses Cases

Character Recognition from Streaming Videos can be used in multitude of applications. In most of the applications, the character recognition technology serves as the means for understanding the context of the Video. Once the context of the video is understood, it can be used create a lot of innovative value-added applications. We list out a few such applications in this section.

8.1 Automatic Classification of Videos for Storage / Retrieval

There are different kinds of programs that are broadcast on TV - News, Sports, Entertainment / Movies etc. It would be of immense help if these videos can be classified automatically based on the content. Possible use cases may include offline recording of TV programs for later analysis and Digital Video Recording (DVR). While each of these videos may have certain underlying properties (Sports Videos are more fast-changing, News Videos contain more static scenes etc.), it is really very difficult to classify the videos reliably in that way. A far more interesting and useful approach lie in trying to detect the texts that are coming embedded inside such videos. Once the texts are detected, the very semantics of the text can give enough clues on the type of the Video. For example detection of a "Breaking News" or Stock Tickers would characterize a News Channel (Fig. 5). Detection of "Score" type text can signify a Sports channel (Fig. 5). Presence of sub-titles can signify a movie channel. Once the videos are classified, it becomes easy to store them with the classification. This in turn results in a faster and easier retrieval mechanism.

Fig. 5. TV screen shots depicting "Stock Ticker" in news channel and "Score" in News Channel

8.2 Advertisement Removal for News Video / Movies

Advertisements can also be characterized by the text embedded in them (Fig. 6). Once they are detected, they can easily be removed during storage. This use case is just an extension of that described in section 8.1, however the end-use objective is slightly different. It should be noted that in order to implement the system in both 8.1 and 8.2, text detection may not be the only technology to be employed – a multi-modal approach of Video Analytics, Audio Analytics and Text Recognition together can provide far better results.

Fig. 6. TV screen shots depicting Advertisement

8.3 Automated Video Indexing for Internet Search

Currently Video Indexing for Search is normally based on File name based indexing. However, texts embedded in the videos can provide far more information about the context of the video. If text recognition engine is run across the complete video, it can yield a set of keywords that best describes the context of the Video (Fig. 7). The complete Search Indexing can be based on these Keywords. Again, this may not be an independent technology, but a complementary one that works hand-in-hand with other Video Indexing Technologies employed to create far more accurate multi-modal implementations.

Fig. 7. TV Video depicting Keyword Texts

8.4 Duplicate News Story Detection

News broadcasts are often accompanied by text tickers that describe the corresponding news event in the video. In applications where video recording is required for multiple TV channels, one can identify duplicate News Stories occurring in multiple channels / repeat broadcasts by just recognizing the accompanying text and comparing the recognized text for duplication (Fig. 8). This is way one can avoid the duplication in recording and save storage space.

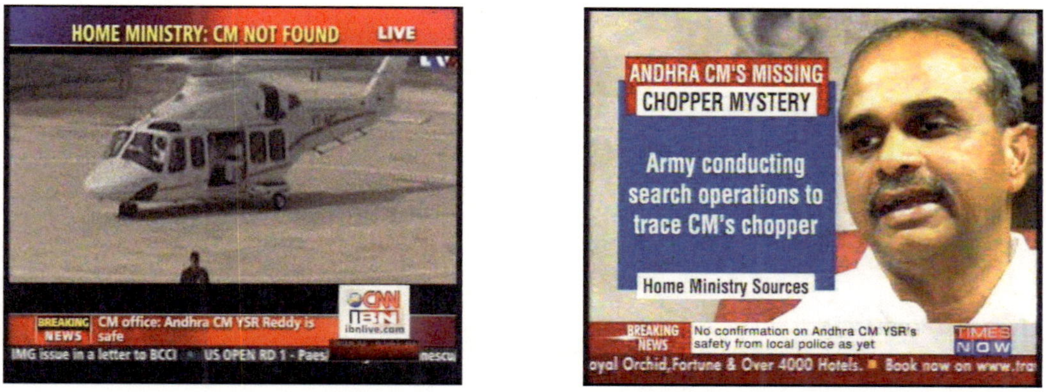

Fig. 8. TV screen shots depicting same texts in two different channel

8.5 Personalized Stock Market Ticker

Normally Stock tickers are embedded into TV broadcast as a continuous stream consisting of all stocks. However, a user may have interest in only a few particular stocks. OCR can be employed in real-time on the stock ticker section of the TV broadcast video and only the stocks of interest can be picked. The picked stock names and their prices can be shown as a separate text overlay ticker on top of the current TV Video (Fig. 9). The Set top Box giving feed to the Television needs to have overlay feature in order to enable this functionality.

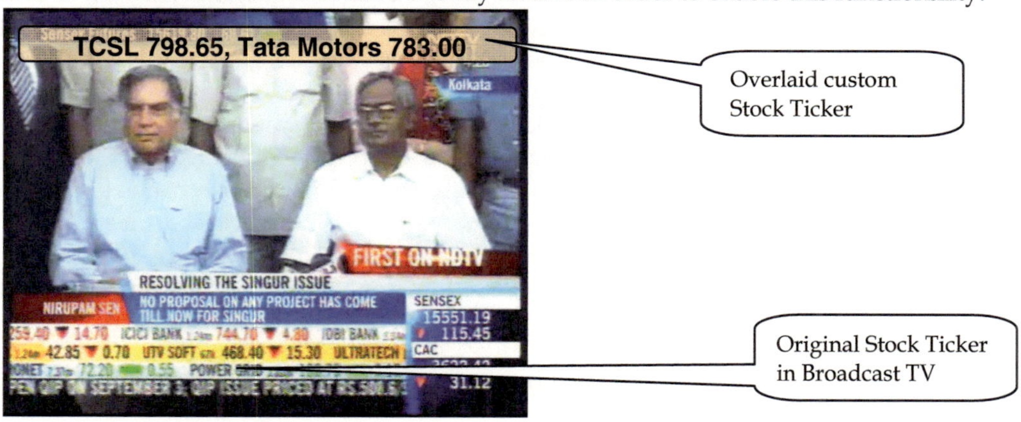

Fig. 9. Intelligent Stock Ticker Overlay on TV

8.6 Personalized Mash-up of Internet News with TV News

As an extension of the same technology described in section 8.5, TV news broadcast that normally has a lot of "Breaking News" text tickers can be a candidate for applying OCR. Once the OCR recognizes the news texts, it can be converted to a set of keywords based on a pre-defined dictionary. These keywords can then be used to fetch related news from Internet by subscribing to different Internet Newsfeed channels. This results in a stream of news information that is contextually related to the news video currently broadcast on TV. The whole process is depicted in Fig. 10. This news information stream can either be overlaid on top of current TV video or can be stored inside the Set top Box for later access by the user.

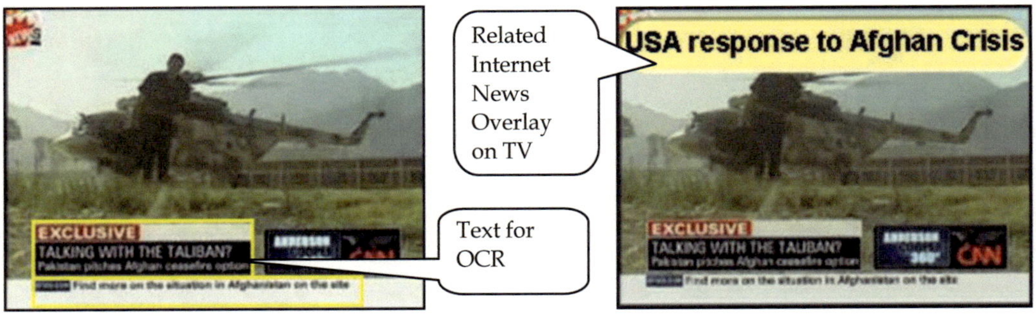

Fig. 10. Intelligent Mash-up of TV News with Internet News

9. References

Alexander G. Hauptmann, Rong Jin, Tobun Dorbin Ng. (2002). Multi-modal Information Retrieval from Broadcast Video using OCR and Speech Recognition, *Joint Conference on Digital Libraries (JCDL '02)*, Portland, OR, pp. 376, July 13-17, 2002

Allen R. Hanson, Edward M. Riseman, and Edward G. Fisher. (1976). Context in word recognition, *Pattern Recognition*, 8:33–45, 1976

C. Emmanouilidis, C. Batsalas, N. Papamarkos. (2009). Development and Evaluation of Text Localization Techniques Based on Structural Texture Features and Neural Classifiers, *Proceedings of 10th International Conference on Document Analysis and Recognition*, pp.1270-1274, 26-29 July 2009

C.-W. Ngo, C.-K. Chan. (2005). Video text detection and segmentation for optical character recognition," Multimedia Systems, vol. 10, No. 3, pp. 261-272, Mar. 2005

Herman Stehouwer, Menno van Zaanen. (2009). Language models for contextual error detection and correction, *Proceedings of the EACL 2009 Workshop on Computational Linguistic Aspects of Grammatical Inference*, pages 41–48, Athens, Greece, 30 March

J. Zhong, W. Jian; S. Yu-Ting. (2009). Text detection in video frames using hybrid features, *Proceedings of International Conference on Machine Learning and Cybernetics*, pp.318-322, 12-15 July 2009

J. Gllavata, R. Ewerth, B. Freisleben. (2004). Tracking Text in MPEG Videos, *Proc. Of ACM*, 2004

Jiangbo Xu; Xiuhua Jiang; Yuxia Wang. (2009). Caption Text Extraction Using DCT Feature in MPEG Compressed Video, *Proceedings of WRI World Congress on Computer Science and Information Engineering*, pp. 431-434, March 31 2009-April 2 2009

K. Jung, K. I. Kim, and A. K. Jain. (2004). Text Information Extraction in Images and Video: A Survey, *Pattern Recognition*, Volume 37, Issue 5, May 2004, Pages 977-997

Karen Kukich. (1992). Techniques for automatically correcting words in text, *ACM Computing Surveys*, 24(4):377–439, December 1992

Kazem Taghva and Eric Stofsky. (2001). OCRSpell: an interactive spelling correction system for OCR errors in text. *IJDAR*, 3(3):125–137, 2001

Kobayashi, Akio Onoe, Kazuo Imai, Toru Ando, Akio. (1998). Time dependent language model for broadcast news transcription and its post-correction, *ICSLP-1998*, paper 0973

Liddy E. D. (2003). Natural Language Processing. In: *Encyclopedia of Library and Information Science*, Editor: Miriam Drake, New York: Marcel Dekker Inc., ISBN: 978-0-8247-2075-9 (hardback) 978-0-8247-2071-1 (electronic)

M. Anthimopoulos, B. Gatos, I. Pratikakis. (2008). A Hybrid System for Text Detection in Video Frames, *Proceedings of The Eighth IAPR International Workshop on Document Analysis Systems*, pp. 286-292, 16-19 Sept. 2008

Martin Chodorow, Joel R. Tetreault and Na-Rae Han. (2007). Detection of Grammatical Errors Involving Prepositions, *Proceedings of the 4th ACL-SIGSEM Workshop on Prepositions*, pages 25–30, Prague, Czech Republic

Okan Kolak, William Byrne, Philip Resnik. (2003). A Generative Probabilistic OCR Model for NLP Applications, *Proceedings of HLT-NAACL*, Main Papers, pp. 55-62, Edmonton, May-June 2003

P. Shivakumara, Q. P. Trung, L. T. Chew. (2009). A Gradient Difference Based Technique for Video Text Detection, *Proceedings of 10th International Conference on Document Analysis and Recognition*, pp. 156-160, 26-29 July 2009

P. Shivakumara, T.Q. Phan, T. C. Lim. (2008). An Efficient Edge Based Technique for Text Detection in Video Frames, *Proceedings of The Eighth IAPR International Workshop on Document Analysis Systems*, pp. 307-314, 16-19 Sept. 2008

P. Shivakumara, T.Q. Phan, T. C. Lim. (2008). Efficient video text detection using edge features, *Proceedings of 19th International Conference on Pattern Recognition*, pp. 1-4, 8-11 Dec. 2008

P. Shivakumara, T.Q. Phan, T. C. Lim. (2009). Video text detection based on filters and edge features, *Proceedings of IEEE International Conference on Multimedia and Expo*, pp. 514-517, June 28 2009-July 3 2009

P. Shivakumara, T.Q. Phan, T. C. Lim. (2009). A Robust Wavelet Transform Based Technique for Video Text Detection, *Proceedings of 10th International Conference on Document Analysis and Recognition*, pp. 1285-1289, 26-29 July 2009

R. Lienhart. (1996). Automatic text recognition for video indexing, *in Proc. ACM Multimedia* Boston, MA, Nov. 1996, pp. 11-20

R. M. K. Sinha. (1990). On partitioning a dictionary for visual text recognition, *Pattern Recognition*, Vol 23, Issue 5, Pages 497-500, 1990

R. M. K. Sinha and Biendra Prasada. (1988). Visual text recognition through contextual processing, *Pattern Recognition*, 21(5):463–479, 1988

Sargur N. Srihari, Jonathan J. Hull, and Ramesh Choudhari. (1983). Integrating diverse knowledge sources in text recognition, *ACM Transactions on Office Information Systems*, 1(1):68–87, January 1983

S. Yu, W. Wenhong. (2009). Text Localization and Detection for News Video, *Proceedings of Second International Conference on Information and Computing Science*, pp. 98-101, 21-22 May 2009

T. Sato, T. Kanade, E. K. Hughes, and M. A. Smith. (1998). Video OCR for digital news archive, in *Proc. IEEE Workshop Content-Based Access Image Video Database*, 1998, pp. 52-60

U. Gargi, S. Antani, and R. Kasturi. (1998). Indexing text events in digital video databases, *Proceedings of 14th Int. Conf. Pattern Recognition*, pp. 916-918, 1998

U. Pal, P. K. Kundu, and B. B. Chaudhuri. (2000). OCR error correction of an inflectional Indian language using morphological parsing, *Journal of Information Science and Engineering*, 16(6):903–922, November 2000

Veena Bansal and R. M. K. Sinha. (2000). Integrating Knowledge Sources in Devanagari Text Recognition System, *IEEE Transactions on Systems, Man and Cybernetics – Part A: Systems and Humans*, Vol. 30, No. 4, July 2000

X. Qian, G. Liu. (2006). Text Detection, Localization and Segmentation in Compressed Videos, *ICASSP*, pp 385-388, 2006

Y. Zhong; H. J. Zhang, A.K. Jain. (1999). Automatic caption localization in compressed video, *Proceedings of International Conference on Image Processing*, pp.96-100, 1999

Y. Su, Z. Ji, X. Song, R. Hua. (2008). Caption text location with combined features using SVM, *Proceedings of 11th IEEE International Conference on Communication Technology*, pp.711-714, 10-12 Nov. 2008

Y. Su, Z. Ji, X. Song, R. Hua. (2008). Caption Text Location with Combined Features for News Videos, *Proceedings of International Workshop on Geoscience and Remote Sensing and Education Technology and Training*, pp. 714-718, 21-22 Dec. 2008

Y.-K. Lim, S.-H. Choi, and S.-W. Lee. (2000). Text extraction in MPEG compressed video for content-based indexing, *Proceedings of Int. Conf. on Pattern Recognit.ion*, pp. 409–412, 2000

Y. Zhong, H. Zhang, and A. K. Jain. (2000). Automatic Caption Localization in Compressed Video, *IEEE Trans. Pattern Analysis and Machine Intelligence*, vol. 22, No. 4, pp. 385-392 Apl. 2000

Y. Jun, H. Lin-Lin, L. H. Xiao. (2009). Neural Network Based Text Detection in Videos Using Local Binary Patterns, *Proceedings of Chinese Conference on Pattern Recognition*, 2009, pp. 1-5, 4-6 Nov. 2009

3

Adaptive Feature Extraction Method for Degraded Character Recognition

Minoru Mori, Minako Sawaki and Junji Yamato
NTT Communication Science Laboratories (NTT Corporation)
Japan

1. Introduction

Most character recognition applications target machine printed and handwritten characters on paper documents. Recently, the recognition of text in videos, web documents, and natural scenes has become an urgent demand; research has intensified because this task is difficult to realize (Antonacopoulos & Hu, 2004; Doermann et al., 2003; Kise & Doermann, 2007; Lienhart & Wernicke, 2002; Lyu et al., 2005; Zhang & Kasturi, 2008). The problems posed by recognizing low quality characters in the above mentioned applications are mainly due to deformation such as the variety of font styles and style effects, as well as image degradation like background noise, blur, and low resolution. A key weakness of most conventional character recognition methods is that they tackle either one problem or the other, not both.

For overcoming image degradation, some methods, e.g. (Ho, 1998; Kopec, 1997; Xu & Nagy, 1999), design templates that reflect the degradation type anticipated. Also a robust discriminant function for recognizing degraded characters was proposed in (Sato, 2000; Sawaki & Hagita, 1998). Unfortunately, these methods are sensitive to shape deformation, since they employ image-based template matching. They fail to effectively handle multiple fonts and several style effects.

On the other hand, geometric features are often used for recognizing multiple fonts. Stroke direction is particularly effective against character deformation (Umeda, 1996). For example, the direction contribution based on stroke run-length is effective (Akiyama & Hagita, 1990; Srihari et al., 1997; Zhu et al., 1997). However, geometric features are not robust against corruption of information due to image degradation. In addition, although geometric features are more robust against deformation than image-based template matching, they are not invariant for deformation such as aspect ratio fluctuation and stroke position shift. Therefore, geometric features are weak against the kinds of deformation that are not present in the training samples.

For overcoming deformation problems mentioned above, nonlinear shape normalized techniques (Tsukumo & Tanaka, 1988; Yamada et al., 1990) have been proposed as a pre-processing method to relocate strokes uniformly. They normalize a pattern by exploiting the distance between strokes (Tsukumo & Tanaka, 1988) and stroke line density (Yamada et al., 1990), and are mainly aimed at the recognition of Kanji characters that consist of many strokes in mostly square patterns. Therefore, applying these methods to the recognition of numerals, alphabets and kana characters, which consist of fewer strokes and are not square shape, is difficult. Also these methods are ineffective for degraded characters with backgrounds noise and blur be-

cause when calculating stroke line density or distance between strokes they basically assume that characters are not degraded.
To reduce the influence caused by image degradation in the recognition based on geometric features, some methods try to compensate for the inaccuracy in the values of discriminant function or geometric feature by assuming the type of degradation and estimating the degree of degradation using local pixel distributions (Mori et al., 2001; Omachi et al., 2000). The method in (Omachi et al., 2000) detects blurred areas using the thinning technique and compensates similarity values in those areas. Another approach (Mori et al., 2001) offsets the feature values using the complexity of pixel distributions. They, however, are counterproductive when the assumption of the degradation type is invalid. This suggests the difficulty of compensating geometric information using local pixel distributions; discriminating noise from the strokes of the character is almost impossible.
To tackle the problems mentioned above, we focus on a category-dependent method with the top-down approach. All category-dependent methods assume the category of an input pattern and adaptively compensates deformation or image degradation by exploiting category-specific information. Category-dependent methods include a shape normalization method that tackles the deformation (Nakagawa et al., 1999; Wakahara & Odaka, 1998). In this chapter we propose a category-dependent method that achieves robustness against both deformation and image degradation (Mori et al., 2005; 2010). Our method estimates the degree of deformation and degradation of the input pattern on the basis of specific information of each category. Exploiting the category information enables us to extract the variation of the aspect ratio and that of the run-length used for computing feature values. The fluctuations in shape and feature values are then offset by the estimated compensation coefficients. To evaluate the proposed method, we apply it to the recognition of video text that is degraded by background noise and blur, and deformed by aspect ratio fluctuations.
The rest of the chapter is organized as follows: Section 2 provides a description of the directional feature and the algorithm of the proposed method. Experimental results gained from video text are reported in Section 3. Section 4 summarizes this chapter.

2. Adaptive Feature Extraction Using Category Information

2.1 Overview

This section describes the geometric feature used and details the algorithm of our method; feature extraction that exploits category-specific information. We use the stroke directional information based on the stroke run-length as the geometric feature. The proposed method tackles deformation and image degradation in two ways. One is adaptive normalization. Adaptive normalization is applied after the classification stage, and yields a normalization size appropriate for the input pattern with fluctuation in aspect ratio by repeating the processes of normalization and classification. The other is feature compensation. Feature compensation is applied to the candidates output by the classification stage, and offsets the feature values corrupted by image degradation to obtain higher recognition accuracy in the final recognition stage. Figure 1 overviews the process flow including the proposed method.

2.2 Directional Feature

Geometric features that extract stroke direction are effective for discriminating multiple fonts. In this chapter we use the stroke directional feature (Akiyama & Hagita, 1990; Srihari et al., 1997; Zhu et al., 1997) that is based on stroke run-length. This feature is extracted as follows:

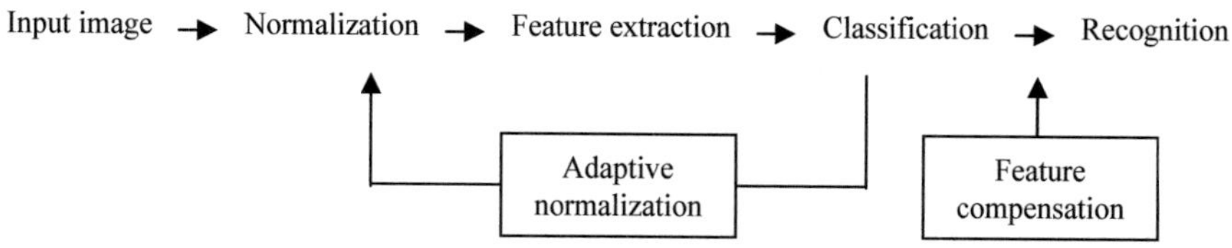

Fig. 1. Overview of processing.

Let l_1, l_2, l_3, and l_4 be the run-lengths on the horizontal, right diagonal, vertical, and left diagonal directions at each black pixel of strokes, respectively. Let $l_{m,i}$ be the run-length yielded by averaging l_i on the m-th block obtained by partitioning a pattern. Let $d_{m,i}$ be the degree of contribution in stroke direction as components of feature vector for the m-th block. $d_{m,i}$ can be computed by the following steps.

Step 1: The input pattern is divided into $N \times N$ blocks.

Step 2: l_i $(i = 1, ..., 4)$ is extracted at each black pixel.

Step 3: $l_{m,i}$ $(m = 1, ..., N \times N)$ is calculated by averaging l_i on each block.

Step 4: $d_{m,i}$ is computed on each block by

$$d_{m,i} = \frac{l_{m,i}}{\sqrt{\sum_{j=1}^{4} {l_{m,j}}^2}}. \quad (1)$$

Here we use $N = 8$. Figure 2 shows each step in the extraction of stroke directional feature from an input pattern.

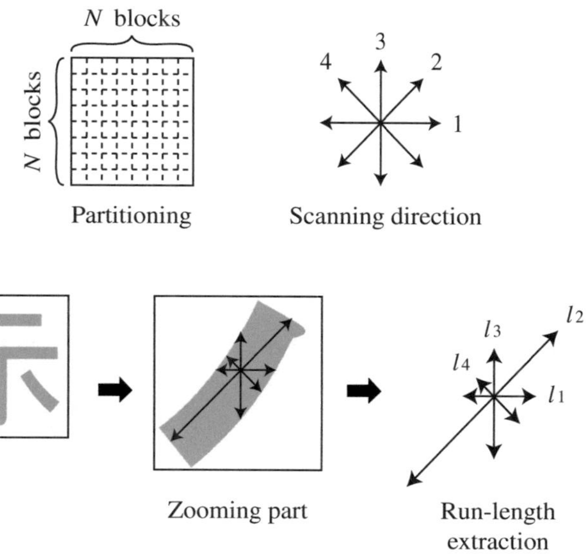

Fig. 2. Directional feature extraction.

2.3 Adaptive Normalization

Characters used in videos or natural scenes come in various fonts and are often deformed when they are superimposed or aligned. The fluctuation in aspect ratio based on these diversities is one of the factors that degrade the recognition accuracy. However Japanese characters contain so many various structures and ratios, that estimating the most appropriate ratio is difficult. The shape normalization to a pre-defined aspect ratio often normalizes a pattern such that it approaches an erroneous category which degrades the recognition accuracy. To normalize a pattern effectively, the shape normalization methods proposed in (Nakagawa et al., 1999; Wakahara & Odaka, 1998) use templates for each category and are effective for normalizing such deformed characters. These methods, however, are too time-consuming because they produce normalized patterns for every each category. Here we propose an adaptive normalization scheme that uses category-specific information; it is simple but effective for compensating aspect ratio fluctuation (Mori et al., 2010). Figure 3 shows the flow of the adaptive normalization scheme.

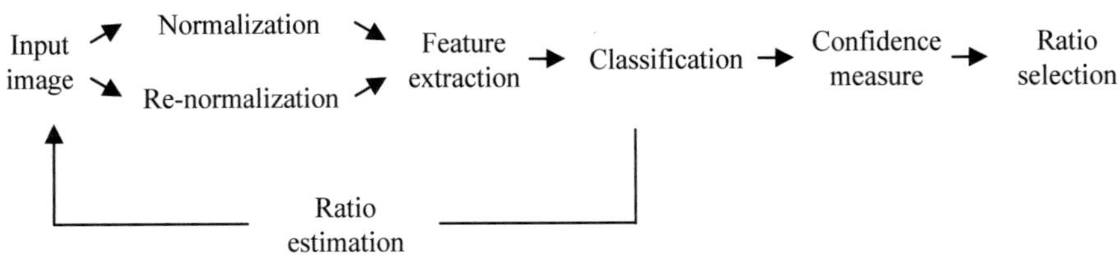

Fig. 3. Flow of adaptive normalization.

Our proposal uses the ratio information of training samples of each category and is applied after the first classification stage as follows: First the input pattern is normalized for the pre-defined size retaining the aspect ratio of the input pattern; Here let r_x^0 and r_y^0 be the horizontal and vertical rectangular size of the input pattern, respectively. Let R be the pre-defined size for pattern normalization, and max(,) be the operation that returns the larger element. The horizontal and vertical rectangular dimensions of the normalized pattern, r_x and r_y, are given by

$$r_x = r_x^0 \cdot R / \max(r_x^0, r_y^0), \tag{2}$$

$$r_y = r_y^0 \cdot R / \max(r_x^0, r_y^0). \tag{3}$$

When $R < \max(r_x^0, r_y^0)$, the input pattern is scaled down so that the longer rectangular size fits pre-defined size R, and otherwise the input pattern is scaled up. Next the normalized pattern is classified and candidate categories are obtained. Let r_x^c and r_y^c be the rectangular sizes for the c-th category obtained by averaging r_x and r_y of training samples in the c-th category, where $c\ (= 1, ..., C)$ denotes the category number. Here we define the new rectangular sizes, r'_x and r'_y, by averaging r_x^c and r_y^c among the top candidates as follows:

$$r'_x = \frac{1}{N1} \sum_{c=1}^{N1} r_x^c, \tag{4}$$

$$r'_y = \frac{1}{N1} \sum_{c=1}^{N1} r_y^c, \tag{5}$$

where $N1$ is the number of the candidate categories used for calculating new rectangular sizes. Finally, the input pattern is re-normalized to fit the size of r'_x and r'_y and re-classified; When $r'_x > r^0_x$, the horizontal rectangular size of the input pattern is enlarged by the factor of r'_x/r^0_x, otherwise shrunk by r'_x/r^0_x times. The new vertical rectangular size is obtained in the same manner. The new candidate categories are obtained by re-classifying the re-normalized pattern.

It should be noted here that when the classification result involves many error candidates, the normalization of input pattern tends to result in an erroneous size or shape. To avoid over-fitting to erroneous sizes and obtain appropriate values, we define the confidence measure, s_{conf}, as follows:

$$s_{conf} = \sum_{c=1}^{N2} dist_1/dist_c, \tag{6}$$

where $dist_c$ is the distances obtained in the classification stage for the c-th candidate category. $N2$ is the number of categories used for calculating the confidence measure. s_{conf} is defined as the summation of the ratio between the 1st candidate's distance and the c-th candidate's one and means the reliability of the classification result. We can select the appropriate normalization pattern using this measure. When s_{conf} obtained using the first normalized pattern is less than that of the re-normalized one, the ratio of the first normalized one is more reliable and so the first normalized pattern is selected as indicating the appropriate rectangular size. Otherwise, the re-normalized pattern is selected. The normalized pattern with the selected aspect ratio is submitted for the following stage.

2.4 Feature Compensation

Feature values extracted from a degraded pattern are often corrupted and cause mis-recognition. To tackle this problem, we introduce a feature compensation technique that estimates the degree of degradation in the input pattern (Mori et al., 2005; 2010). Figure 4 shows the flow of feature compensation technique.

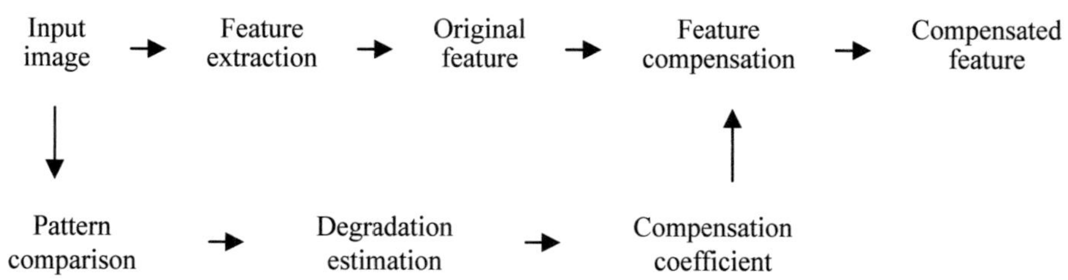

Fig. 4. Flow of feature compensation.

Feature values extracted from parts degraded like background noise or blur and those extracted from strokes are generally combined. In other words, the influence of degradation appears as a weight that depends on the degree of degradation. Therefore, by estimating the degree of degradation, we can acquire the compensation coefficient needed to compensate the degraded feature values. This estimation thus enables us to obtain the most approximate feature vector by compensating the degraded feature vector.

The key to estimating the degree of degradation is using the variation in run-length distribution of the input pattern. The variation of run-length basically depends on the degree of degradation. Therefore, the degree of degradation can be estimated by extracting the degree of variation in run-length distribution of the input pattern. However, as mentioned in Section 1, it is impractical to estimate the variation from just pixel distribution in the input pattern. To realize this estimation, we exploit the template of each category as category-specific information. Comparing the input pattern to the template of each category enables us to calculate the variation of run-length against the focused category.

It should be noted that using a run-length distribution extracted from just one localized region tends to result in failure. The reason is that local parts of different categories often have similar properties, particularly when the input pattern is degraded. Therefore, we estimate the degree of degradation from the total pattern, not just the local regions. Adjusting the local estimation against the global estimation provides an appropriate compensation coefficient for the focused part. In summary, combining local and global estimations, both based on pattern comparison, enables us to extract an approximate feature vector even from strongly degraded characters by compensating the fluctuation in feature values.

As the template of each category, we use the directional stroke run-length. The templates for each category are obtained as follows: The averaged stroke run-length $l_{m,i}$ is calculated using same steps given in Section 2.2. The run-length vectors used as the template for the c-th category, $\bar{l}^c_{m,i}$, are then obtained by averaging $l_{m,i}$ from training samples of the c-th category.

Next we define the degree of degradation as the average of the degree of degradation from blocks obtained by partitioning the input pattern. The degree of degradation on focused block, $p^c_{m,i}$, is calculated as the ratio between the run-length distribution of the input pattern, $l_{m,i}$, and that of the c-th category's template, $\bar{l}^c_{m,i}$, as follows:

$$p^c_{m,i} = \begin{cases} (l_{m,i} - \bar{l}^c_{m,i})/l_{m,i} & \text{if } (l_{m,i} > \bar{l}^c_{m,i}) \\ (\bar{l}^c_{m,i} - l_{m,i})/\bar{l}^c_{m,i} & \text{otherwise.} \end{cases} \tag{7}$$

$p^c_{m,i}$ approaches 1 as the focused block of the input pattern become more degraded or more dissimilar. $p^c_{m,i}$ becomes 0 for the comparison of identical patterns. Also, the degree of degradation over the pattern against the c-th category, g^c, is defined by

$$g^c = \frac{\sum_{m=1}^{N^2} \sum_{i=1}^{4} p^c_{m,i}}{4 \cdot N^2}. \tag{8}$$

g^c approaches 1 as the input pattern become degraded or dissimilar. g^c becomes 0 if we are comparing the identical patterns.

The compensation coefficient is then calculated. First the compensated run-length, $l'_{m,i}$, an indication of the compensation amount, is computed using the above degree of degradation by

$$l'_{m,i} = l_{m,i} \cdot (1 - g^c) + \bar{l}^c_{m,i} \cdot g^c. \tag{9}$$

The compensation coefficient $w^c_{m,i}$ is computed from $l'_{m,i}$ in each block by

$$w^c_{m,i} = (l_{m,i} - l'_{m,i})/(l_{m,i} - \bar{l}^c_{m,i}). \tag{10}$$

Finally, a new feature value against the c-th category, $d^c_{m,i}$, is obtained by compensating $d_{m,i}$ with coefficient $w^c_{m,i}$ as follows:

$$d^c_{m,i} = d_{m,i} \cdot (1 - w^c_{m,i}) + \bar{d}^c_{m,i} \cdot w^c_{m,i} \tag{11}$$

where $\bar{d}^c_{m,i}$ is the mean vector of the c-th category. C feature vectors are obtained by repeating the above procedure for every category and the input pattern is recognized by calculating distances between the vector from the input pattern and the reference vector of each category. Figure 5 shows the flow of the feature extraction and the recognition stage in the proposed method and the conventional one.

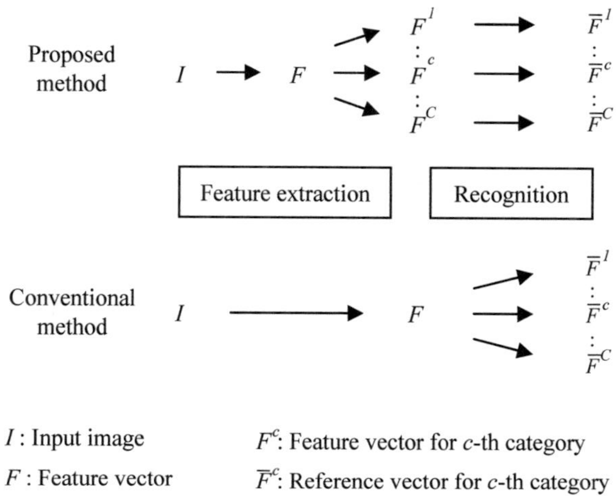

Fig. 5. Flow in feature extraction and recognition.

Figure 6 visualizes the feature values obtained using compensation technique and those of the original feature for the character with background noise. Darker block represents higher contribution strength in each stroke direction. Figure 6 shows that the compensated feature yielded by the proposed method still retains stroke direction while suppressing the influence of background noise.

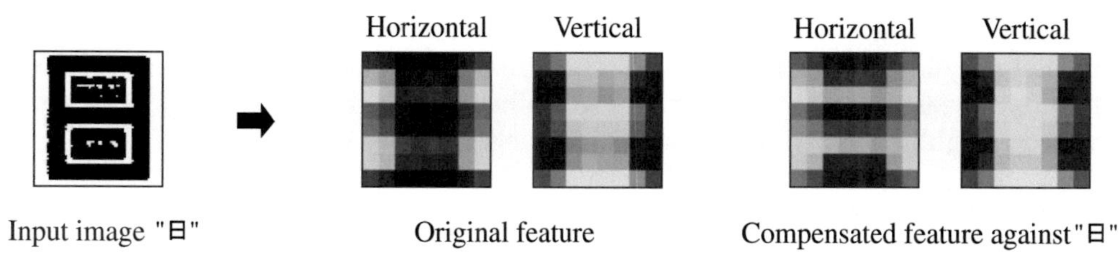

Fig. 6. Examples of feature values.

3. Recognition Experiments

3.1 Data

To confirm the proposed method's robustness against degradation and deformation, we used the characters in videos as the experimental data. Characters extracted from binarized video frames suffer from several types of degradation and deformation; Fluctuation in aspect ratio, background noise, and blur are the main causes of poor recognition accuracy. Ratio fluctuation comes from the variety of fonts used and shape adjustment caused by aligning characters in fixed space when superimposing them. Background noise is caused by misjudging the background region as character region due to similar properties such as color or size. Blur is derived from the low spatial resolution of the image and inappropriate thresholds used in binarizing the video frame. Figure 7 shows typical characters extracted from binarized frames using the method proposed in (Kuwano et al., 1997). Characters with varied aspect ratio are shown on the upper row (a) and characters with background noise or blur are shown on the lower row (b). On the upper low, each value of "Origin. ratio" indicates the original aspect ratio (horizontal size/vertical size) of the each sample, and each value of "Ave. ratio" indicates the averaged aspect ratio of training data mentioned below in each sample's category. These values show that the aspect ratio of these samples are strongly fluctuated.

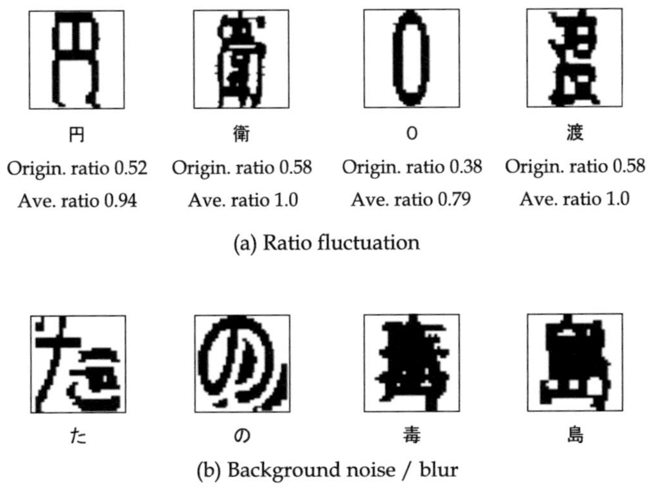

Fig. 7. Characters extracted from video.

We used the following data in the recognition experiments. As the training data set, we used 67 fonts of machine-printed Japanese characters from 3,190 categories. As the test data set, 9,980 samples were selected from samples we gathered; They contained 7,841 clean / ratio-fluctuated / slightly noisy characters and 2,139 noisy / blurred ones.

3.2 Experimental Conditions

Normalization size for each sample was $R = 64$ pixels. Each feature vector consisted of 256 dimensional components (8×8 blocks $\times$ 4 directions). The dictionary was constructed by averaging features from the training samples for each category. The following Euclidean distance was used as the classifier

$$dist^c = \sqrt{\sum_{m=1}^{64} \sum_{i=1}^{4} (d^c_{m,i} - \bar{d}^c_{m,i})^2}. \quad (12)$$

In the adaptive normalization process, the adaptation iteration was set to the 1 time. $N1$ and $N2$ were decided through a preliminary experiment. We used $N1 = 128$ for the aspect ratio estimation and $N2 = 16$ for the recognition confidence measure.

3.3 Experimental Results

First, we compared the adaptive normalization technique to conventional fixed normalization; the input pattern was normalized using a pre-defined aspect ratio. In this chapter we applied the following two normalization flows as conventional techniques; In the first one (Fixed normalization 1), multiply the shorter rectangular length by the normalization parameter, $rt(= 1.0 \sim 1.6)$, so that the input pattern becomes more square. For example, when $r_x^0 < r_y^0$, r_x and r_y are given by

$$r_x = r_x^0 \cdot R / \min(r_x^0 \cdot rt,\ r_y^0), \tag{13}$$

$$r_y = R, \tag{14}$$

where min(,) is the operation that returns the smaller element. When $r_x^0 > r_y^0$, the operation is applied to r_y^0 in the same manner. Normalization with $rt = 1.0$ yields the normalized pattern retaining the original aspect ratio of the input pattern as the standard normalization method. On the other hand, the second conventional method (Fixed normalization 2) normalizes the input pattern to a square shape; the horizontal and vertical lengths of the normalized pattern are R and the aspect ratio is constant at 1.0.

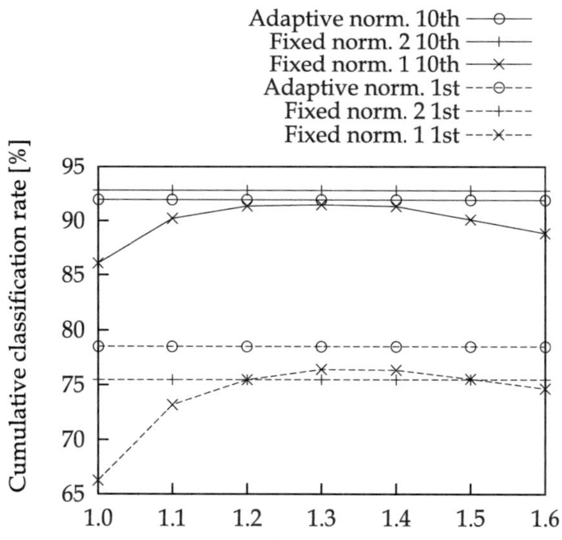

Fig. 8. Classification rates versus normalization parameter

Figure 8 shows the 1st and 10th classification rates of the adaptive normalization method and the two conventional techniques for all test data. The horizontal axis shows the normalization parameter rt for fixed normalization 1. Figure 8 indicates that the adaptive normalization yielded 12.3% better rates for the 1st classification rates and 5.8% better rates for the 10th rates than the standard normalization, $rt = 1.0$. Also the best result of the 1st and 10th classification rates obtained by $rt = 1.3$ in fixed normalization 1 and the 1st classification rate of fixed normalization 2 are lower than that offered by the adaptive normalization. These results show that the proposed adaptive normalization accurately estimates and determines the rectangular

sizes for each input pattern in the presence of aspect ratio fluctuation. On the other hand, the 10th classification rate obtained by the fixed normalization 2 is only slightly higher than that of the proposed adaptive normalization method. From these results, square normalization by fixed normalization 2 seems to offset some degree of the ratio fluctuation in the compulsory normalization method. However, this method deforms patterns of different categories to a similar shape and so degrades the 1st classification rate.
Next, we examined the effectiveness of the proposed feature compensation technique. The conventional method consists of the original directional feature without compensation technique. Adaptive normalization was applied to both features. Figure 9 shows the classification rates of these methods for a data set containing only background noise and blur. The compensated feature achieved about 8% better classification rates than the original one for all candidate orders. In particular, for the top ten candidates, the compensated feature obtained 7.7% higher rates than the original one; that means our proposed method yielded 28% fewer errors than the original one. This result proves that the proposed feature compensation effectively achieves robustness against image degradation such as that caused by background noise and blur.

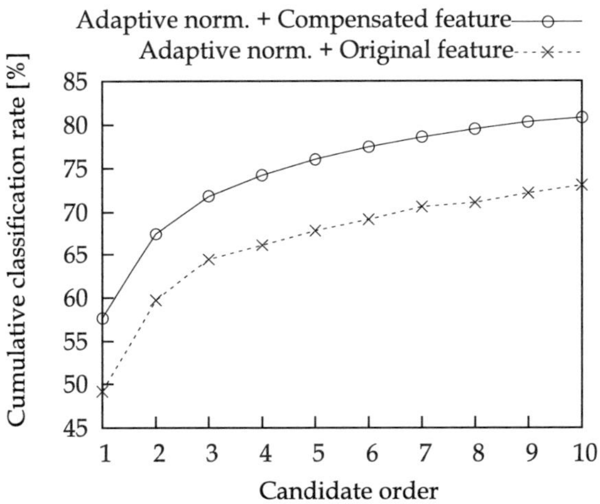

Fig. 9. Classification rates for each feature.

Finally, we evaluated the overall performance of the proposed method using all test data including clean and degraded data. Figure 10 shows the classification rates for each method. We used $rt = 1.0$ in fixed normalization 1 as the standard method retaining the original aspect ratio of the input pattern. Figure 10 shows that adaptive normalization offers significantly higher rates for every candidate order than the normalization method that holds the original aspect ratio of the input pattern. Moreover, the compensated feature yields about 2% higher classification rates than the original one for both fixed and adaptive normalization. This advantage proves that our method can effectively offset the variation in features caused by degradation without lowering the recognition accuracy for clean data. The results shown in Figure 10 mean that our proposed method is effective for both fluctuation of aspect ratio as deformation and background noise and blur as image degradation.

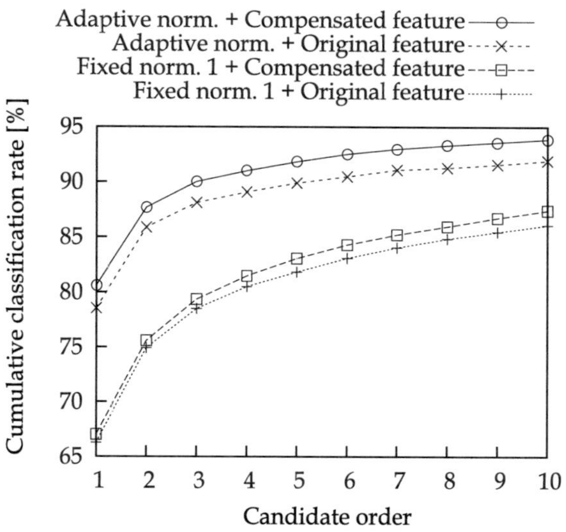

Fig. 10. Classification rates for all test data.

3.4 Discussion

We first evaluated the effect of ratio selection using the confidence measure. Table 1 shows the classification rates with/without the ratio selection. From Table 1, the use of ratio selection raised the recognition accuracy for both 1st and 10th rates. This shows that the proposed confidence measure and ratio selection procedure are effective for avoiding over-fitting to erroneous sizes.

	1st rate	10th rate
With ratio selection	78.53%	91.93%
Without ratio selection	75.20%	90.56%

Table 1. Classification rates with/without ratio selection.

Next, we compared the classification rates obtained by adaptive normalization to those obtained by fixed normalization 1 using ratio selection between $rt = 1.0$ and $rt = 1.3$ to examine the effectiveness of aspect ratio estimation. Table 2 shows the 1st and 10th classification rates for each method. From Table 2, the aspect ratio estimation yielded more appropriate ratios automatically and so raised the recognition accuracy. It should be noted that it's difficult to know parameter $rt = 1.3$ for the best rates in fixed normalization 1 in advance.

	1st rate	10th rate
Adaptive norm.	78.53%	91.93%
Fixed norm. 1 with ratio selection	78.12%	91.34%

Table 2. Classification rates using adaptive normalization and fixed normalization 1 with ratio selection.

Then, we examined the classification rates in repeating the adaptive normalization for validating the effect of the normalization iteration. Figure 11 shows the 1st and 10th classification rates for each iteration with the adaptive normalization. When the iteration time, $N1$, is more than 1, the classification rates for both 1st and 10th are saturated. This result indicates that the adaptive normalization effectively estimates the rectangular sizes but has also limited ratio estimation ability.

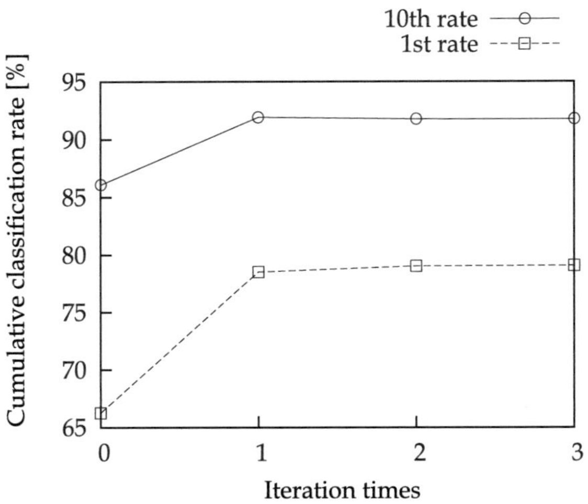

Fig. 11. Classification rates for each iteration time.

Moreover, we compared the CPU run time required for the recognition with adaptive normalization to that with fixed normalization. The system resources and development environment are as follows:

- CPU: Core2 Duo E6600 2.4GHz
- Memory: 1.5GB
- OS: Windows XP
- Language: C/C++

Table 3 shows the CPU run time per sample for each normalization method. The process assessed ran from pattern normalization to classification, and the CPU run time was computed by averaging the time taken to process each sample in the complete test data set. Table 3 shows that adaptive normalization has consumes more CPU run time. The increase is caused by the repetition of feature extraction and classification and the addition of the ratio selection process. However, this increase in time is offset by the increase in recognition accuracy.

	CPU run time
Adaptive normalization	3.13 msec
Fixed normalization	1.97 msec

Table 3. CPU run time with each normalization method.

Figure 12 shows examples recognized correctly by the proposed method which were recognized erroneously by the conventional one (correct result ← erroneous result). Figure 12 (a) shows examples with ratio fluctuation and Figure 12 (b) shows examples with background noise or blur. The upper row in (a) expresses first normalized patterns and their aspect ratios. The lower one in (a) expresses adaptive normalized patterns and their aspect ratios. "Ave. ratio" means the averaged aspect ratio of training data. Those examples show that the proposed normalization method well handles aspect ratio fluctuation and can estimate the most appropriate aspect ratios. With regard to the examples in (b), the proposed method effectively compensated the feature fluctuation, and so suppressed errors.

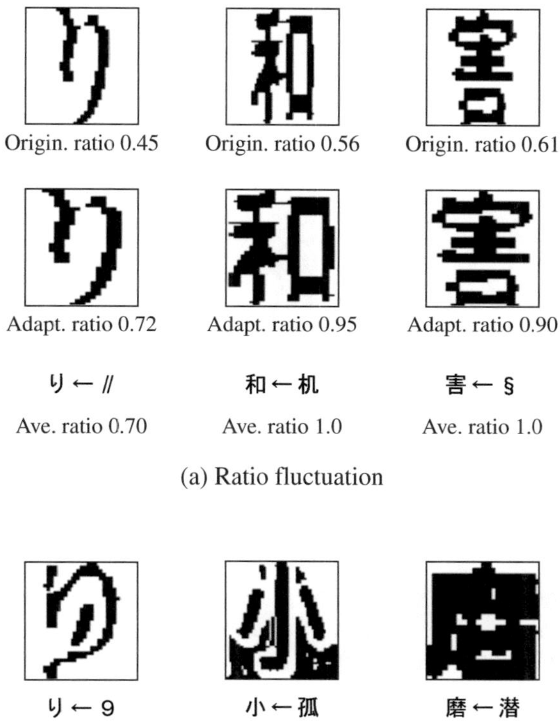

(b) Background noise / blur

Fig. 12. Examples of correct recognition.

Figure 13 shows examples recognized correctly by the original feature that were recognized erroneously by the compensated one for the first candidate (correct category → erroneous result). The errors in (a) are caused by the mis-normalization of the aspect ratio of the input pattern, it approaches erroneous category's ratio, and the failure of ratio selection using the confidence measure. The errors in (b) are caused by the compensation of feature values on the blocks deemed to be strongly degraded.

4. Conclusion

We have proposed a feature extraction method that is based on category-dependent processing for the recognition of characters exhibiting both deformation and degradation. Our

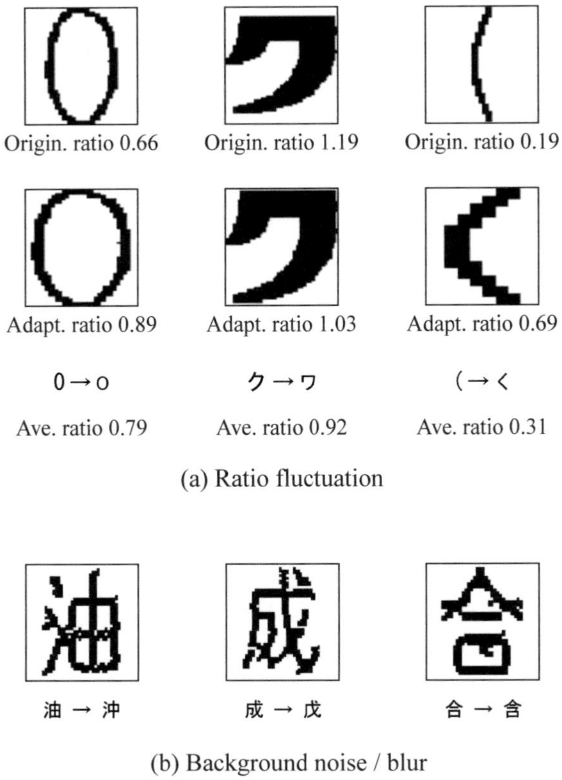

Fig. 13. Examples of mis-recognition.

method estimates the degrees of deformation and degradation of the input pattern by exploiting category-specific information. The estimation realizes adaptive compensation of aspect ratio fluctuations and feature value corruption caused by image degradation. Recognition experiments with video texts exhibiting varying levels of deformation and degradation showed that our method achieves higher classification rates than the conventional method.

5. References

Akiyama, T. & Hagita, N. (1990). Automated entry system for printed documents, *Pattern Recognition* **23**(11): 1141–1154.

Antonacopoulos, A. & Hu, J. (eds) (2004). *Web Document Analysis: Challenges and Opportunities*, World Scientific Press.

Doermann, D., Liang, J. & Li, H. (2003). Progress in camera-based document image analysis, *Proceedings of 7th International Conference on Document Analysis and Recognition*, Vol. 1, pp. 606–616.

Ho, T. (1998). Bootstrapping text recognition from stop words, *Proceedings of 14th International Conference on Pattern Recognition*, Vol. 1, pp. 605–609.

Kise, K. & Doermann, D. (eds) (2007). *Proceedings of 2nd International Workshop on Camera-Based Document Analysis and Recognition*.

Kopec, G. (1997). Supervised template estimation for document image decoding, *IEEE Transactions on Pattern Analysis and Machine Intelligence* **19**(12): 1313–1324.

Kuwano, H., Kurakake, S. & Odaka, K. (1997). Telop character extraction from video data, *Proceedings of Workshop on Document Image Analysis*, pp. 82–88.

Lienhart, R. & Wernicke, A. (2002). Localizing and segmenting text in images and videos, *IEEE Transactions on Circuits and Systems for Video Technology* **12**(4): 256–268.

Lyu, M., Song, J. & Cai, M. (2005). A comprehensive method for multilingual video text detection, localization, and extraction, *IEEE Transactions on Pattern Analysis and Machine Intelligence* **15**(2): 243–255.

Mori, M., Sawaki, M. & Hagita, N. (2005). Video text recognition using category-dependent feature extraction based on feature compensation, *Systems and Computers in Japan* **36**(10): 1–8.

Mori, M., Sawaki, M., Hagita, N., Murase, H. & Mukawa, N. (2001). Robust feature extraction based on run-length compensation for degraded handwritten character recognition, *Proceedings of 6th International Conference on Document Analysis and Recognition*, pp. 650–654.

Mori, M., Sawaki, M. & Yamato, J. (2010). Robust character recognition using adaptive feature extraction method, *IEICE Transactions on Information and Systems* **E93-D**(1): 125–133.

Nakagawa, M., Yanagida, T., & Nagasaki, T. (1999). An off-line character recognition method employing model-dependent pattern normalization by an elastic membrane model, *Proceedings of 5th International Conference on Document Analysis and Recognition*, pp. 495–498.

Omachi, S., Sun, F. & Aso, H. (2000). A noise-adaptive discriminant function and its application to blurred machine-printed kanji recognition, *IEEE Transactions on Pattern Analysis and Machine Intelligence* **22**(3): 314–319.

Sato, A. (2000). A learning method for definite canonicalization based on minimum classification error, *Proceedings of 15th International Conference on Pattern Recognition*, Vol. 2, pp. 199–202.

Sawaki, M. & Hagita, N. (1998). Text-line extraction and character recognition of document headlines with graphical designs using complementary similarity measure, *IEEE Transactions on Pattern Analysis and Machine Intelligence* **20**(10): 1103–1109.

Srihari, S., Hong, T. & Srikantan, G. (1997). Machine-printed japanese document recognition, *Pattern Recognition* **30**(8): 1301–1313.

Tsukumo, J. & Tanaka, H. (1988). Classification of handprinted chinese characters using non-linear normalization and correlation methods, *Proceedings of 9th International Conference on Pattern Recognition*, Vol. 1, pp. 168–171.

Umeda, M. (1996). Advances in recognition methods for handwritten kanji characters, *IEICE Transactions on Information and Systems* **79**(5): 401–410.

Wakahara, T. & Odaka, K. (1998). Adaptive normalization of handwritten characters using global/local affine transformation, *IEEE Transactions on Pattern Analysis and Machine Intelligence* **20**(12): 1332–1341.

Xu, Y. & Nagy, G. (1999). Prototype extraction and adaptive OCR, *IEEE Transactions on Pattern Analysis and Machine Intelligence* **21**(12): 1280–1296.

Yamada, H., Yamamoto, K. & Saito, T. (1990). A nonlinear normalization method for handprinted kanji character recognition – line density equalization, *Pattern Recognition* **23**(9): 1023–1029.

Zhang, J. & Kasturi, R. (2008). Extraction of text objects in video documents: recent progress, *Proceedings of 8th International Workshop on Document Analysis Systems*, pp. 5–17.

Zhu, J., Hong, T. & Hull, J. (1997). Image-based keyword recognition in oriental language document images, *Pattern Recognition* **30**(8): 1293–1300.

4

Hybrid of HMM and Fuzzy Logic for Isolated Handwritten Character Recognition

Azizah Suliman
College of Information Technology
Universiti Tenaga Nasional
Malaysia

1. Introduction

Handwriting is a skill that is personal to individuals. The term "handwriting" is defined to mean as a surface consisting of artificial graphic marks conveying some message through the mark's conventional relation to language (Plamondon & Srihari, 2000). Handwriting recognition is the task of producing the symbolic form, from the stored information of the handwriting data. Handwriting data is captured and stored in its digital format either by scanning the writing on paper or by writing with a special pen on an electronic surface such as a digitizer combined with a liquid crystal display. The two approaches are respectively distinguished as off-line and on-line handwriting. On-line systems for handwriting recognition are available in hand-held computers such as PDAs with acceptable performance (Plamondon & Srihari, 2000). Off-line systems are less accurate than on-line systems due to their less informative data capturing device, which is usually the scanner. However, they are now good enough that they have a significant economic impact in specialized domains such as interpreting handwritten postal addresses on envelopes and reading courtesy amounts on bank cheques (Plamondon & Srihari, 2000).

Comparing the achievements of various researches in this field is quite difficult as the databases and general approaches might differ. Testing done with different databases would give differing results as variations and complexity of the data in the databases are not the same. Similar issues are also with approaches. Approaches would differ in recognition of characters, digits, words, cursive, non-cursive, with or without post-processing. Even though research in the area are extensive many more can be done at not necessarily in improving the percentage of accuracy but also at attempting to reduce complexity of its pre-processing techniques, its classifier, its post-processing and also the need for huge databases for trainings.

In this paper a hybrid approach of recognition is investigated with the fusion of Hidden Markov Model and Fuzzy Logic. The motivation behind this is to incorporate the syntactical nature of a fuzzy logic with the statistical approach of an HMM.

2. Handwritten Character Research

According to (Arica & Yarman-Vural, 2001) in their article that reviews the research of character recognition (CR), the CR systems have evolved in three ages. The early ages are in the period of 1900-1980. The beginning of Optical Character Recognition (OCR) was said to have started with the objective of developing reading machines for the blind. In these early systems of automatic recognition of characters, area of concentrations are either in machine-printed text or upon small set of well-distinguished handwritten text or symbols. Machine printed character recognition at that time used template matching in which an image was compared to a library of images. Statistical classifiers were mainly used for handwritten text, whereby feature vectors which were extracted using low-level image processing techniques on the binary image were fed to it.

In the second period of development in the era of 1980s -1990s, the explosion of information technology has helped a rapid growth in the area of OCR. Structural approaches were introduced in many systems in addition to the statistical methods (Belaid & Haton, 1984; Shridhar & Badreldin, 1985). The CR research was focused basically on the shape recognition techniques without using any semantic information. Although an upper limit in the recognition rate was achieved, it was not sufficient in many practical applications. Reviews of character recognition research and development during this period for off-line can be found in (Mori et.al., 1992) and in (Suen et.al., 1990) for on-line cases.

The 1990s period and onwards are referred as the advancements era, where the real progress in OCR systems is achieved. With the continuous growth in information technologies, new development tools and methodologies are utilized. In the beginning of this period, image processing and pattern recognition techniques were efficiently combined with artificial intelligence (AI) methodologies. Complex algorithms for character recognition systems were developed. With powerful computers and more accurate electronic equipments (e.g. scanners, cameras, and electronic tablets), efficient and modern use of methodologies such as neural networks (NNs), hidden Markov models (HMM), fuzzy set reasoning and natural language processing are possible. In recent systems for machine-printed off-line (Avi-Itzhak et.al., 1995; Bazzi et.al. 1999) and limited vocabulary, user-dependent on-line handwritten characters (Hu et.al., 2000; Meyer, 1995; Plamondon & Srihari, 2000) recognition rate are quite satisfactory for restricted applications. There is, however, still a long way to go in order to reach the ultimate goal of machine simulation of fluent human reading, especially for unconstrained on-line and off-line handwriting (Arica and Yarman-Vural, 2001).

2.1 Methodologies of OCR Systems

The methodologies that will be the topic of focus here are the methodologies of the off-line handwriting recognition. The sequence of approach for most of OCR systems would be to start the process from the pixel level and ending up with a meaningful text. This approach varies a great deal, depending upon the type of CR system and the methodology used. The literature review in the field of OCR indicates that these hierarchical tasks are grouped in the stages of preprocessing, segmentation, representation, training and recognition and postprocessing. In some methods, some of the stages are merged or omitted; in others a feedback mechanism is used to update the output of each stage. The three common alternative structures of word recognition systems are presented in Fig.1.

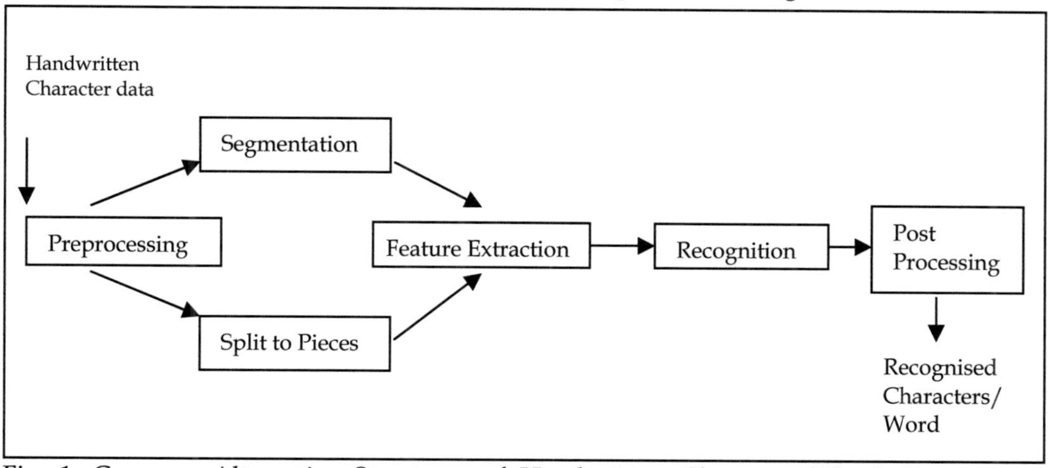

Fig. 1. Common Alternative Structures of Handwritten Characters/Words Recognition Systems

3. The Problem

In constructing systems such as a classifier, in general there are two kinds of information available: numerical information from a measuring instrument and the linguistic information from a human expert. As the problem of handwritten character recognition deals with lots of variations and complexity of data, most of the time to use a purely statistical method would be too risky. In 1965, Zadeh introduced a modified set theory namely known as fuzzy sets (Zadeh, 1965). Fuzzy logic deals with fuzzy sets that classify using unsharp boundaries. Since the data of some of the handwritten characters are sometimes vaguely distinguishable, a fuzzy inference seems to be a very logical way to deal with the recognition. Fuzzy rule-based systems utilize linguistic variables and changing numerical data of an image into its linguistic form can be very challenging. Furthermore one of the major drawbacks of fuzzy logic is the lack of learning capabilities, unlike in neural networks and HMM, where its parameters can be trained. There have been efforts in this area where neuro-fuzzy systems are introduced. HMM has been used in a lot of the handwritten character/word recognition as a classifier of characters/words and as a hybrid approach with other methods (Wierer and Boston, 2007; Gilloux et. al, 1993). In this research project, HMM will instead be use in the preparation of linguistic variables of a fuzzy rule based recogniser.

3.1 The Problem Solution

A HMM model is a very useful tool to be incorporated into a fuzzy logic rule based system. It provides an approach that is compatible to the needs of a fuzzy system. The calculation of probabilities by a statistical model such as HMM provides a solid base for the more syntactical approach of a fuzzy system. HMM yields a more accurate assessment of probabilities for the linguistic variables of a fuzzy system. However the nature of fuzziness in the data captured for the offline handwritten characters recognition research makes a pure statistical approach a little inappropriate. Fuzzy logic has been used in many of the offline researches, giving an impressive result (Bouslama, 1997; Hanmandlu, 2003). There are many ways of using fuzzy classifier into the problem of handwritten character recognition and this paper proposes a method that does not need huge training sets and that is computationally simpler.

Linguistic variables which are considered an important descriptive element in a fuzzy rule based system are prepared and trained by using HMM (Suliman et. al, 2007). Since the linguistic variables are just used at identifying strokes and curves from the input image not much training data will be needed as it would to train the HMM in identifying the strokes that made up the characters. This is in line with the motivation of this research as one of it is to minimize training data. Hence by incorporating HMM and fuzzy logic, it seems to be an idea worth investigating.

In making the research more manageable, the area of concentration is scoped down to the recognition of isolated handwritten lowercase characters. The database used is The IRESTE On/Off (IRONOFF) Dual Handwriting Database, developed by researchers from University of Nantes, France. The IRONOFF database can be obtained by contacting: Christian VIARD-GAUDIN: cviard@ireste.fr).

3.2 The Proposed System Structure

The structure of the whole system is illustrated in Fig. 2. The task of recognizing and classifying the characters from an image file, goes through a few processes as illustrated by the figure. The input image file is preprocessed using minimum preprocessing functions like binarization and thinning. The thinned image will then undergo a feature extraction process of chain-coding.

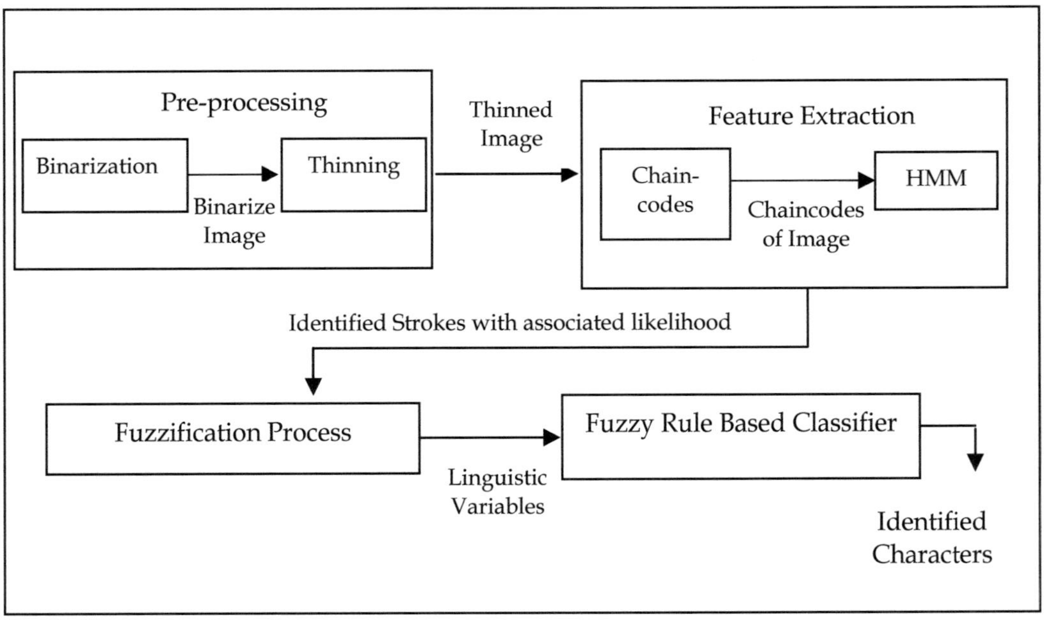

Fig. 2. The System Structure

The chain-coded image kept in a file, is then passed through a Hidden Markov Chain. The HMM will be processing the chain-codes and the output produced would be the identified strokes and its associated log-likelihood. These log-likelihood values are then converted to probabilities and pass through fuzzification process producing meaningful linguistic terms for the variables. The linguistic variables will then be used by a set of fuzzy rules to classify the character accordingly.

4. Hidden Markov Model

HMM is a doubly statistical process with an underlying Markov process that is not directly observable (hidden), but can only be observed through another set of statistical processes that produce the sequence of observed symbols (Rabiner, 1989; Kundu & He, 1991). The HMM is characterized by a finite-state Markov chain and a set of output distributions.

Following are the notations introduced by (Rabiner, 1989). The elements of the first-order HMM for character recognition are formally defined as follows.

i) *N*, the number of states in the model. Even though the states are usually hidden often there are some physical significance attached to the states or to set of states of the models.

ii) *M*, the number of distinct observation symbols per state. The observation symbols correspond to the physical output of the system being modeled. The individual symbols are denoted as $V = \{v_1, v_2, \ldots.. v_m\}$.

iii) The state transition probability distribution $A = \{a_{ij}\}$ where ,

$$a_{ij} = P[q_{i+1} = S_i \mid q_t = S_i], \quad 1 <= i,j <= N$$

iv) The observation symbol probability distribution in state j, $B = \{b_j(k)\}$, where

$$b_j(k) = P\left[v_k \text{ at } t \middle| q_t = S_i\right] \qquad 1 \le j \le N$$

$$1 \le k \le M$$

v) The intial state distribution $\pi = \{ \pi_i\}$, where

$$\pi_i = P[q_1 = S_i], \quad 1 \le i \le N$$

Given appropriate values of N, M, A, B and π, the HMM can be used as a generator to give an observation sequence,

Hence, a model can be denoted by a parameter set λ = (A, B, π).
As according to (Rabiner, 1989), there are three basic problems of interest in an HMM. Problem 1 is the evaluation problem, namely given a model and a sequence of observations, how do we compute the probability that the observed sequence was produced by the model. This problem allows the model that best matches the observation be chosen. Problem 2 is where we attempt to uncover the hidden part of the model, i.e. to find the 'correct' state

sequence. Problem 3 is the one in which we adjust the model parameters so as to best describe how a given observation sequence comes about. The observation sequence used to adjust the model parameters is called a training sequence since it is used to "train" the HMM. The training problem is a crucial one for most applications of HMMs, since it allows us to optimally adapt model parameters to observed training data – i.e. to create best models for real phenomena. This is part of machine learning.

Since our problem would be an evaluation problem whereby, given a model and a sequence of observations, how do we compute the probability that the observed sequence was produced by the model or also viewed as one of scoring how well a given model matches a given observation sequence. In our view point we are considering a case in which we are trying to choose among several competing models, the model which best matches the observations. As such Problem 1 will be of our concern. Problem 3 will also be needed as we need to first train the model parameters to the observed training data. With this we would be incorporating the concept of machine learning into the system. Since the two problems will be used in this research work, both of the solutions to the problem are elaborated below.

<u>Solution to Problem 1</u>

As we wish to calculate the probability of the observation sequence $O = O_1, O_2, \ldots, O_T$ given the model λ, i.e. $P(O \mid \lambda)$, a more efficient procedure to use would be the forward procedure (Kundu and He, 1991). Consider the following forward variable $\alpha_t(i)$ defined as

$$\alpha_t(i) = P(O_1 O_2 \ldots O_t, q_t = S_t \mid \lambda),$$

$\alpha_t(i)$ may then be solved inductively as follows ,

1. Initialization,

$$\alpha_1(i) = \pi_i b_i(O_1), \qquad 1 \le i \le N$$

2. Induction :

$$\alpha_{i+1}(j) = \left[\sum_{i=t}^{N} \alpha_t(i) a_{ij} \right] b_i(O_{t+1}), \qquad 1 \le t \le T-1$$

$$1 \le j \le N$$

3. Termination :

$$P(O \mid \lambda) = \sum_{i=1}^{N} \alpha_T(i),$$

In modelling the problem to an HMM, the observation sequence would be the extracted chain-codes of the hand-written characters images. The chain codes will then be fed to the appropriate HMM of strokes to be identified. The codes will be 'churned' by the HMM and as a result strokes will be identified together with its associated probabilities. The strokes as identified will go through a fuzzification algorithm that will change it to linguistic variables which will then be utilized by a fuzzy classifier.

Solution to Problem 3

The third problem is the most difficult as it is to determine a method to adjust the model parameters (A, B, π) to maximize the probability of the observation sequence given the model. There is no known way to analytically solve for the model which maximizes the probability of the observation sequence. However we can choose λ = (A, B, π) such that P(O| λ) is locally maximized using an iterative procedure such as Baum-Welch method or equivalent. Here the iterative procedure of Baum-Welch will be discussed as a solution for problem 3.

To implement the solution we will first need to define the variable $\gamma_t(i)$ the probability of being in state S_i at time t and then define $\xi_t(i,j)$ the probability of being in state S_i at time t and state S_j at time *t+1*, given the model and the observation sequence, i.e.:

$$\gamma_t(i) = P(q_t = S_i \mid O,\lambda) = \frac{\alpha_t(i)\beta_t(i)}{P(O\mid\lambda)}$$

$$\xi_t(i,j) = P(q_t = S_i, q_{t+1} = S_j \mid O,\lambda) = \frac{\alpha_t(i)a_{ij}b_j(O_{t+1})\beta_{t+1}(j)}{P(O\mid\lambda)}$$

Now we have,

$$\sum_{t=1}^{T-1} \xi_t(i,j) = \text{expected number of transition made (from } S_i \text{ to } S_j\text{)}$$

$$\sum_{t=1}^{T-1} \gamma_t(i) = \text{expected number of transition from } S_i.$$

The Baum-Welch re-estimation formulas for *A,B* and π are

$$\bar{\pi}_i = \gamma_1(i)$$

$$\bar{a}_{ij} = \frac{\sum_{t=1}^{T-1} \xi_t(i,j)}{\sum_{t=1}^{T-1} \gamma_t(i)}$$

$$\bar{b}_j(k) = \frac{\sum_{t=1,\ s.t.O_t=v_k}^{T} \gamma_t(j)}{\sum_{t=1}^{T} \gamma_t(j)}$$

Iterative application of these formulas will converge to a local maxima of $P(O\mid\lambda)$.

5. Fuzzy Logic

Fuzzy logic refers to all of the theories and technologies that employ fuzzy sets, which are classes with unsharp boundaries. Not as in a classical set theory, the concept in fuzzy sets does not have a well defined natural boundary. A representation of the concept closer to human interpretation is to allow a gradual transition. In order to achieve this, the notion of membership in a set needs to become a matter of degree. This is the essence of fuzzy sets.

A fuzzy logic system would usually consist of the following:

a) A fuzzification unit which maps the measured inputs, which might be in the form of crisp values, into the fuzzy linguistic values used by the fuzzy reasoning mechanism.

b) A knowledge based which is the collection of the expert control rules (knowledge) needed to achieve the control goal.

c) A fuzzy reasoning mechanism which performs various fuzzy logic operations to infer the control action for the given fuzzy inputs.

d) A defuzzification unit which converts the inferred fuzzy control action into the required crisp control value.

In this research it is to the first part of the fuzzy logic system that an HMM Model is introduced to. The fuzzy linguistic values are extracted and quantified by an HMM Model. As previously mentioned, the extracted chain-codes of the hand-written character images will then be fed to a few HMM models of strokes to be identified. As a result, strokes will be identified together with its associated log likelihoods which may in turn be used derive to probabilities. The strokes as identified will go through a fuzzification algorithm that will change it to linguistic variables which will then be utilized by a set of fuzzy rules to determine the class of the character.

6. The Pre-processing Phase

The raw data of handwritten characters, no matter how it is acquired, will be subjected to a number of preprocessing steps to make it useable. The preprocessing phase aims to extract the relevant textual parts and prepares them for segmentation and recognition. The main objectives of preprocessing are i) noise reduction, (ii) normalization of data and (iii) compression in the amount of information to be retained. In noise reduction alone there are hundreds of available techniques which can be categorized into three major groups of filtering, morphological operations and noise modelling (Serra, 1994; Sonka & Boyle, 1999). Filters can be designed for smoothing (Legault & Suen, 1997), sharpening (Leu, 2000), thresholding (Solihin & Leedham, 1999), removing slightly textured background (Lee & Fan, 2000) and contrast adjustment process (Polesel et. al., 1997). Various morphological operations can be designed to connect broken strokes (Atici & Yarman-Vural, 2001), decomposed the connected strokes (Chen et. al., 1994), smooth the contours, prune the wild points, thin the characters (Reinhardt & Higgins, 1996), and extract boundaries (Yang & Li, 1995).

In this research work a minimal number of preprocessing processes are used. The preprocessing steps are shown in Fig. 3. An image file of handwritten character will first be read and binarized. Then reference line of upper and lower base line of the character will be estimated. The estimation of the upper and lower base line will be used to classify the characters into its three groups of either ascenders (e.g. *h, l, t, f, d, b*), descenders (e.g. *g, p, q, y*) or neither (e.g. *a, c, e, i, m, n* etc.) . The subsequent sections will explained further the pre-processing phase undertaken in this research.

Pre-processing Steps	
Step 1:	Binarize the character image. Input: An image file of the character in .bmp format Results: A matrix of the character image in 0's (for background) and 1's (for the foreground that makes up the character contour).
Step 2:	Estimate Reference Line to classify the three groups of characters (ascenders, descenders, neither). Input: The character matrix from Step 1. Results: A classification of the character into its 3 groups. To be used as one of the character features in the fuzzy inference system.
Step 3:	Thinned the image into edges of one pixel thick. Input: The character matrix from Step 1. Results: A character matrix with all (or at least most of) its edges with one pixel thickness only.

Fig. 3. Pre-processing Steps

6.1 Binarization

When an image is captured, it is stored in the form of pixel density value, which means each pixel has the value of a 0-255 (for a gray scaled image). Many researchers choose to work with a binarize image where all the grey value will be threshold and converted to either 0 for white (background) and 1 for black (foreground). This process is known as binarization.
The method used to binarize is known as thresholding. In thresholding, the gray-scale or color images are represented as binary images by picking a threshold value. The two categories of thresholding are global and local thersholding. In global thresholding, one threshold value is used for the entire document image which is often based on an estimation of the background intensity level with that of the image using an intensity histogram (Chen et. al., 1994). Local or adaptive thresholding use different values for each pixel according to the local area information (Saula & Pietikainen, 2000). Local thresholding is commonly used in works that involve images that are of varying level of intensities, such as pictures from satellites cameras or medical scanned images. For simple images like handwriting, where the characters are written on a white background, using a global threshold would suffice to distinguish the background and the foreground. Fig. 4 displays an image of the character 'e' in its image file format of .bmp and the same character after it had been binaries and save in a text (.txt) file.

```
000000000011111111000000000
000000000111111111100000000
000000001111111111100000000
000000001111100111110000000
0000000111100000001110000000
0000000111000000001110000000
0000001110000000001110000000
0000001110000000011100000000
0000001110000000011100000000
0000001111000000111000000000
0000001111000011110000000000
0000000111111111100000000000
0000001111111111100000000000
0111111111111111000000000000
0111111111111110000000000000
0010111111111000000000000000
0000000111110000000000000000
0000000011110000000000000000
0000000011111000000000000000
0000000001111100000000000000
0000000000111110000000000000
0000000000011111000000000000
0000000000011111100000000000
00000000000011111111000000111
0000000000000111111111111111
00000000000000011111111111110
```

Fig. 4. The character "e" in its image file format (.bmp) and in its binarize text file format

6.2 Reference Line Estimation

One preprocessing technique that has been particularly helpful in determining features in a word is reference line estimation. (Bozinovic & Srihari, 1989) referred to it as, the task of locating such lines as the lower line, lower baseline, upper baseline and the upper line. To determine these lines, an approach based on that proposed by (Bozinovic & Srihari, 1989) is considered. The approach however was for a word image and in such images the reference lines are more distinguishable as the input are larger.

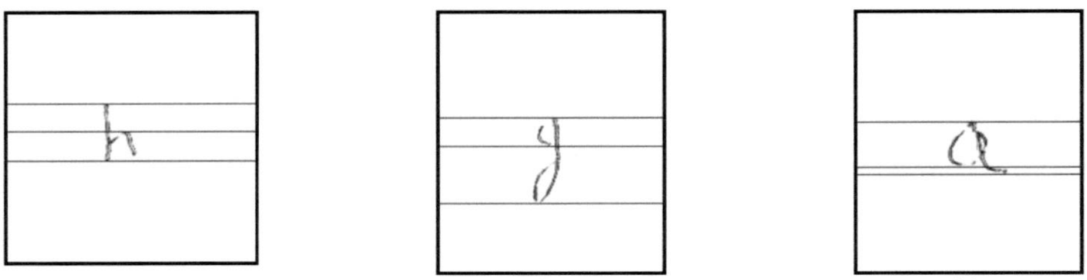

(a) (b) (c)

Fig. 5. Examples of characters after line referencing (a) an ascender, (b) a descender, and (c) neither an ascender nor descender.

With a little improvisation the similar approach was implemented for character image. Examples of the line referencing used in this research are shown in Fig. 5. The first step would be to generate a horizontal density histogram for the character image. This was done based on a black pixel count in each row (horizontal direction at each position on the y-axis). From the top, the first row count that have more than a minimum threshold (in this case a pixel count of 2 is used) and an upper line is found. Next, traversing from the bottom of the image or the last row in the image, the first row count that is more than the minimum threshold would indicate the lower line. Estimating the middle line is slightly more complex. First we have to access roughly if the image is denser in lower or the upper zone. This is estimated by first determining the mid line, i.e. the average of upper line and lower line. Then the pixels density of the upper and the lower zones are calculated. If the upper zone is denser then we start traversing from the mid line to the upper line, otherwise we traverse from the mid line to the lower baseline. Taking a threshold T, that is the average density of the character, we scan through density vector and the first line that have a density value that is lower than T, would be consider as the middle line. The middle line produced was a better option than the mid line gotten from the average of the lower and the upper lines. This estimate of the middle line was favourable enough for the next step.

```
Gap1 = upper line - middle line
Gap2 = middle line - lower line

If Gap1 is small or Gap2 is small
    Alphabet is Neither
else
  if density in upper zone > density in lower zone
          Alphabet is Descender
Else
          Alphabet is Ascender
```

Fig. 6. Algorithm for grouping characters

Once the upper, middle and lower lines had been placed, the character will be heuristically categorized into an ascender, a descender or neither. The algorithm for the simple heuristic technique used in the research is given Fig. 6. The grouping of the characters into the 3 groups are utilized directly by the recognition phase and if grouped correctly it would have scoped down the classification phase from the 26 possibilities (26 alphabets of a .. z) to about a third lesser of possibilities.

The heuristic technique was compared to an HMM model created to group the character using the vertical density of the image. Relying on the fact that some of the characters in a certain group would be denser in the upper zone than the lower zone and so on, the result of the grouping using the heuristic method is given in Table 1. The heuristic technique yield a correct grouping rate of 70.35% while the HMM technique yields a correct grouping rate of 64.3%.

	Classified group			
Actual Group	*Neither*	*Ascenders*	*Descenders*	*Total*
Neither	***94.39***	*3.57*	*2.04*	*100.0*
Ascender	*21.43*	***63.09***	*15.48*	*100.0*
Descenders	*27.38*	*19.05*	***53.57***	*100.0*

Table 1. Confusion matrix of the three groups of characters

6.3 Thinning

There are a number of algorithms available for the thinning process. Thinning algorithms has to satisfy among others the following two constraints:

- Connectivity must be maintained at each iteration. Removal of border pixels must not cause discontinuities.
- The end of the thinned shape limbs must not be shorten.

Since the image of handwritten words are relatively small and less elaborate and less convex than an image of other objects, a slightly simpler version of a thinning algorithm would suffice. The thinning process used in this research is a one pass thinning algorithm that has been slightly modified to ensure connectivity and at the same time to repair any repairable discontinuities. An example of a binarize image of the same character 'e' as in Fig. 4, which is before thinning procedure, is shown in Fig. 6 after it had been thinned. The chain-coded version of the same 'e' is in Fig. 7 and will be explained in the next section.

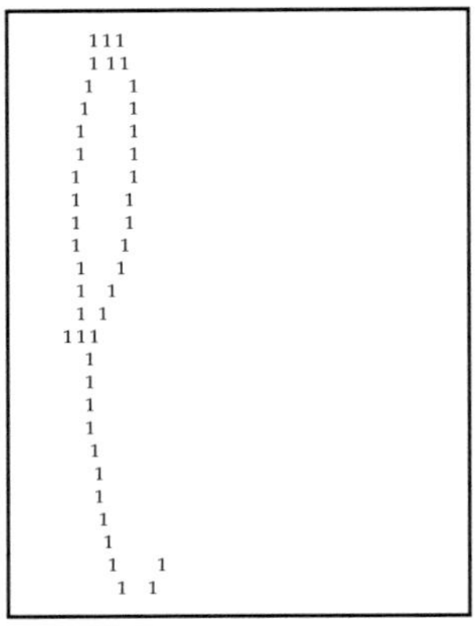

Fig. 6. A thinned binarize image of 'e'

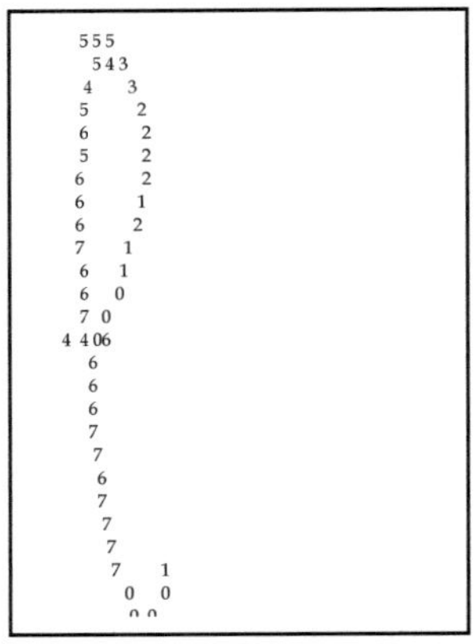

Fig. 7. An image of chain-coded "e"

With the process of thinning where pixels are removed, sometimes the image can get broken or disjointed. To cater for such cases, images that had been thinned will be passed through a special function that would check and repair simple disjointed edge that was caused by thinning.

7. The Feature Extraction Phase

The feature extraction phase in a handwriting recognition system is agreed by many (Suen, 1986; Impedovo et. al., 1991; Arica & Yarman-Vural, 2001) to hold a very important role. Feature extraction can be defined as the process of extracting distinctive information from the matrices of digitized characters. In OCR applications it is important to extract those features that will enable the system to discriminate between all the character classes that exist. A suggested reading on the survey of feature extraction methods for handwriting recognition would be (Oh et. al. 1999).

Geometrical and topological representation is one of the many feature extraction methods used in the OCR research. This method has proven to be the most popular feature extraction method amongst researchers (Blumstein & Verma, 1999). This type of representation is able to encode some knowledge about the structure of the object or may provide some knowledge as to what sort of components make up that object. There are hundreds of topological and geometrical representations than can be grouped to a few categories (Arica & Yarman-Vural, 2001).

One popular category in geometrical and topological representation of features is by extracting and counting topological structures. Common primitive structures that are searched from a character or word image are strokes which may be as simple as lines and arcs or as complex as curves and splines. Characters and words can be successfully represented by extracting and counting many topological features such as the extreme points, maxima and minima, cusps above and below a threshold, openings, cross points (x), branch points (T), line ends, loops and many more (Madhvanath & Govindaraju 1999; Madhvanath et. al., 1999).

Coding is a category where the strokes of the character are mapped into chain-codes. One of the most popular coding schemes is Freeman's chain code (Freeman, 1974) even though there are many versions of chain coding. Fig. 9. shows a directional guide of a Freeman Code. The following section will discuss the process of chain coding as used in this research work.

Once the image has been pre-processed and chain-codes of the character to be classified had been stored, it is now ready for the feature extraction phase. The feature extraction phase is just as important as the classification phase. In this research work the feature extracted will be used solely as the input for the classification phase. This component is regarded as very important because the focal point of the research lies in the success of the features extracted. Fig. 8 gives an account of the steps in the feature extraction phase.

Feature Extraction Steps	
Step 1:	Decode the one-pixel thinned image into chain codes using the Freeman code of directions.
Step 2:	Examine the segments of chain codes that made up the character, to decide which HMM Models to call.
Step 3:	Call the appropriate HMM Models for the segments. This will produce log-likelihood values of the strokes identified. Take the possibilities of all strokes that are above its lower threshold value.
Step 4:	Change the log-likelihood values of the strokes into numbers between 0 to 1 to reflect the probability values.

Fig. 8. Feature Extraction Steps

7.1 Chain coding

The one-dimensional model of the image is obtained by tracing the contour edges of the character image and representing the path by Freeman chain codes. The objective of the edge tracing would be to get chain codes that would traverse an image of a handwritten character as naturally as it would as it was written. The challenge of the chain-coding process would lies very much on the way the image would be traverse and the starting point of the traversing method. A same image will produce a different chain-code if it starts from a different point or traverse in a different direction. Consistency is required in order to minimize variations in chain-codes of the same character.

The image is traversed using the connected component analysis algorithm. It then performs a traversal of the skeleton, segmenting it into strokes separated by points that have one or more than three neighbours (since these points are either endpoints or junctions where different strokes meet). The general steps followed in traversing the image are given in Fig. 10. The algorithm is implemented as a recursive function in C codes. It will traverse a body of connected components recursively and return to the calling function once all the pixels in the connected component have been cleared. It will be called again if there are still connected components left in the image.

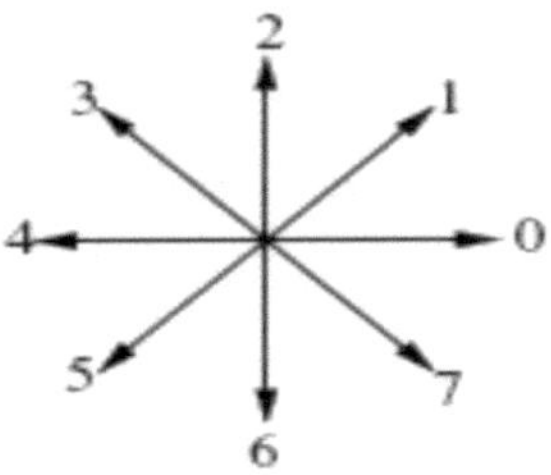

Fig. 9. Freeman's Directional Guide

```
While there are still edges to be traverse
Begin
   Find the starting point to traverse.
   From starting point till junction point or end  point
   Begin
          Find and store the direction code of the point
          by investigating its neighbour position.
         Once done, cleared pixel from image.
   End
End
```

Fig. 10. Algorithm for Traversing the Image

An example of an image of character "e", the same character used in Fig. 4 and Fig. 6., is shown in Fig. 7, after it has been chain coded. From the chain codes of the character, features such as the type of strokes will be extracted. The strokes will be identified with a set of probabilities. How these features are extracted by means of HMM and later used by a fuzzy inference system for classification is the other novelty of this research work.

7.2 Extracting Features from Chain-codes

After a careful study of the different types of stroke directions in a character set a few types are selected and thought to have distinguishing factors to identify a character class. Table 1 shows the types of strokes that are used to distinguish the characters. In order to simply the strokes without needing to consider the way it might be traverse, codes that visually produced the same, the directions are usually combined. For example, in identifying a vertical stroke, if the image is traverse from bottom up then the direction will be North and if it is traverse top to bottom the directions will be South. Of course the traversing method is meant to be consistent and it will always traverse the same way, but just in case, the directions are disregarded and both will be considered as a vertical stroke. Hence are true for the Horizontal stroke, the Right Slant and the Left Slant.

The other two obvious strokes are named as the C-curve and the D-curve. The last two strokes will be given the highest priorities in the investigation of strokes. In the case where the curve might be broken and not too distinguishable then the normal NSEW directions will be investigated. The combination of these smaller identifiable strokes can still make a good set of features for producing linguistic variables. The C-curve would be a prominent feature in characters like a, c, d, e etc., and the D-curve in characters like b, p, etc. Some of the characters may have the combinations of both curves and some may have a fuller curve than others. All these differences are projected in the linguistic that will describe the strokes.

The codes that form the strokes and the visual examples of some of the strokes investigated are shown in Table 2 and Fig. 11.

Types of Strokes Identified	Corresponding Direction Codes
Horizontal lines	4 or 0
Vertical lines	2 or 6
Right Slant	1 , 2, 0 or 5, 4 , 6
Left Slant	3, 2, 4 or 7, 6, 0
Loop	6, 5, 4, 7, 0, 1, 2, 3
Right Hook	6, 7, 0 1
Left Hook	6, 5, 4, 3
C - curves	7, 6 , 4, 5 or 1, 2, 4, 3
D-curves	5, 6, 0, 7 or 3, 2, 0, 1

Table 2. Among the types of strokes identified from the character image

Fig. 11. Visual examples of some of the strokes identified (from left to right: Right hook, Left hook, C-curve, D-curve, U-curve).

From the chain codes of the character, features such as the type of strokes will be extracted. The strokes will be identified with a set of probabilities. HMM as mentioned before will be used for this purpose. In addition to the standard left-right model, null transitions are used for state skipping, which allows the model to tolerate omissions of some features, whereas self loops are used for modelling the repetition of features. Most of the strokes shared the same model topology. It was tested during development of the models, that increasing the number of states in the model does not improve the probabilities too much. This is probably because the strokes are all relatively very simple. However it is found that the best is to have models for as many strokes variation rather than having one and conclude its variations from the emerged log-likelihood values. For example, rather than have one model for vertical line, we tend to have a few such as for right slant, left slant, very tall vertical and small vertical lines. Since types of stroke played a distinguishing factor in the classification phase, its identification is considered very important.

The major drawback of using chain codes as the features for the HMM model is the observation symbols (which are the Freeman direction codes) are usually common and appear in more than one stroke models. One very important observation made during the development of the HMM models for the various strokes is, it is difficult to distinguish strokes that have similar observation symbols. If we were to pass the chain codes for Vertical_Lines to both the C_curve's HMM Model and the Vertical_Lines's HMM Model, it will be recognized by both and sometimes the log-likelihood values alone would not be enough to ascertain which model fits the chain codes better. In order to minimize confusion that might occur in the identification of the strokes, the of list chain codes to be processed would first be scanned through for two purposes. The first intent is to clean the list from any spurious direction codes that might appear in the strokes. This is done by removing any symbols that appear only once in a list of chain codes that is longer than 5. The second purpose is to determine which HMM model to be invoked and thus reduce the degree of confusion to ascertain the types of strokes through its log-likelihood values alone. The general algorithm for the above mentioned tasks is given in Fig. 12. The decision to determine which HMM models to be called is by examining the number of different symbols that occurred in the chain codes. For a list of chain codes that have the occurrence of 4 or more different symbols, it is assumed that the stroke are complex and as such it will fit the description of a curve or loop, and so the corresponding HMM model would be called. For a list of chain codes that is made of less than 4 symbols would be considered as simple strokes and the appropriate model will be called.

```
Procedure for Determining Which HMM Model to invoke

        Create and initialize an array to hold the count for each of the 8 possible
        observation symbols in a list of chain codes

        Count the occurrence of each symbol in the list of

        Clean the list from any spurious symbols that might appear in the chain codes,
        i.e. any symbols that only occur once in a list that is longer than 4 will be
        removed.

        Count the number of different symbols that appear in the chain codes

        If (Count is more than 3)
                Call HMM Models for curves and loop
        Else
                Call HMM Models for N,S,E,W and other simpler strokes
```

Fig. 12. Algorithm to Determine HMM Models to be invoked

7.3 Preparing Input for Linguistic Variables

A linguistic variable enables its value to be described both qualitatively by a linguistic term (i.e. a symbol serving as the name of a fuzzy set) and quantitatively by a corresponding membership function (which express the meaning of the fuzzy set). Linguistic term is used to express concepts and knowledge in human communication, whereas membership function is useful for processing numeric input data.

In this research the classification component of the system which is based on the concept of fuzzy logic is developed purely using Mathlab Toolbox of Fuzzy Logic. This component will be discussed in the next section. Since we will be utilizing Mathlab for this purpose all the fuzzification process of the linguistic variables and the inference for the classification are just a matter of invoking the functions in the toolbox. The fuzzy inference system, or FIS as it is known in Mathlab, however accepts probabilities of the input variables in order to change it to its corresponding linguistic variables. Since the HMM models of the strokes, give as an output the log-likelihood of the strokes fitting the model λ = (A, B, π), it is our task to change the log-likelihood values to a value resembling probability (value between 0 and 1). The log-likelihood values, which computation is based on a series of intensive calculations of forward and backward variables and then re-estimation in the training part, and this values will then be used in the calculation of the forward variable again in the testing part inclusive of scaling in order to avoid the values going too small and to infinity, would usually gives a value that is very unlike a probability. In order to change these values to more meaningful probability values a simple method is employed.

During testing, the most perfect and the least perfect strokes of each type will be carefully selected and tested. The term "perfect" in describing any type of strokes would be a stroke that is most prominent in visibility of the image to resemble the contour of the stroke in question. For example for a vertical line (South), that would be the tallest and the most vertical of lines, such as in the character "p" or "d" or "l" and so on. The description of "least perfect" would be strokes that have minimum features to fit the category, e.g. in this example would be a very short vertical line. The log-likelihood value of the perfect stroke, named it x, would be used as an upper threshold and the log-likelihood value of the least perfect stroke, named it y, will be used as a lower threshold, i.e. the threshold of acceptance.

Log-likelihood of the current stroke being investigated name it m,

To illustrate the idea further, assumed the example below.

Assuming the following chain codes of a south stroke (6 6 6 6 6 7 6 6 6 7 6 6 6 7 6 6 7), yields a log-likelihood of, named it m, -18.357026. Assume x = -31.981509 and y = -3.427863. So, the probability of the chain codes above fitting the South model would be,

$$\frac{m}{y} = \frac{-18.357026}{-31.981509} = 0.5739887$$

The threshold for acceptance of any strokes for this category would be,

$$\frac{y}{x} = \frac{-3.427863}{-31.981509} = 0.1071826$$

As such, anything below this threshold value would not be accepted. Of course this upper and lower threshold values differ from stroke to stroke. These probability values need only to be fed to the FIS designed for the classification task for it to be fuzzify into its corresponding linguistic variables and be used in the classification task.

8. Classification Phase

A HMM model is a very useful tool to be incorporated into a fuzzy logic rule based system. It provides an approach that is compatible to the needs of the system. The derivation of probabilities by a statistical model such as HMM provides a solid base for the more syntactical approach of a fuzzy system. HMM yields a more accurate assessment of a log-likelihood which may in turn be used to derive probabilities for the linguistic variables of a fuzzy system. The set of steps employed in the classification phase is given in Fig. 13.

Classification Phase: Steps in Fuzzy Inferencing	
Step 1:	Fuzzification of the input variables: Determine to which degree the input variables belong to each of the appropriate fuzzy sets via membership functions.
Step 2:	Application of the fuzzy operator (AND or OR) to multiple part antecedents: Using as input two or more membership values from fuzzified input variables, a single truth value will emerge as output. The output is the degree of support for the rule.
Step 3:	Application of implication method from the antecedent to the consequent: Using the single value from the antecedent which is the degree of support for the entire rule to shape the output fuzzy set. If the antecedent is only partially true, (i.e., is assigned a value less than 1), then the output fuzzy set is truncated according to the implication method.
Step 4:	Aggregation of the consequents across the rules: Testing is done on all rules in the FIS, and so the rules outputs must be aggregated to make a decision. The inputs to this process are the outputs from each rule's antecedent and the output is one fuzzy set for each output variable.
Step 5:	Defuzzification: The fuzzy set from the aggregated output is defuzzify to produce a single number output from the set.

Fig. 13. Classification Phase: Steps in Fuzzy Inferencing

The classification phase of the system is based on the concept of fuzzy rules developed using Mathlab (Version 7.4.0). The fuzzy inference system (FIS) was built using Mathlab GUI tools from its Fuzzy Logic Toolbox.

A fuzzy rule has two components, an if-part (referred as the antecedent) and a then-part (referred to as the consequent). The structure of fuzzy rule is identical to that of a conventional rule in artificial intelligence. The main difference is the antecedent of a fuzzy rule is described by a linguistic variable and a membership function. A linguistic variable is like a composition of symbolic variable and a numeric variable. Numeric variables are frequently used in science, engineering, mathematics, medicine and many other disciplines while symbolic variables play an important role in AI and decision sciences. Using the notion of the linguistic variable to combine these two kinds of variables into a uniform framework is one of the main reasons that fuzzy logic has been successful in offering intelligent approaches in engineering and many other areas that deal with continuous problem domain.

The features extracted by the HMM yields a very good medium for further conversion of the linguistic variables. The strokes as identified, together with its probability will go through the process of fuzzification. The triangular and the trapezoidal membership functions were used to change the strokes probability into its linguistic variable forms. The two membership functions were chosen due to their simple formulas and computational efficiencies. Examples of the linguistic variables used are : "Very Tall Right_Slant", "Very Tall Vertical_Line", as in l's, or as in some of d's or b's. "Tall C_curve" as in c's, "small C_curve" as appear in d's, a's and so on. When the HMM models were used with the fuzzy rules to recognize the handwritten characters, a favorable results was achieved.

8.1 Fuzzy Rule Based

The fuzzy rule-based is comprised of fuzzy if-then rules that are used to formulate the conditional statements that comprise fuzzy logic. A single fuzzy if-then rule assumes the form,

if x is A then y is B,

where A and B are linguistic values defined by fuzzy sets on the ranges (universes of discourse) X and Y, respectively. The if-part of the rule "x is A" is called the antecedent or premise, while the then-part of the rule "y is B" is called the consequent or conclusion. If the antecedent is true to some degree of membership, then the consequent is also true to that same degree.

The antecedent of a rule can have multiple parts, in which case all parts of the antecedent are calculated simultaneously and resolved to a single number using the logical operators as described in the preceding section. Example of such rule as in the rule-based is as below:

If descender is certain and RightCurve is medium and VerticalLine is tall then Char_p is definite

Another example of one the rule from the fuzzy rule-based that describes character 'd' is:

If ascender is certain and LeftCurve is medium and Vertical_line is tall then Char_d is definite

The rule above gives a perfect description of character 'd'. There are other rules that describe all the combination of the linguistic variables that gives the description that would match the character to various degrees. The consequent of a rule can also have multiple parts, in which case all consequents are affected equally by the result of the antecedent. The consequent specifies a fuzzy set be assigned to the output. The implication function then modifies that fuzzy set to the degree specified by the antecedent. The most common ways to modify the output fuzzy set are truncation using the *min* function (where the fuzzy set is chopped off) or scaling using the prod function (where the output fuzzy set is squashed).

The algorithm of fuzzy rule-based inference consists of three basic steps and an additional original step. These steps are : (i) Fuzzy matching: Calculate the degree to which the input data match the condition of the fuzzy rules. (ii) Inference: Calculate the rules conclusion based on its matching degree. (iii) Combination: combine the conclusion inferred by all fuzzy rules into a final conclusion. (iv) Defuzzification: for outputs that need a crisp output and additional step is to convert a fuzzy conclusion into a crisp one. By using the FIS of Mathlab for the purpose mentioned above, the outcome of the inference will be used to determine the classification of the characters.

9. Experimental Results

For all reported results, the following definitions of recognition rate, error rate, rejection rate and reliability rate are used.

Let *B*, be a test set with character images. If the classifier system rejects, N_{rej}, classifies correctly, N_{rec} and misclassifies the rest, N_{err}, then,

$$\text{Recogniton rate} = \frac{N_{rec}}{N_B} \times 100$$

$$\text{Error rate} = \frac{N_{err}}{N_B} \times 100$$

$$\text{Rejection rate} = \frac{N_{rej}}{N_B} \times 100$$

$$\text{Reliability rate} = \frac{\text{Recognition Rate}}{\text{Recognition Rate} + \text{Error Rate}} \times 100$$

The recognition rate, error rate and rejection rate will all summed up to 100%. The calculation of these rates as used by Oliveira (Oliveira et. al., 2002) is felt to be very reflective of the needs of a handwriting recognition system when applied to real applications. The reliability of the system can be demonstrated by the above equation for a given error rate.

The result of the following experiment is based on the recognitions of characters from the IRONOFF database. A sample of not more than 1000 handwritten characters with variability in handwriting is used from that database. Characters chosen from the database are based on its legibility. That means characters that could not be recognize by the naked eye and those written too cursively would be dropped from the test samples. This is because some of the characters in the database are written in a cursive manner and without context it would be quite difficult to be recognized. About 20 to 30 samples of each character are used in the testing. An overall recognition rate of 80.19% is recorded for the system. Table 3 shows all the rates measured for the classification of the lowercase characters in the data set. Table 4 gives the recognition rate grouped by the categories of the characters which is used as one of the distinguishing features in the fuzzy rules.

The features extracted by the HMM yields a very good medium for further conversion of the linguistic variables. The strokes as identified, together with its probability will go through the process of fuzzification. The triangular and the trapezoidal membership functions were used to change the strokes probability into its linguistic variable forms. The two membership functions were chosen due to their simple formulas and computational efficiencies. Examples of the linguistic variables used are : "very tall right slant", "very tall vertical line", as in l's, or as in some of d's or b's. "Tall C-curve" as in c's, "small C-curve" as appear in d's, a's and so on.

When the HMM models were used with the fuzzy rules to recognize the handwritten characters, a favorable results was achieved. Bearing in mind that comparing the achievements of various researches in this field is quite difficult as the database and general approaches might differ. Testing done with different databases would give differing results as variations and complexity of the data in the databases are not the same. Similar issues are also with approaches. Approaches would differ in recognition of characters, digits, words, cursive, non-cursive, with post-processing or not. Even though research in the area are extensive many more can be done at not necessarily in improving the percentage of accuracy but also at attempting to reduce complexity of its pre-processing techniques, its classifier, its post-processing and also the need for huge databases.

Data Group	Recognition Rate	Error Rate	Rejection Rate	Reliability Rate
Overall Classification	80.19	8.28	11.53	89.4

Table 3. Recognition, Error, Rejection and Reliability Rate of all characters

Characters grouped in categories of ascender, descender or neither	Recognition rate
Ascenders (e.g. b, d ,f, h, k, l, t)	86.55
Descenders (e.g. g, j, p, q, y)	81.62
Neither (e.g. a, c, e ,i, m, n, o, r, s, u, v, w)	72.40
Average %	80.19

Table 4. Recognition rate of characters in groups

10. Conclusion

The success of the fuzzy rule-based system that is used in recognizing the characters would be quite heavily depended on the accuracy of the features extracted and the way the rules are structured. The work presented by (Lazzerini & Marcelloni, 2000) uses a purely linguistic fuzzy recognizer on handwritten character digit with a recognition rate of 69.5%. Even though it might seem comparatively lower than other methods, the method presented has the novelty in other areas of importance.

With a reasonable rate of recognition on a more difficult database of lower-case characters, HMM model is proven to be a very useful tool to be incorporated into a fuzzy logic rules based system. It provides an approach that is compatible to the needs of the system. The calculation of probabilities for each observation by a statistical model such as HMM provides a solid base for the more syntactical approach of a fuzzy system. HMM yields a more accurate assessment of probabilities for the linguistic variables of a fuzzy system. However the nature of fuzziness in the data captured for the offline handwritten characters recognition research makes a pure statistical approach a little inappropriate. Fuzzy logic has been used in many of the offline researches, giving an impressive result (Wierer & Boston, 2007; Hanmandlu et. al. 2003; Bouslama, 1997). There are many ways of using fuzzy classifier into the problem of handwritten character recognition and this paper proposes a method that does not need huge training sets and is computationally simpler.

The tasks of digit recognition and upper-case character recognition have proven to be simpler than lower-case character recognition. For comparison purposes, some character classifiers recognize some 97% for digits (Lee, 1996; Shouno et. al., 1999), 97% for upper-case letters and 80% for lower-case letters (Heutte, 1998). However, these results are obtained by using complex image processing techniques ((Lee, 1996), or combination feature types, e.g. a combination of structural and statistical features (Heutte, 1998) or complex classifiers (Shouno et. al., 1999). Even though much lower recognition accuracy is achieved by our method comparatively with other methods but on the whole the objective of the research is met. This is to investigate the compatibility of an HMM with a fuzzy rule-based system as the recognizer.

11. References

Atici, A. & Yarman-Vural, F. (2001). "A Heuristic Method for Arabic Character Recognition", *Signal Process*, vol. 62, pp. 87-99.

Arica, N., & Yarman-Vural. F. T. (2001). An Overview of Character Recognition Focused on Off-line Handwriting, *IEEE Trans. On Systems, Man, and Cybernetics*, Vol. 31. No. 2. pp. 216-233.

Blumstein, M. & Verma, B. (1999). A new segementation algorithm for handwritten word recognition, *Proc. of the Int. Joint Conf. on NN, IJCNN '99*, Washington D.C., 878-882.

Bouslama, F. (1997). Arabic character Recognition by Fuzzy Techniques, *in Proc. EUFIT*, Aachen, Germany, pp. 1940-1944.

Bozinovic, R. M. & Srihari, S. N. (1989). Off-Line Cursive Script Word Recognition, *PAM1*, 11, pp. 68-83.

Chen, M. Y.; Kundu, A. & Zhou, J. (1994). Off-Line Handwritten Word Recognition using HMM type Stochastic Network, *IEEE Transactions of Pattern Analysis and Machine Intelligence*, 16, 481-496.

Freeman, H. (1974). *Computer Processing of Line-Drawing Images*, ACM Computing Surveys, 6(1): 57-98 March.

Hanmandlu, M.; Murali-Mohan K. R.; Chakraborty, S.; Goyal, S., & Choudhury, D. R. (2003). Unconstrained Handwritten Character Recognition based on Fuzzy Logic, *Pattern Recognition*, Vol. 36, Issue 3, March, 603-623.

Heutte, L., Paquet, T., Moreau, J.V., Lecourtier, Y., Olivier, C. (1998) A structural/statistical feature based vector for handwritten character recognition, *Pattern Recognition Letters* 19, pp. 629-641.

Impedovo, S.; Ottaviano, L. and Occhinegro, S. (1991). Optical Character Recognition - A Survey, *International Journal of Pattern Recognition & Artificial Intelligence*, 5, 1-24.

Kundu, A. & He, Y. (1991). On optimal order in modeling sequence of letters in words of common language as a Markov chain, *Pattern Recognition*, vol. 24, no. 7, pp. 603-608.

Lazzerini, B. & Marcelloni, F. (2000). A Linguistic Fuzzy Recogniser of Off-line Handwritten Characters, *Pattern Recognition Letters*, 21, pp. 319-327.

Lee, W.L. & Fan, K.C. (2000). Document image preprocessing based on optimal Boolean filters, *Signal Process*, Vol. 80, no. 1, pp. 45-55.

Legault R. & Suen, C.Y. (1997). Optimal local weighted averaging methods in contour smoothing, *IEEE Trans. Pattern Anal. Machine Intell.*, July vol. 18, pp. 690-706.

Leu, J.G. (2000). "Edge Sharpening through ramp width reduction", *Image Vision Computing*, vol. 18, no. 6-7, pp. 501-514.

Madhvanath, S. & Govindaraju, V. (1999). References lines for holistic recognition of handwritten words, *Pattern Recognition*, vol. 32, no. 12, 2021-2028.

Madhvanath, S.; Kim, G. & Govindaraju, V. (1999). Chaincode contour processing for handwritten word recognition, *IEEE Pattern Anal Machine Intell.* , vol. 21, 928-932, September.

Mori, S.; Suen C.Y. & Yamamoto, K. (1992). Historical Overview of OCR Research and Development, *Proceedings of the IEEE*, 80, pp. 1029-1058.

Oh, I.S.; Lee, J.S. & Suen, C.Y., (1999) Analysis of class separation and combination of class-dependent features for handwriting recognition, *IEEE Trans. Pattern Anal. Machine Intell.*, vol. 21, pp. 1089-1094, October.

Oliveira, L. S., Sabourin, R., Bortolozzi, F., & Suen, C. Y., (2002). Automatic Recognition of Handwritten Numerical Strings: A Recognition and Verification Strategy, *IEEE Trans. Pattern Anal. Machine Intell.*, Vol. 24, No. 11, November.

Plamondon, R. & Srihari, S.N. (2000). On-line and Off-line handwriting Recognition: A Comprehensive Survey, *IEEE Transactions on Pattern Analysis and Machine Intelligence*, 22, pp. 63-84.

Polesel, A., Ramponi, G., & Mathews, V. (1997). "Adaptive unsharp masking for contrast enhancements", *in Proc. Int. Conf. Image Process*, vol. 1, pp. 267-271.

Rabiner, L.R. (1989). A Tutorial on Hidden Markov Models and Selected Applications in Speech Recognition, *Proceeding of the IEEE*, Vol. 77, No. 2, February.

Reinhardt, J.M. & Higgins, W.E. (1996). Comparison between the morphological skeleton and morphological shape decomposition, *IEEE Trans. Pattern Anal. Machine Intell.*, vol. 18, pp. 951-957, Sept.

Saula, J. & Pietikainen, M. (2000). Adaptive document image binarization, *Pattern Recognition*, vol. 33, no. 2, pp. 225-236.

Serra, J. (1994). "Morphological Filtering: An Overview", *SignalProcess*, vol. 38, no. 1, pp. 3-11.

Shridhar M. & Badreldin, A. (1985) High accuracy syntactic recognition algorithm for handwritten numerals, *IEEE Trans. On Systems, Man, and Cybernetics*, Vol. 15, pp. 152-158, January.

Shouno, H., Fukushima, K., Okada, M. Recognition of handwritten digits in the real world by a neocognitron, in Jain L.C., Lazzerini, B., Knowledge-Based Intelligent Techniques in Character Recognition, CRC Press, Florida, 1999, pp. 19-46.

Solihin, Y. & Leedham C.G. (1999). "Integral ratio: A new class of global thresholding techniques for handwriting images", *IEEE Trans. Pattern Anal. Machine Intell.*, vol.21, August, pp. 761-768.

Sonka, M., Hlavac V. & Boyle, R., (1999). Image Processing, Analysis and Machine Vision, 2nd ed. Pacific Grove CA:Brooks/Cole.

Suen, C. Y. (1986). Character Recognition by Computer and Applications, *in Handbook of Pattern Recognition and Image Processing*, ed. Young T.Y., Fu, K.S., Academic Press Inc., San Diego, CA, pp. 569-586.

Suen, C. Y.; Tappert, C.C. & Wakahara, T. (1990). The state of the art in on-line handwriting recognition, *IEEE Trans. Pattern Anal. Machine Intell.*, Vol. 12, pp. 7877-808.

Suliman, A.; Sulaiman, M. N.; Othman, M. & Wirza, R. (2007). Extracting Features for the Lingusitic Variables of Fuzzy Rules Using Hidden Markov Model, *International E-Conference on Computer Science (IeCCS),* 9-11 July, Greece, AIP Conference Proceedings.

Wierer, J. & Boston, N. (2007). A Handwritten Digit Recognition Algorithm Using Two-Dimensional Hidden Markov Models for Feature Extraction, *IEEE International Conference on Acoustics, Speech and Signal Processing ICASSP,* Vol. 2, April.

Yang, J. & Li, X. B. (1995). Boundary Detection using mathematical morphology, Pattern Recognition Letters, vol. 16, no. 12, pp. 1287-1296.

Zadeh, L. A., (1965). Fuzzy sets, *Information and Control,* Vol. 8, pp. 338-353.

5

Development of a recognizer for Bangla text: present status and future challenges

Saima Hossain, Nasreen Akter,
Hasan Sarwar and Chowdhury Mofizur Rahman
United International University
Bangladesh

1. Introduction

Optical Character Recognition (OCR) System, by virtue of its usefulness, has emerged as a major research area since 1950. Now it is becoming a more challenging issue all over the world to have efficient and more accurate recognizers. There are many widely spoken languages in the world like Chinese, Arabic, Hindi, English, Spanish, Bangla, Russian, Japanese etc. Bangla is one of the most widely spoken languages, ranking 5th in the world. 21st February is observed as the international mother language day to pay homage to the martyrs fought for the establishment of Bangla as the mother tongue of Bangladesh. With the automation everywhere, it is a burning issue to digitize huge, volume of Bangla documents by using an efficient OCR. However as of today there is no such good recognizer available for Bangla compared to other languages. From 80s, it took huge interest and now becomes as a major research area particularly in Bangladesh and India. Lots of works have been done in different sections of pattern recognition tasks (i.e, pre-processing, segmentation, feature extraction, classification) but there is a lack of synchronization between these works. That is why we put our effort into a comprehensive review of the current status of research to develop an all-inclusive Bangla OCR which will enable one to understand the difficulties and challenges involved, to know how much progress has been done and to estimate what more to be done to come out with a successful Bangla OCR.

2. Overview

This chapter includes introduction to Bangla language which provides a brief description on it, present status on the development of Bangla OCR and some comparative analysis of several proposed methods on Noise Reduction, Skew Detection and Correction, Segmentation, Feature Extraction, Classification published in different articles. Future works in this field explaining the futures challenges are summarised at the end of this chapter.

3. Introduction to Bangla Language

Bangla is an eastern Indo-Aryan language and evolved from Sanskrit (Barbara F. Grimes, 1997). The direction of the writing policy is left to right. Bangla language consists of 50 basic characters including 11 vowels and 39 consonant characters and 10 numerals. In Bangla, the concept of upper case or lower case letter is not present. Bangla basic characters have characteristics that differ from other languages. Bangla character has headline which is called matraline or matra in Bangla. It is a horizontal line and always situated at the upper portion of the character. Among basic characters, there are 8 characters which are with half matra, 10 characters with no matra and rest of them with full matra. All consonants except ঙ ঞ ণ ড় ঢ় য় ৎ ং ঃ ঁ are used as the starting character of a word whereas, vowels are used everywhere. Vowels and consonants have their modified shapes called vowel modifiers and consonant modifiers respectively. Both types of modifiers are used only with consonant characters. There are 10 vowels and 3 consonant modifiers which are used before or after a consonant character, or at the upper or lower portion of a consonant character or on the both sides of a consonant character, likewise, খা খি খু খে খৌ ক্য র্ক ক্র. In Bangla, some special characters are there which are formed by combining two or more consonants and acts as an individual character. These types of characters are known as compound characters. The compound characters may further be classified as touching characters and fused characters. Two characters placed adjacent contact to each other produce a touching character. Touches occur due to horizontal placement of only two characters and/or vertical placement of two or more characters. About 10 touching characters are there in Bangla. Fused characters are formed with more than one basic character. Unlike touching characters, the basic characters lose their original shapes fully or partly. A new shape is used for the fused characters. In sum, there are about 250 special characters in Bangla except basic and modified characters. Table 3.1 illustrates different types of Bangla characters.

Vowels	অ আ ই ঈ উ ঊ ঋ এ ঐ ও ঔ
Consonants	ক খ গ ঘ ঙ চ ছ জ ঝ ঞ ট ঠ ড ঢ ণ ত থ দ ধ ন প ফ ব ভ ম য র ল শ ষ স হ ড় ঢ় য় ৎ ং ঃ ঁ
Vowel Modifiers	া ি ী ু ূ ৃ ে ৈ ো ৌ
Vowel Modifiers attached with consonants	খা খি খী খু খূ খৃ খে খৈ খো খৌ
Consonant Modifiers	্য র্ ্র
Consonant Modifiers attached with consonants	ক্য র্ক ক্র

Compound Characters: Horizontal Touching Characters	ড + ড = ড্ড ব + ব = ব্ব হ + ব = হ্ব চ + চ = চ্চ চ + ছ = চ্ছ ধ + ব = ধ্ব ট + ন = ট্ন ঠ + ন = ঠ্ন
Compound Characters: Vertical Touching Characters	ষ্ম ক্ম ঙ্ক ঙ্গ জ্জ ন্ত ত্ম ন্দ দ্ম ড গ্ব ত্ত্ব প্ত ন্ড ক্ল ল্ফ ক্স ষ্ফ স্থ স্ন স্ফ ক্ক গ্ন শ্ব গ্ল প্ল ঞ্চ ঙ্ক ক্ল ম্ল ব্ক ম্ল ব্ল ল্ল স্ক শ্ল স্ব ম্ভ জ্ব ঘ্ন ট্ব থ্ব ত্ব ম্ব ক্ব ল্ব স্ব জ্জ্ব জ্ঝ ত্ন ন্ত প্ন স্ত্ব গ্ন ক্ল ক্ষ হ্ন ম্ল ন্ন ম্ভ
Compound Characters: Fused Characters	ট্টু ষ্ম ক্ত ক্র ষ্ক ণ্দ ত্ত ধ্ঙ ঞ্ছ ত্র ত্ত থ্ব ল্ট ঞ্জ ণ্ট ঙ্খ ঙ্গ ষ্ঠ ড ন্স ণ্ট ল্ফ শ্চ ক্স ন্ট ক্ক ল্স জ ব্দ ভ্র ষ্ফ হু হ্র ম্ফ শ্ছ হ্ন ষ্ট ষ্ঠ ট্ট ম্ব দ্ধ ত্ব ন্ধ ব্ধ
Numerals	০ ১ ২ ৩ ৪ ৫ ৬ ৭ ৮ ৯

Table 3.1. Different types of Bangla characters. A subset of 112 compound characters out of about 250 characters (B.B. Chaudhuri, 1998) is shown here.

The occurrence of vowels and consonants are larger compared to special characters in most of the Bangla documents. A statistical analysis, shown in Table 3.2, took 2 sets of data populated with 100,000 words from Bangla books, newspapers and 60,000 words from Bangla dictionary respectively (B.B. Chaudhuri, 1998).

Global characteristics	1st set of data	2nd set of data
Vowel characters	38.70%	37.10%
Consonant characters	61.30%	62.90%
Compound characters	4.10%	7.20%
Entropy of the alphabet	4.07 (bits/char)	3.54 (bits/char)
Average word length	5.73 (char)	4.99 (char)
Words with suffix	69.80%	0.00%

Table 3.2. Statistical analysis on the occurrence of different characters

Some of the modifiers are there which are used on top of the character (basic or special character) as well as a few in the bottom of the character. Again some basic characters also have upper portion which is treated as a part of the character. So it can be said that the construction of Bangla characters require 3 zones named upper zone, middle zone and lower zone. Upper portion from matra line is called upper zone. Middle portion that is situated under the matraline is called middle zone. As some modifiers are used at the bottom of the middle zone, this portion is called lower zone. Most of the characters are situated in the middle zone. Fig. 3.1 shows a simple example explaining the construction of a Bangla word.

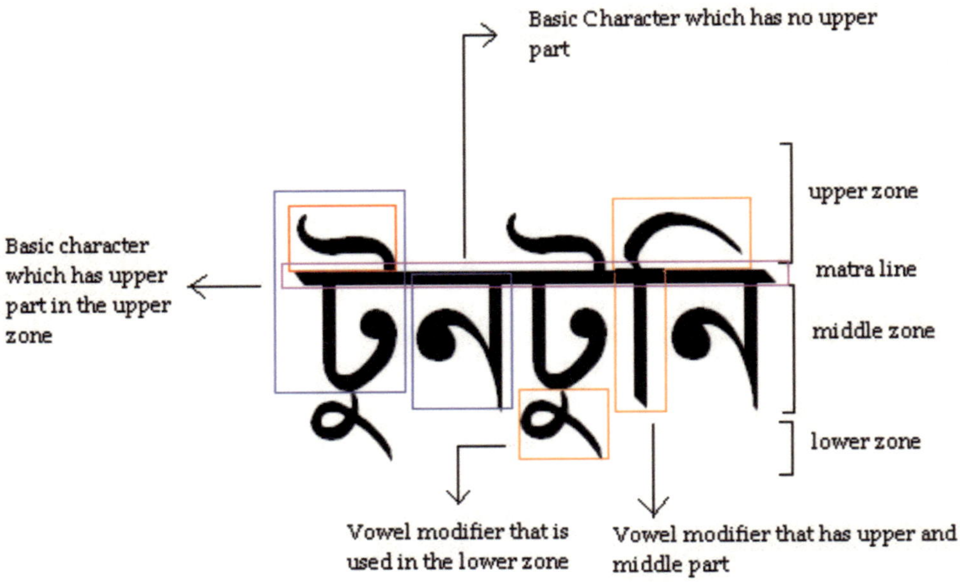

Fig. 3.1. Dissection of a Bangla Word

4. Scanning and Image Digitization

Before going into the ocr process, one must scan the paper through a flat-bed scanner. It is better not to use hand-held scanner, which may create local fluctuation for hand movement (B.B. Chaudhuri, 1998). It is crucial to have good quality printed document scanning. If the quality is poor and the color contrast is too low, it will be hard for the OCR software to read the text and to make correct interpretation. The scanned image is stored, for example, as a jpeg/bmp format file which is converted to a binary image. In order to improve the quality of the image to make the OCR correct interpretation, noise reduction and elimination and skew detection and correction processes are performed.

5. Noise Detection and Removal

Noise is naturally added during scanning process. When documents or papers are scanned, some noises are added automatically into it. There are two different types of noises known as background noise and salt and pepper noise which are given most importance. A histogram-based thresholding approach is used to convert gray tone into two-tone images

(B.B. Chaudhuri, 1998). The histogram shows two prominent peaks corresponding to white and black regions. The threshold value is chosen as the midpoint of the two histogram peaks. The two-tone image is converted into 0-1 labels where 1 and 0 represent object and background, respectively. Authors also claim that their approaches are better than J. N. Kapur, P. K. Sahoo and A. K. C. Wong (J. N. Kapur, 1985), and N. Otsu (N. Otsu 1979). However, salt and pepper noise is not mentioned here. Different authors have suggested for applying noise elimination process at different stages of Preprocessing or Segmentation. (B.B. Chaudhuri, 1998) and (A. Roy, 2002) used it during binarization of the image.

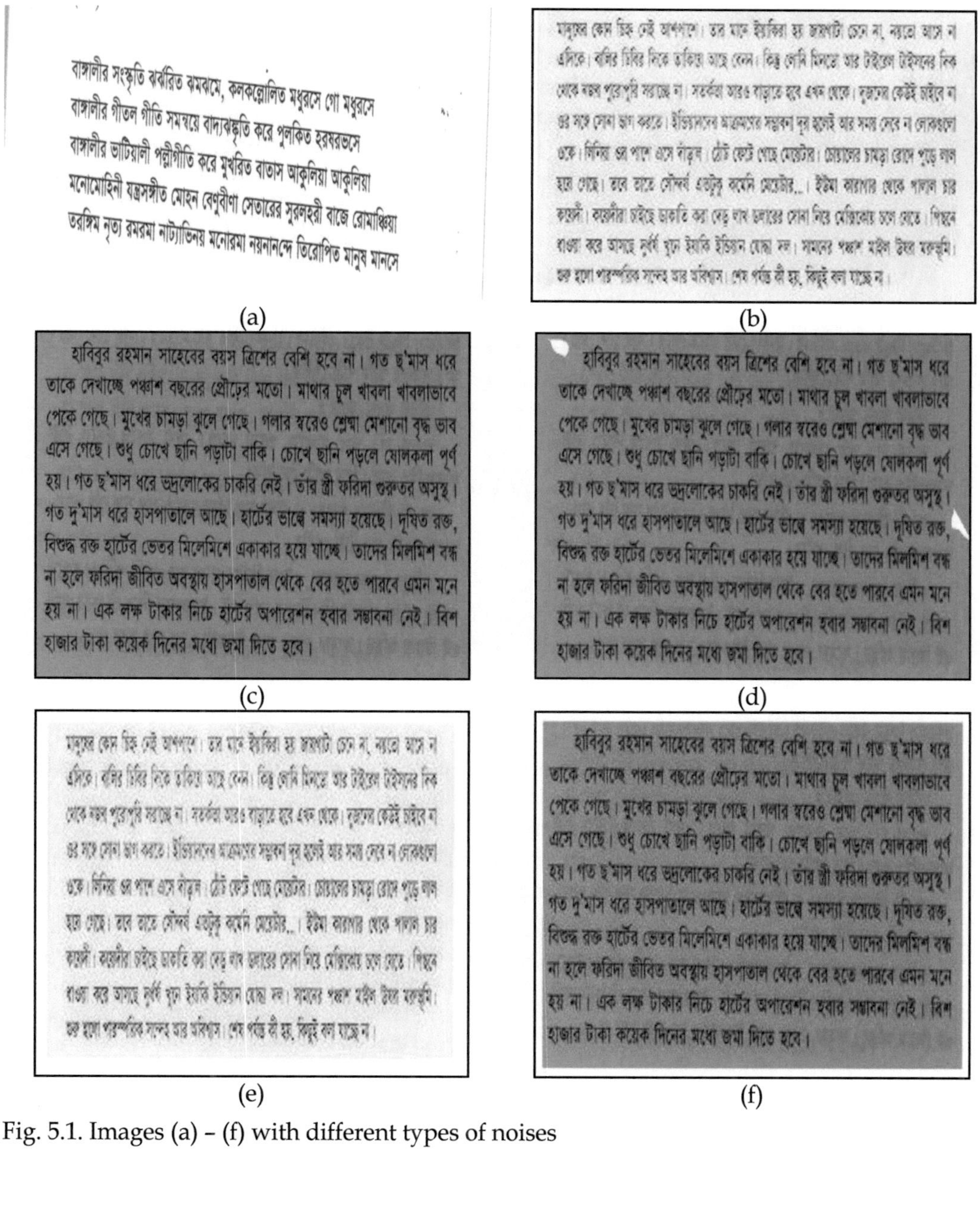

Fig. 5.1. Images (a) – (f) with different types of noises

In (A. Roy, 2002), gray-level images are median filtered and then Otsu's thresholding algorithm is used to binarize the images of word. The binary images are then filtered to obtain smooth images. In (Jalal Uddin Mahmud, 2003), noise is removed from character images. Noise removal includes removal of single pixel component and removal of stair case effect after scaling. Stair case effect occurs when the scaled characters have junctions so thin that inner and outer contour required for chain code representation cannot be found. Each pixel has been replaced by a filtering function to avoid such effect. However, this does not consider background noise and salt and pepper noise. In (Md. Abul Hasnat, 2007), the authors used connected component information and eliminated the noise using statistical analysis for background noise removal. For other type of noise removal and smoothing they used wiener and median filters (Tinku Acharya, 2005). Connected component information is found using boundary finding method (such as edge detection technique). Pixels are sampled only where the boundary probability is high. This method requires elaboration in the case where the characteristics change along the boundary. A comparative performance study in Table 5.1 is given below for some of the images shown in fig. 5.1.

Papers	Fig. 5.1a	Fig. 5.1b	Fig. 5.1c	Fig. 5.1d	Fig. 5.1e	Fig. 5.1f
B.B. Chaudhuri, 1998	yes	yes	x	x	yes	x
A.Roy, 2002	yes	yes	yes	yes	yes	x
Jalal Uddin Mahmud, 2003	yes	yes	Yes	yes	yes	x
Md. Abul Hasnat, 2007	yes	yes	yes	yes	yes	x

Table 5.1. Applicability of different techniques on noisy images shown in fig. 5.1

6. Skew Detection and Correction

Skew is basically an angle that is created due to an angular placement of document in the scanner. (B.B. Chaudhuri, 1998) says that it can be corrected in two steps, i) estimation of skew angle θ_s and ii) rotation of image by θ_s in the opposite direction. Many skew detection and correction algorithms are available. B.B. Chaudhuri (1998) suggests an approach suitable for Bangla scripts. Basically, it tries to detect the head line of document words. Head line is a straight line given on the upper side of a character when used in words. It has been found that average length of Bangla words is six characters (R. M. Bozinovic, 1989), 30-35% of characters are vowel modifiers having very little contribution to head word, 5% is compound character. In Bangla, 41 characters can appear in the first position, of them 30 characters have headlines. Probabilistic analysis reveals that, in 99.39% cases, there will be at least one character with head line in a Bangla word. In this process, firstly a bounding box (an upright rectangle containing a word/component) is defined. The mean box width is b_m and the standard deviation is b_s. Components having boundary box equal to b_m and less than b_m +3b_s are retained, others are discarded, which fall into categories like dots, punctuation marks, isolated characters and characters without headlines. Next, upper envelop of selected component, G, is found. From each pixel of the uppermost row of the bounding box, a vertical scan is performed until a pixel labelled G is encountered; it is converted into U label, known as the upper envelope. Hough transform technique may be

applied on the upper envelopes for skew estimation. (B.B. Chaudhuri, 1998) has suggested a new idea which is faster, robust and accurate compared to Hough transform. The idea is based on Digital Straight Line (DSL). The upper envelope may contain non-linear parts which require deletion, for which chain code representation has been used. Conditions for straightness of chain code digital arc are given in (J. N. Kapur, 1985).
A subset of DSL is known as SDSL. SDSL consists of runs of pixels in at most two directions which differ by 45^0. For runs of two directions, the run lengths in one of the directions are always one. The run length in the other direction can have at most two values differing by unity. An example is shown in fig-6.1. Here, the angle between two directions d1 and d2 is 45° and run lengths in d1 direction are two (n) or three (n+1) occurring alternately.

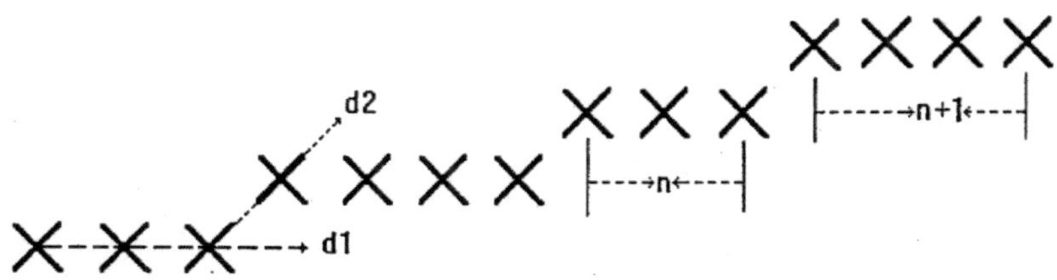

Fig. 6.1. Example of a digital straight line (DSL). Here, "X" denotes DSL pixel

A reasonable number of SDSLs can be used to find the average estimate of skew angle, which is formed between the first and last pixel of every SDSL with horizontal direction. To get a better estimate, clusters of SDSLs are found. Each line of text contains a number of SDSLs, which are grouped into a cluster. The SDSLs that have equal normal distances from a reference point are considered to be members of same cluster. The leftmost and the rightmost pixels of each cluster is taken and considered as the leftmost and rightmost coordinate of a line represented by that cluster. The Skew estimation algorithm is:

- STEP 1: Find connected components in the binary document image and find the mean b_m and standard deviation b_s of their bounding box widths.
- STEP 2: Choose the set S of connected components having bounding box width greater than or equal to b_m and less than $b_m+ 3b_s$.
- STEP 3: For each component in S find the upper envelope described above. From each envelope component, find the SDSLs. If more than one SDSL is found choose only the longest one and form the subset R_1. Let the longest SDSL in R_1 be C_L.
- STEP 4: From the line C_L or its continuation, find the normal distances to the leftmost pixel of other SDSLs of R_1.
- STEP 5: Cluster the SDSLs of R_1 corresponding to individual text lines and find the leftmost and rightmost pixel of each cluster, as described above.
- STEP 6: For each cluster find the angle of line joining the leftmost and rightmost pixels (e.g., A and B in Fig. 6.2d) with horizontal direction.
- STEP 7: Average of such angles over all clusters (e.g., text lines) gives an accurate estimate of the skew angle.

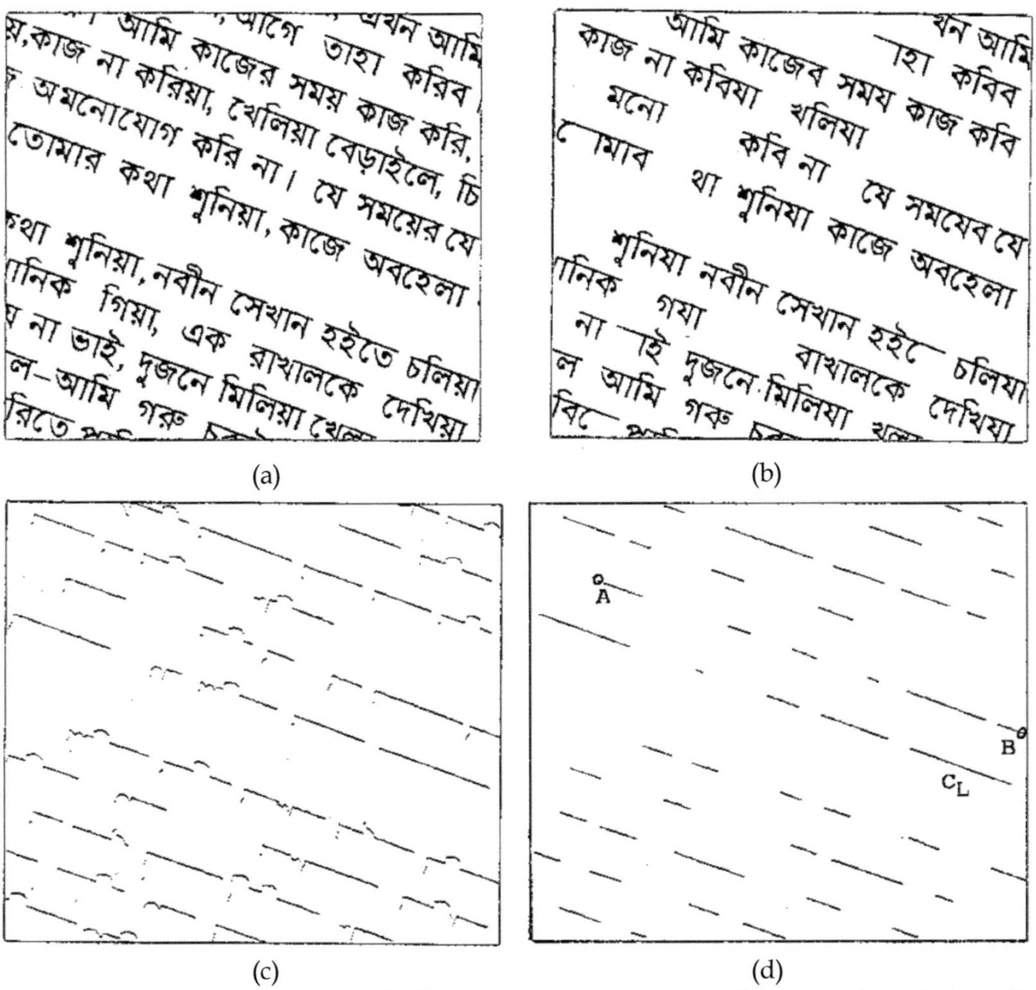

Fig. 6.2. Skew detection approach (Bangla). (a) An example of Bangla skewed text; (b) Selected components from fig. 6.2a; (c) Upper envelope of selected components of fig. 6.2b; (d) SDSL components of fig. 6.2c.

The efficiency of the above described method (A3) in table 6.1 has been measured and compared with Hough transform applied on original document (A1) and on SDSLs (A2), shown in that table. The average execution times for a document of 512X512 pixels on a SUN 3/60 (with Microprocessor MC68020, and SUN O.S. Version 3.0) machine are 620, 312, and 17.80 seconds for methods A1, A2 and A3, respectively shown by (B.B. Chaudhuri, 1997). It is shown that the methods A2 and A3 are statistically equally accurate. However method A3 takes less execution time.

True skew angle (in deg.) (manual)	Mean and SD of estimated skew angles using method					
	A_1		A_2		A_3	
	mean	SD	mean	SD	mean	SD
40	40.396	0.285	40.034	0.256	39.889	0.301
20	20.174	0.439	20.049	0.3162	20.047	0.242
10	10.271	0.393	10.166	0.201	10.112	0.323
5	5.064	0.458	4.962	0.213	5.188	0.233
2	1.986	0.396	2.151	0.234	2.054	0.307

For each true skew angle the statistics is computed over 20 document images.

A_1: Hough transform over total image.

A_2: Hough transform over SDSLs of upper envelop.

A_3: Proposed quick method.

Table 6.1. Mean and Standard Deviation (SD) of Estimated Skew Angles Obtained by Different Methods shown by (B.B. Chaudhuri, 1997)

7. Segmentation

This is the most vital and important portion for designing an efficient Bangla OCR because feature extraction and recognition process depends on this phase to make the recognition process successful. The output of this phase consists of individual images of basic, modified and compound characters. Segmentation process includes the following steps. They are:

1. Line Detection
2. Matraline or Headline detection
3. Baseline Detection
4. Word Segmentation
5. Character Segmentation

7.1 Line Detection Process

Generally, a document is written in multiple lines considering one or more than one columns. In this chapter, one columned document is considered. The lines of a text block are detected by finding continuous white pixels between two consecutive matralines. Fig: 7.1.1 shows the result.

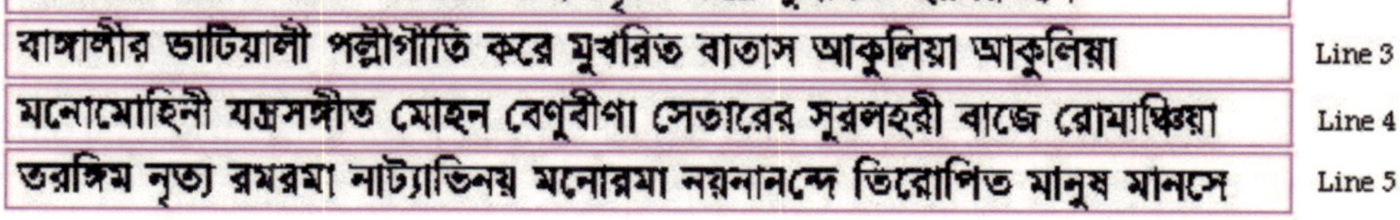

Fig. 7.1.1. Text line detection in a document image

7.2 Matraline or Headline Detection Process

Matraline or headline is an important and distinct feature in bangla. It connects the bangla components together. The matraline consists of highest number of black pixels compared to the upper, middle and lower zone. Under the matraline, the basic shapes of the characters are found. So, if matraline can be detected correctly, it helps to segment the characters in a more flexible way. The row with the highest frequency of black pixels is detected as matraline or headline. It is observed that the height or thickness of the matraline increases in case of larger font size. In those cases we get more rows having similar frequency or nearly close to the row of highest frequency. In order to detect the matraline with its full height, the rows with those frequencies are also treated as matraline (Jalal Uddin Mahmud, 2003). Thus we can say that matraline consists of matra upper line and matra bottom line. Fig. 7.2.1 shows the detection of matarline for different images, (a) and (b).

(a)

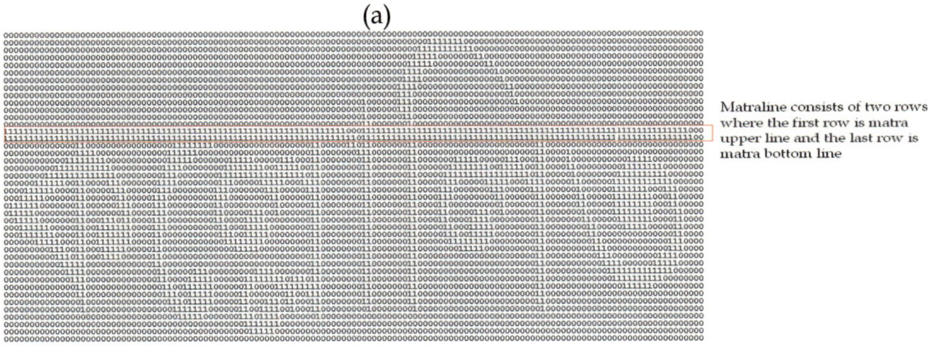

(b)

Fig. 7.2.1. Matraline detection process for different mages (a) - (b)

7.3 Baseline Detection Process

A line has a baseline, also named as an imaginary line, which is a row from where the middle zone ends and lower zone starts i.e. a separator between middle and lower zone. Baseline gets equal to end row of the line when the line does not have any lower modifier(s). It is the row where an abrupt change occurs between the previous and next row (S.M. Milky Mahmud, 2004). In a general document, it is observed that about 70% lines hold baseline i.e., 30% lines do not have lower modifiers. So detection of baseline is very important for bangla. Some characters particularly some modifiers are situated here and they are needed to be recognized. Baseline can be detected efficiently searching from lower position of the middle zone to the end row of a line. This is to find out the position from where the black pixels start to increase while they are decreasing in the middle zone. That position is denoted as baseline (Nasreen Akter, 2008). Fig. 7.3.1 shows the baseline.

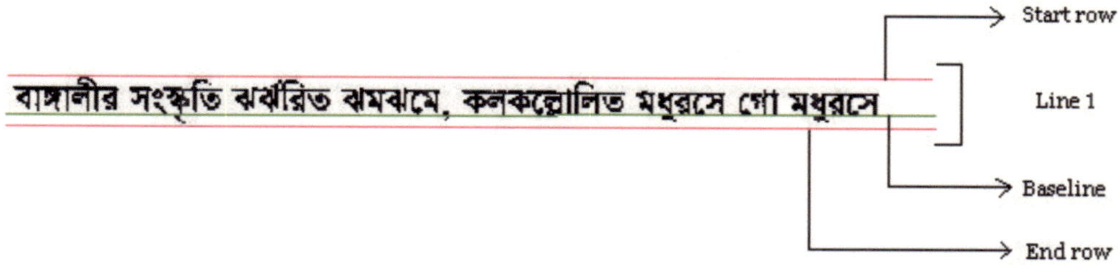

Fig. 7.3.1. Process of baseline detection

7.4 Word Segmentation Process

There are always some white spaces between two words in a text line. Using vertical scan, words are separated by treating the white spaces as a separator. Fig. 7.4.1 shows the word segmentation process.

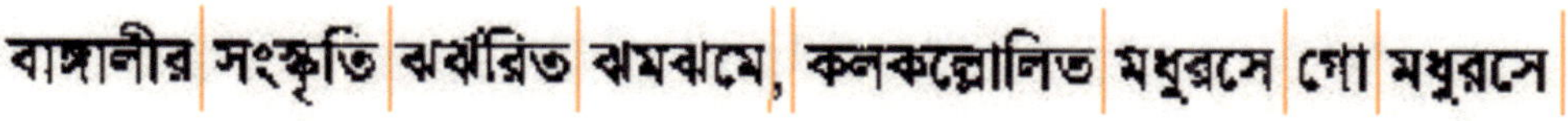

Fig. 7.4.1. Process of word segmentation

During the word segmentation process, peculiar situations occur when some matraless character is used in a word (fig. 7.4.2). These situations create some false separators which cause the word to be broken into small pieces. So the process of word segmentation becomes faulty. To avoid this error, widths of each separator in a line is calculated and an average of them is found. Separators which have widths greater than or equal to the half of the average are considered to be true separator (Nasreen Akter, 2008). (B.B. Chaudhuri, 1998) used the midpoint of a run of at least k_1 consecutive 0s (i. e., white pixels) if the run exits in a vertical projection profile of a line.

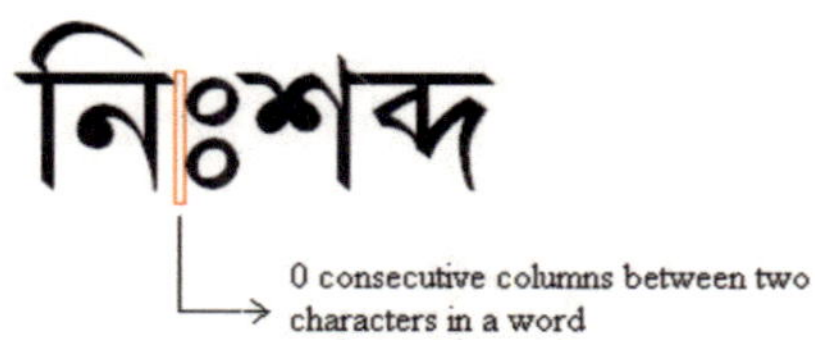

Fig. 7.4.2. Word with 0 consecutive columns between two characters

7.5 Character Segmentation Process

It is the most difficult and challenging part to build printed Bangla OCR. As Bangla is an inflectional language, the ornamentation of the characters in a word causes many peculiarities and makes the segmentation difficult. Many works have been done in order to solve those problems. A word can be constructed either with only taking the basic characters or basic characters and modifiers or basic and compound characters or basic, modified and compound characters. The main parts of all the characters are situated in the middle zone. So the middle zone area is considered as the character segmentation portion. Since matraline connects the characters together to form a word, it is ignored during the character segmentation process to get them topologically disconnected (B.B. Chaudhuri, 1998).

A word constructed with basic characters is segmented into characters in a way by scanning vertically, starting from just beneath the lower row of the matraline to the baseline, considering a column of continuous white pixels as the separator, shown in fig. 7.5.1, between the characters (B.B. Chaudhuri, 1998, Jalal Uddin Mahmud, 2003, Md. Abdus Sattar, 2007, Md. Al Mehedi Hasan, 2005, Nasreen Akter, 2008, S.M. Milky Mahmud, 2004). In this technique, the two characters, গ and ণ, get split into two pieces due to ignoring matraline. This problem is overcome by joining the left piece to the right one to make an individual character by considering the fact that a character in the middle zone always touches the baseline (B.B. Chaudhuri, 1998).

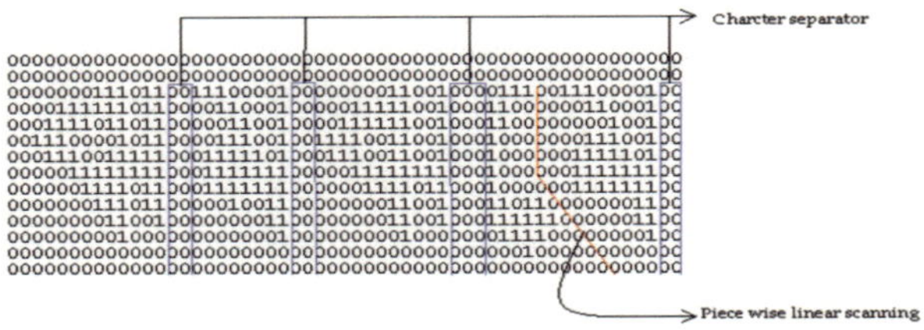

Fig. 7.5.1. Character segmentation ignoring matraline

There are four kinds of modifiers based on their uses. One kind of modifiers, used only in the middle zone, is called middle zone modifiers, for example া, ৗ, ে and the modifiers which are used only in the lower zone, such as, ু. ূ. ৃ - are called the lower zone modifiers. Another kind of modifiers is there which consists of both upper and middle zone. They are like ি . ী . ৗ, ৈ. The last kind of modifier is called the upper zone modifier, such as .

The four modifiers, ি . ী . ৗ, ৈ - have middle part as well as upper part. Some basic characters are there which also have upper portion of their own, for example, ই ঈ উ ঊ ট ঠ ঐ ঔ. The portions of these characters are found by a set of characteristic functions Md. Al Mehedi Hasan, 2005) or initiating a greedy search from a pixel in order to find a whole character (Jalal Uddin Mahmud, 2003). When the above modifiers, especially ি . ী . ৗ - are used with basic characters, many combinations like কি. কী. টি. ঠি. টী. ঠী. কৌ. টৌ. ঠৌ. In case of কি . কী . কৌ - these three modifiers have been used with those basic characters that have no upper portion of their own. As there is a separator, shown in fig. 7.5.2, in the middle zone for each of them, the thickness of the left and right portion of the separator determines which portion is for the modifier. A horizontal scan applying in immediate upper row of the matra upper line from left to right or right to left determines that the basic character does not have the upper part of its own (as because a row of white pixels is found from the scan). After that, the characters, কি . কী . কৌ - are got segmented keeping their original shapes (Nasreen Akter, 2008). In the time of টি. ঠি. টী. ঠী. টৌ. ঠৌ, a row of white pixels is not found during the horizontal scan. In টি and ঠি, the first found black pixel determines whether there is ট or ঠ and then টি is segmented to ি and ট in the way shown in fig. 7.5.2 and ঠি is segmented by calculating the gap in the upper zone and the thickness of the upper part of the basic character (Nasreen Akter, 2008).

In order to segment টী and ঠী, more than one gaps are found in the immediate upper row of the matra upper line for ঠী which determines there is ঁ. Then টী is segmented into characters by finding the cutting point in the first and second half of the upper zone and ঠী is by the thickness column (Nasreen Akter, 2008). Although ঠী has one gap, it does not get mixed up with টী since no cutting point is found in the first half of the upper zone. The segmentation process of ঠী is similar with the segmentation process of ষি only differing with the scan direction (Nasreen Akter, 2008). টী is segmented by finding the cutting point (Nasreen Akter, 2008).

More peculiarities are formed if the modifer র্ or ঁ gets included with those situations. These issues have not been addressed yet by researches. However, modifier, র্ with basic character, which is used in the upper zone, is detected by considering its distinct feature which is, it always makes a regular angle with matra (Md. Abdus Sattar , 2007).

Three other modifiers are there, ু. ূ. ৃ, which are used in the lower zone. They are extracted by doing DFS (Depth first search) below the baseline ((Jalal Uddin Mahmud, 2003) or finding a column of white pixels after the first black pixel is found (Nasreen Akter, 2008). Sometimes a small part of a middle zone character exceeds the baseline. They are distinguished from lower zone modifiers since they don't touch the end row of the line as the characters in the lower zone always touch that row (Nasreen Akter, 2008).

Rests of the modifiers are used in the middle zone and both of them are segmented as the regular way. However, sometimes basic character and modifier or two basic characters or two modifiers get into each others' region. If the middle zone modifiers and basic characters get into each others' region, a piecewise linear scanning is applied on them to segment the characters (B.B. Chaudhuri, 1998, Jalal Uddin Mahmud, 2003). Above all, during the character segmentation time, sometimes group of characters do not get segmented as they enter each others' region and seems to act like a character. A piece wise linear scanning, shown in fig. 7.5.1, is done to segment those characters (B.B. Chaudhuri, 1998).

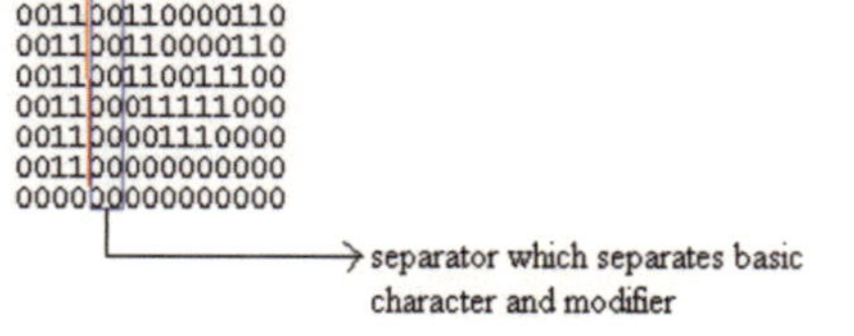

Fig. 7.5.2. Segmentation process of টি

8. Feature Extraction

Feature extraction is an important and challenging part for any character recognition process. Selection of good features leads to improved recognition rate. Many feature extraction algorithms are proposed for both printed and handwritten bangla document. Some of the potential algorithms are described below with comparative analysis.

8.1 Feature extraction algorithm for printed bangla character

(a) (Jalal Uddin Mahmud, 2003) proposed the following procedure to extract feature from bangla text. In Bangla language, more than one connected components are present. Here, at first, all the connected components of an isolated character are detected using DFS (Depth First Search). Then center of mass has been calculated for each connected component. Center of mass for i th connected component is (X_i, Y_i). Where

$$X_i = \sum_{j=1}^{N_i} P_{ij} / N_i \quad (1)$$

$$Y_i = \sum_{j=1}^{N_i} Q_{ij} / N_i \quad (2)$$

Here,
N_i = Number of Black pixels in connected component i.
P_{ij} = x Coordinate of the jth Black pixel in i^{th} connected component.
Q_{ij} = y Coordinate of the jth Black pixcl in i^{th} connected component.

Then a bounded rectangle of each component is calculated by its minimum and maximum span in x direction and y direction. The freeman chain code is calculated by dividing each component into four regions depending on the center of mass of that component shown in fig. 8.1.1.

Fig. 8.1.1. Four Regions for a connected component

Freeman Chain code is based on the observation that each pixel has eight neighborhood pixels. The 8 transitional positions defined by freeman chain code are then divided into 4 transitional zones in order to keep the correct order of searching. Fig. 8.1.2 describes the freeman chain code.

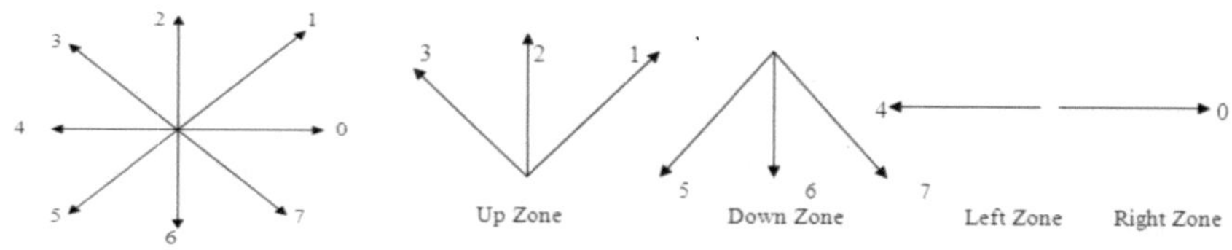

(a) (b)

Fig. 8.1.2. (a) Slope Convention for Freeman Chain code, (b) 8 directional slopes divided into 4 direction zones for searching.

Maintaining an anti clock wise order of searching, zonal information is used to modify the chain coded position of the next selected pixel. The algorithm selects the next pixel if it fulfils all of the following criteria:

- The pixel is Black, i.e., it is a part of the character.
- The pixel is within the bounded rectangle of the connected component.
- The pixel is still not visited.
- The pixel is in a zone.

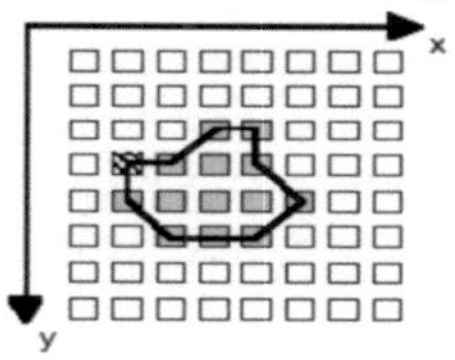

Zone	Searching Order
DOWN	3,4,5,6,7,0,1,2
RIGHT	5,6,7,0,1,2,3,4
UP	7,0,1,2,3,4,5,6
LEFT	1,2,3,4,5,6,7,0

(a) (b)

Fig. 8.1.3. (a) Chain code generation for an image, (b) Searching order in the four zones

Fig. 8.1.3 (a) shows the chain code generation of an image marked by gray pixels. When the algorithm starts from the hatched pixel (absolute coordinate, x=1, y=3), it marks the current black pixel as visited and initiates its directional zone as DOWN zone. So it searches for an unvisited black pixel in the directional order: 3,4,5,6,7,0,1,2 (Searching order is shown in Fig. 8.1.3 (b) for each zone). In this way the process continues and finally produces the chain code, 06700132454.

The frequency of each directional slope at each region is recorded and updated during the traverse. A total of 32 directional slopes or local features for each component are found. Then they are normalized to 0-1 scale. In Bangla, as there are more than one components in a character, the normalized features for each connected components are then averaged. The calculation of normalized slope distribution is as follows:

If $a_1, a_2, a_3, \ldots\ldots\ldots, a_8$ are 8 directional slopes in region 1, then normalizing constant for region 1 is,

$$N_1 = \sqrt{(a_1 * a_1 + a_2 * a_2 + \ldots\ldots\ldots + a_8 * a_8)} \qquad (3)$$

So, normalized slope in region i = $S_{i,j} / N_i$, where i = 1 to 4 and j = 1 to 8

$S_{i,j}$ = Frequency of jth directional slope in i^{th} region.

N_i = Normalizing constant in i^{th} region.

(b) (Abu Sayeed Md. Sohail, 2005) demonstrated a method where a large two dimensional vector is converted into a small one dimensional vector. Here, initially, character images of fixed resolution are separated from original text and digitized into a large two dimensional vector, later converted into a small one dimensional vector. The algorithm they used is:

i. Find center of the image by Center_x = (width)/2, Center_y = (Height + 1)/2
ii. For each black pixel, a radius is calculated as $r = \sqrt{(Center\_x - x)^2 + (Center\_y - y)^2}$
iii. Sum all pixels within same radius (sum_r_max,..........., sum_r_min)
iv. Calculate the membership for each circle or disk using the membership function, $m\_f(bp) = e^{-(|\,|bp - rbp)/total\_pixels}$

This technique is used for the recognition of a single isolated character. It has not been tested for all the characters in a document or at least in a word.
The technique has been used with ANN (Artificial Neural Network). The advantage of this technique, shown by the authors, is that the extracted features are same even if the original character is rotated with rotation angles from 5 to 350 degree having a little bit of distortion. Non rotated characters are recognized with more than 90% of efficiency while rotated characters are recognized over 80- 89% efficiency depending upon the angle of rotation.

(c) (B.B. Chaudhuri, 1998) showed that compound characters occupy only 4-6% of the text corpus. In order to introduce fast, accurate and robust technique, basic, modifier and compound characters are distinguished and identified by the following 3 features listed below.

i. Feature f_1 - Bounding box width.
ii. Feature f_2 - Number of border pixels per unit width, which is computed by dividing the total number of character border pixels by the width of the character.
iii. Feature f_3 - Accumulated curvature per unit width.

They have used a feature-based approach for basic and modifier character recognition and a combination of feature-based and template-matching approach for the compound character recognition.
The authors considered a few stroke features for initial classification of the basic characters by a tree classifier. Apart from them, some other features are also used at some nodes of the tree classifier. In fig. 8.1.4, the principal set of chosen stroke features is shown.

Fig. 8.1.4 Stroke features used for character recognition. (Shaded portions in the character represent the features)

It is mentioned that most of the cases, the strokes, 1, 2, 3, 4, 5 and 8 are correctly detected.

8.2 Feature extraction algorithm for Bangla handwritten characters

(a) (Subhadip Basu, 2005) has used a set of 76 features which includes 24 shadow features, 16 centriod features and 36 longest- run features, computed taking 64 x 64 pixel size binary images.

Shadow features are calculated by dividing the image into 8 octants within minimal square. Lengths of all projections on each of the 24 sides of all octants are summed up to produce 24 shadow features, shown in fig. 8.2.1.

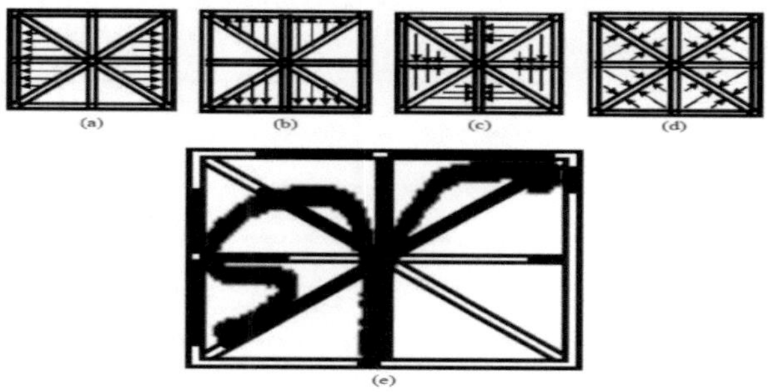

Fig. 8.2.1. An illustration for shadow features. (a-d) Direction of fictitious light rays as assumed for taking the projection of an image segment on each side of all octants. (e) Projection of a sample image

Coordinates of centriods of black pixels in all 8 octants of a digitized image, shown in fig. 8.2.2, are considered to add 16 centriod features.

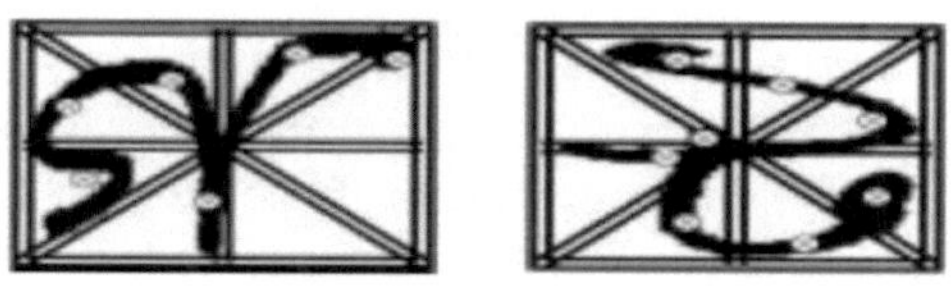

Fig. 8.2.2. Centriod features of two different characters (a)-(b)

Longest- run features are computed dividing the square into 9 overlapping regions and for each, 4 longest-run features are calculated respectively by row wise, column wise along 2 of its diagonal. Thus 36 features are produced (fig. 8.2.3).

1	0	1	1	1	1
1	0	0	1	1	0
1	0	0	1	1	0
1	0	0	0	1	0
0	1	0	0	1	0
0	0	1	1	0	0

(a)

						Length of the Longest Bar
1	0	4	4	4	4	4
1	0	0	2	2	0	2
1	0	0	2	2	0	2
1	0	0	0	1	0	1
0	1	0	0	1	0	1
0	0	2	2	0	0	2
					Sum =	12

(b)

Fig. 8.2.3. An illustration for computation of the row wise longest-run feature.(a) The portion of a binary image enclosed within a rectangular region.(b) every pixel position in each row of the image is marked with the lenght of the longest bar that fits consecutive black pixels along the same row.

(b) (Mohammad Badiul Islam, 2005) suggested various stroke feature generation for handwritten bangla characters (fig. 8.2.4). Stroke identification is performed using curve fitting algorithm and curvature analysis. The equation of curve fitting is, $x=a+by+cy^2$. The point on the stroke that has maximum curvature, k, is calculated with the formula, $k= x_2/(1+x_1^2)^{3/2}$ where $x_1 = dx/dy$ and $x_2 = d^2x/dy^2$. If $k >= 0.9$ then the stroke is a curve otherwise a straight line. Finally, the code is given using the slope equation, $x = a + by$.

Stroke	Characteristics	Numeric Code
	Horizontal line	1
	Positive sloping line	2
	Vertical Line	3
	Negative sloping line	4
	Vertical concave curve	5
	Vertical convex curve	6
	Rejected stroke	0

Fig. 8.2.4. Strokes used for Bangla character Recognition.

(c) (T.K. Bhowmik, 2003) constructed a feature vector of lengths ((2L + 1) + 3) as:
$f_L = (D_L, P_i, H_v, H_{Run})$, generated for those points whose lower bound and upper bound cardinalities are greater than or equal to L excluding that point.
Where, $D_L = \{d_{i-1}, d_{i-1+1}, \ldots, d_{i-1}\} \cup \{d_i\} \cup \{d_{i+1}, d_{i+2}, \ldots d_{i+1}\}$
P_i = (height of x_i with respect to middle zone) / height of the middle zone
H_v = (value of vertical histogram of x_i) / height of the middle zone
H_{Run} = value of black pixel run of x_i
Then the feature vector, f_L, is normalized to $f_L^N = (D_L/8, P_i, H_v, H_{Run}/\delta)$ where, δ is a constant.

8.3 Comparative analysis on different types of features

In section 8.1 and 8.2, a total of six features are discussed. The technique given in section 8.1b is used for the recognition of a single isolated character. It has not been tested for all the characters in a document or at least in a word. Using stroke feature technique (section 8.1c), a set of characters are found in most of the leaves of the decision tree (fig. 9.1) which needs further care to extract feature for identification of individual character. Chain code feature generation, discussed in section 8.1a, helps to produce a distinct feature set of 32 slopes for each component of the segmented characters. Shadow, centriod and longest-run feature set illustrated in section 8.2a, provides a total of 76 feature values for each characters. Although these two techniques produce distinct feature sets for each character, significant difference is observed between these two techniques among the samples of different sized characters.

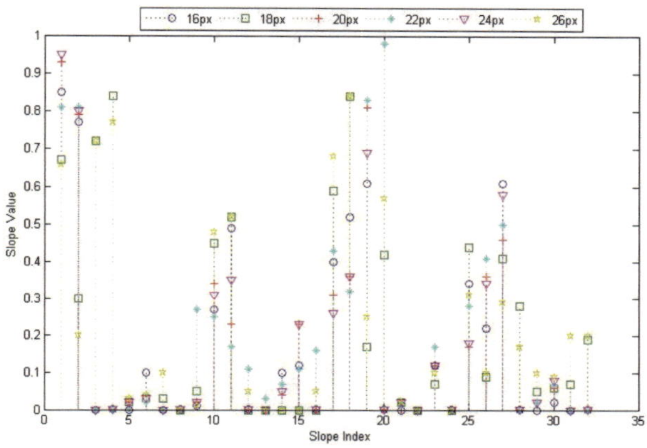

(a) Slope values for letter Aa

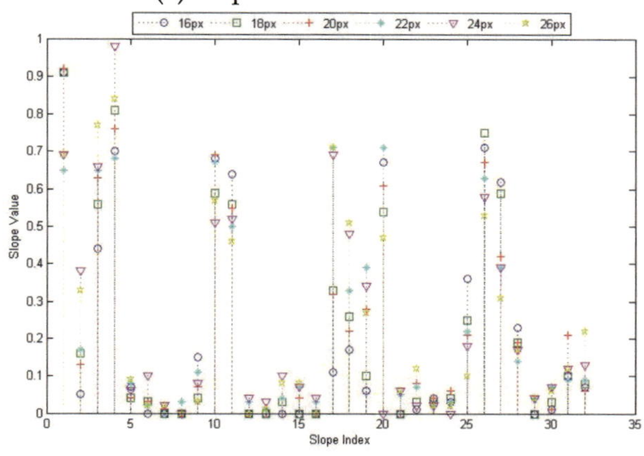

(b) Slope values for letter Kha

Fig. 8.3.1. Slope produced by chain code (a)-(b)

Fig. 8.3.1a and fig. 8.3.1b display 32 slope values for character Aa (আ) and Kha (খ) respectively. Six different sizes of fonts, namely 16, 18, 20, 22, 24 and 26 pixel font sizes have been considered for both cases. All these fonts have been resized into 64 x 64 pixels. In some cases, a slope value for each of the font size is same, for example, slope values at index 7 for

Aa (আ) while slope values at index 26 differ by a significant amount. Same type of result is found in fig. 8.3.2. On the other hand, similar analysis is performed with shadow, centriod and longest run features. We considered 68 feature values from them used in (Subhadip Basu, 2005). Values of these 68 features for letter 'Aa' and 'Kha' are presented in fig. 8.3.2. We have considered 6 font sizes for both these characters. It is seen in the figure that each value for all sizes deviates among themselves in a lesser amount than that of chain code representation.

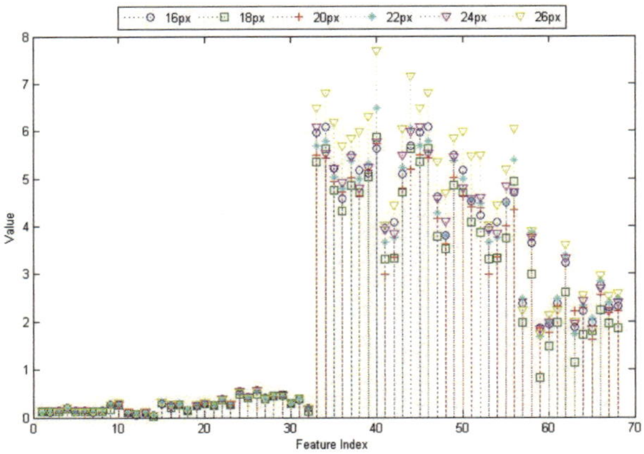

(a) Letter Aa

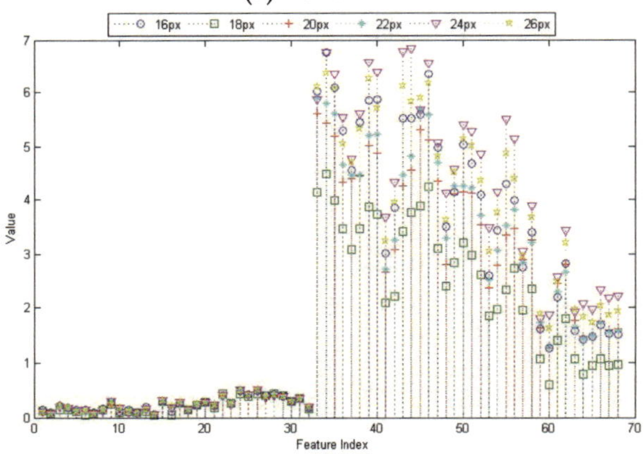

(b) Letter Kha

Fig. 8.3.2. Shadow, centriod and longest run feature values (a)-(b)

9. Classification

This is the last phase of the whole recognition process. Several approaches have been used to identify a character based on the features extracted using algorithms described in previous section. However, there is no benchmark databases of character sets to test the performance of any algorithm developed for Bengali character recognition (Angshul Majumdar, 2009). Each paper has taken their own samples for training and testing their proposals. In choosing classification algorithms, use of Artificial Neural Network (ANN) is a popular practice because it works better when input data is affected with noise. Since a detailed definition of different Neural Network is outside the scope of this chapter, the readers are suggested to see established literature for detailed description of these methods. However a brief overview is provided for Decision tree and MLP classifier with some other neural networks.

9.1 Decision tree

(B.B. Chaudhuri, 1998) used a binary tree classification. Only one feature is tested at each non terminal node. The decision rules are mostly binary e.g. presence or absence of the feature. Here, the features are positional strokes. As one goes down the tree, the number of features to choose from gets reduced. Most basic characters can be recognized by the principle features alone. In some cases, more than one characters share the same non-terminal node of the tree. To separate them, some additional features are used (likewise, ক and ফ - vertical line touches headline or not, ণ and ন, a vertical line at center position cross ন 3 times while ণ is 4 times).

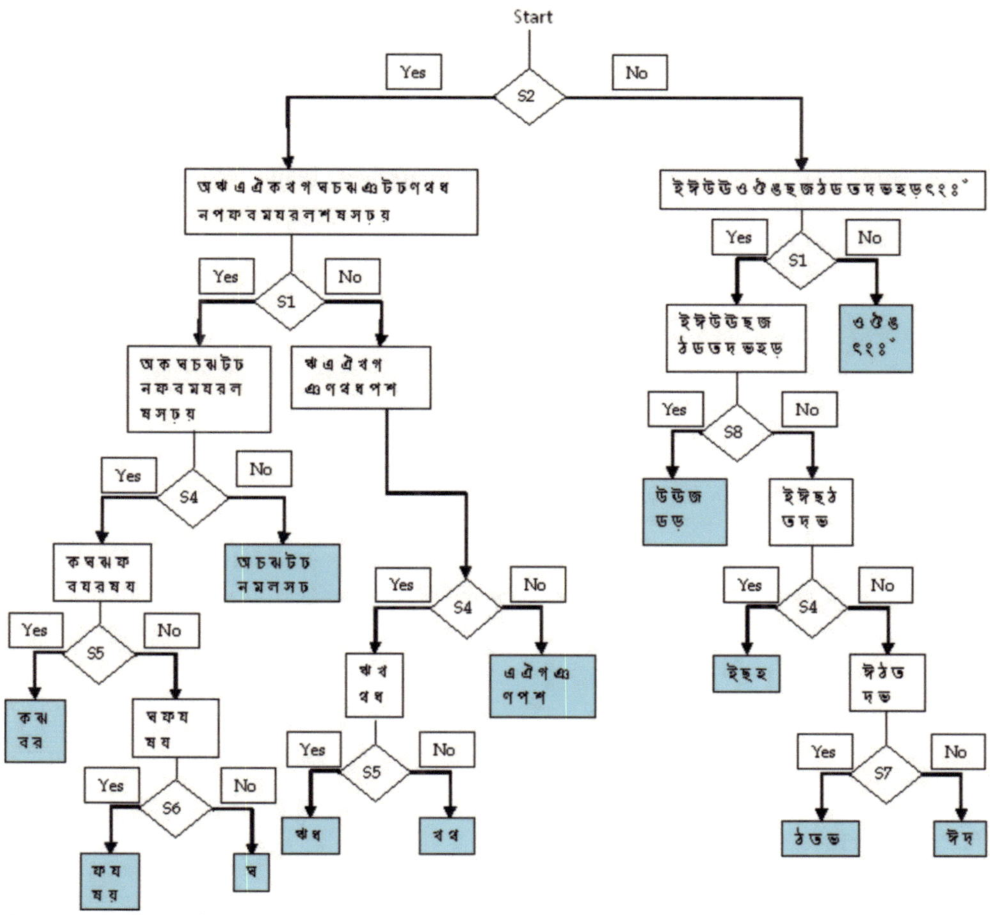

Fig. 9.1. A flow chart representation of a certain portion of tree classifier for basic character recognition

Compound character recognition is done in 2 stages. In the first stage, the characters are grouped into small subsets by a feature-based tree classifier. At the second stage, characters in each group are recognized by a sophisticated run-based template matching approach. The features used in the tree classifier are headline, vertical line, left slant (i.e., features 1, 2, 3 of fig. 8.1.4), boundary box width, presence of signature in upper zone etc. A terminal node of this tree corresponds to a subset of about 20 characters. These character templates are ranked in terms of their bounding box width and stored during the training phase of the classifier. When a character reaches the terminal node in search phase, firstly bounding box width is matched, then a matching score is completed by superimposing the candidate on the template. Different algorithms have been prescribed to compute matching score. In this process, a reasonable amount of character size variation can be accommodated by rescaling. If templates for 12 point character size are stored, it was found that characters from size ranging from 8 to 16 points can be matched by rescaling the candidate without appreciable error. Fig. 9.1 depicts an elaborated decision tree for basic character recognition.

9.2 MLP

(Subhadip Basu, 2005) has used Multi-Layer Perceptron (MLP) classifier to classify handwritten alphabetic characters. It is a special kind of ANN, a feed-forward neural network with artificial neurons. An MLP consists of one input layer, one output layer and a number of hidden layers. The output of each neuron is connected to each neuron of the immediate next layer as input. Neurons in the input layer are used to simply pass the information to the next layer. Supervised training is applied. Back Propagation has been used here which minimizes the sum of square error for the training samples by conducting a gradient descent search in weight space. It is found that the recognition performance is increased as the number of neurons in the hidden layer is increased (Table 9.2.1). A training set of 8000 samples and a test set of 2000 samples of optically scanned handwritten characters of 50 alphabetic symbols have been used to train and test the network. All these samples were scaled to 64x64 pixel images first and then converted to binary images through thresholding. The Back Propagation algorithm with learning rate 0.8 and momentum term 0.7 were executed. (fig. 9.2.1)

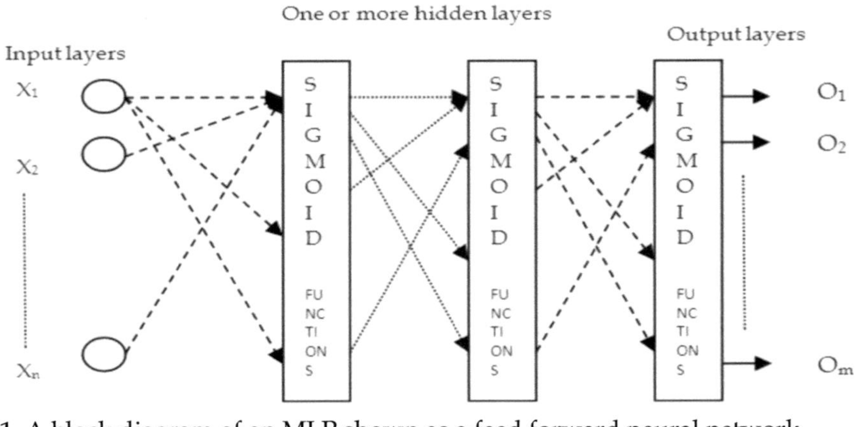

Fig. 9.2.1. A block diagram of an MLP shown as a feed forward neural network

No of Hidden Neurons	35	40	45	50	55	60	65	70	75
Percentage recognition rate on the training samples	80.35	80.93	82.8	84.7	85.70	86.46	87.36	86.69	85.65
Percentage Recognition rate on test samples	70.35	70.70	71.6	73.15	74.2	75.05	73.65	74.7	72.00

Table 9.2.1. Recognition Performance of the MLP with different numbers of neurons in the hidden layers

9.3 Kohonen Neural Network (KNN)

KNN (Adnan Mohammad Shoeb Shatil, 2007) differs from the feed forward back propagation neural network architectures. The first difference is that the Kohonen network (fig. 9.3.1) does not contain hidden layers; secondly, training and recognition processes are significantly different, that is, it is trained in unsupervised mode; thirdly, it does not use an activation function, and finally, the Kohonen Network does not use any bias weight in the network. For a particular feature vector of a given pattern, a single neuron will be fired. Input data is first resized to 250x250 pixels, regardless of whether the input image is a single word or character. Skew detection was not taken into consideration. Both computer generated image and scanned image have been used to train the network. A character is converted into a vector of length 625, which also determines the number of input neurons. This work considered 10 Bangla digits, 11 vowels, 36 consonants, in total, 57 characters. Authors have reported the performance of kohonen network given in Table 9.3.1 based on different scopes of character/words i. e., trained, untrained similar, scanned documents and irregular font. A comparison on accuracy rate between kohonen and neural network is found in Table 9.3.2.

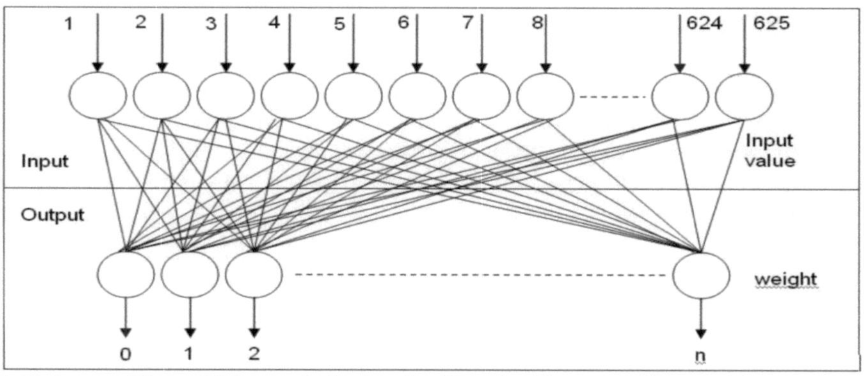

Fig. 9.3.1. Kohonen Neural Network design for Bangla Character Recognition

Character/Words	Rate of accuracy with kohonen network
Trained	100%
Untrained similar	99%
Scanned documents	99%
Irregular font	98%

Table 9.3.1. Accuracy rates corresponding to different sectors

Typeface	Accuracy rate	
	Kohonen network	Neural network
Sutonny	97.6%	94.37%
Sulekha	96.2%	91.25%

Table 9.3.2. Performance comparison between Kohonen Network and Neural Network

9.4 Nearest Subspace Classifier

The concept of Nearest Subspace Classifier has been applied in a different way in (Angshul Majumdar, 2009). The assumption is - samples from each class lie on a subspace specific to that class. As per the assumption, the training samples of a particular class span its subspace. The problem is to determine to which subspace it belongs to. Therefore, any new test sample belonging to a class can be represented as a linear combination of the test samples i.e.

$$v_{k,test} = \sum_{i=1}^{n_k} \alpha_{k.i}.v_{k.i} + \varepsilon_k$$

Where $v_{k,test}$ is the test sample for k^{th} class, $v_{k,i}$ is the ith test sample for the kth class and ε_k is the approximation error for the kth class

The error term is written as

$$\varepsilon_k = ((V_k^T V_k)^{-1} V_k^T - I)v_{k,test}$$

The expression in brackets (the orthoprojector) can be computed beforehand since it does not depend on test sample. The algorithm is as follows:

Training - For each class 'i', compute the orthoprojector (the term in bracket of the above equation)

Testing - Calculate the error for each class 'i' by hitting the test sample by the orthoprojector. Classify the test sample to the class having the minimum error.

During experimentation, each image is normalized to 16x16 pixels. Two different scenarios, namely pessimistic and optimistic scenarios have been considered. There were 12 different fonts of 5 different sizes of each. For the pessimistic scenario 5 different datasets were created by randomly splitting the font types into groups of 9 for training and 3 for testing (Table 9.4.1). For optimistic scenario, 3 different datasets were created by randomly splitting the font sizes into groups of 3 for training and groups of 2 for testing (Table 9.4.2). The authors have shown that this classifier gives better performance than Nearest Neighbour, Sparse Classifier and Support Vector Machine.

Set No.	KNN	Proposed	SC	SVM
1	0.1529	0.0667	0.1085	0.1200
2	0.3660	0.2157	0.2967	0.3507
3	0.4065	0.2549	0.3098	0.3720
4	0.4157	0.3150	0.3699	0.3853
5	0.2706	0.2065	0.2314	0.2507

Table 9.4.1. Recognition Error for Pessimistic Scenario

Set No.	KNN	Proposed	SC	SVM
1	0.0253	0.0074	0.0114	0.0204
2	0.0376	0.0082	0.0188	0.0302
3	0.0596	0.0245	0.0384	0.0474

Table 9.4.2. Recognition Error for Optimistic Scenario

9.5 Heuristics Neural Network

Heuristics on Neural Network (Golam Sarowar, 2009) showed that variation in implementing Back Propagation (BP) algorithm can significantly affect a Neural Network's performance. Even better preprocessing and feature extraction may fail to give better accuracy if the recognition process (both training and testing) is incompetent. The rate of convergence of BP depends on the learning rate. Learning rate is reduced when a new train sample increases error after weight adjustment of NN and rate is increased when a new train sample decreases the error in classification. BP with momentum method is such a method where both the weight change at the previous step and the gradient at the current step are used to determine the weight change for the current step. With momentum, a network can slide through a local minimum which otherwise get stuck. In conjugate gradient algorithms, search is performed along conjugate directions, not in the steepest descent direction (negative of the gradient), which generally produces faster convergence. Some conjugate gradient algorithms are Fletcher-Reeves Update, Polak-Ribiere update, Powell-Beale restarts and scaled conjugate gradient. Some heuristics have also been applied to the above variations of BP. Antisymmetric activation or transfer function quickens the learning. Maximum possible information content in the training set can be ensured by introducing a training set that results largest training error. Desired response of a neuron at the output layer is offset by some amount to prevent the free parameters of the network being driven to infinity. Each input variable should have a zero-mean. It is useful to reduce the dimension of input vectors. Use of crossvalidation (B. Yegananarayana, 2008) may be used to prevent overfitting a common problem with neural network training. Table 9.5.1 and 9.5.2 show performance variations in case of different versions of BP algorithm with and without heuristics.

Algorithm	Performance Error	Epoch	Mis-classification	Accuracy %
Backpropagation with momentum	0.021	1251	115	83.57
Backpropagation with adaptive learning rate	0.07	102	180	74.29
Powell-Beale restarts	0.0121	80	86	87.26
Polak-Ribiere update	0.02	74	95	86.43
Scaled Conjugate Gradient	0.021	150	110	84.29

Table 9.5.1. Accuracy without heuristics

Algorithm	Performance Error	Epoch	Mis-classification	Accuracy %
Backpropagation with momentum	0.40114	3163	102	85.43
Backpropagation with adaptive learning rate	0.69554	62	224	68
Powell-Beale restarts	0.405388	65	78	88.86
Polak-Ribiere update	0.4180	43	84	88.00
Scaled Conjugate Gradient	0.399	81	97	86.14

Table 9.5.2. Accuracy with heuristics applied

The authors mentioned that the main issue with recognition of Bengali characters is the scarcity of samples. Typically, parametric classifiers like Artificial Neural Network (ANN) and SVM perform well when there is a lot of training data available; otherwise the parameters used in classification over-fit. In such a case it is logical to use a non-parametric classifier such as the KNN.

10. Future Challenges and Conclusion

Despite so many attempts to solve problems on several aspects of an OCR, a fully fledged solution is still unavailable for Bangle language. Problems that we have identified are summarized below.
Little data are available as sample. So rigorous testing of an implementation is not possible. Each author has used their own set of data. As a result, comparative analysis does not produce a really meaningful result. Some authors addressed noise detection and cleaning phase in their works. However, a comprehensive solution for elimination of all types of noise is not available. The reader has already understood that Bangla has not only basic characters; it is rich with modifiers and compound characters. Placement of modifiers may happen on the upper, lower, left or right side of original characters which generates a lot of complications. Rarely authors could confidently claim that a particular segmentation and classification scheme has dealt with all of them. Again lack of standard or benchmark samples do not allow one to make a comprehensive testing of their application. Investigation of the phases of pattern recognition deserves special attention to be considered. We have done some component level implementation on Intel® Core™2 Duo processor with 4 GB RAM. Fig. 5.1a has been used as a sample image for binarization, segmentation, feature extraction, and classification. The total time length required for all the activities took from 1 minute to 10 minutes depending on the choice of algorithms. This suggests that careful investigation would reveal the best possible combination of algorithms and processes for all the phases of Bangla OCR. It is evident that a full commercial OCR is a demand of the time in this era of digitization.

11. References

A. Ray Chaudhuri, A Mallick, D. Singh, M. Nasipuri & D.K. Basu (2005). Bangla Document Image Analysis, Recognition and Reconstruction, NCCPB, Bangladesh, pp.276-284

A. Roy, T.K.Bhowmik, S.K.Parui & U.Roy (2005). A New Approach to Skew Detection and Character Segmentation for Handwritten Bangla Words, Proceedings Of The Digital Imafing Computing: Techniques And Applications, IEEE

Abu Sayeed Md. Sohail, Md. Robiul Islam, Boshir Ahmed & M A Mottalib (2005). Improvement in Existing Offline Bangla Character Recognitions Techniques Introducing Substainability to Rotation and Noise, NCCPB, Bangladesh, pp. 163-170

Adnan Mohammad Shoeb Shatil and Mumit Khan (2007). Computer Science and Engineering, BRAC University, Dhaka, Bangladesh

Al-Sakib Khan Pathan, Md. Mahbub Alam, Mostafa Monowar, Forhad Rabbi, Sabbir Ahmed & Tareq Hasan Khan. 12-Segment Display for Bengali Numerical Characters

Angshul Majumdar & Rabab K. Ward (2009). Nearest Subspace Classifier: Application To Character Recognition

Angshul Majumdar (1999). Bangla Basic Character Recognition Using Digital Curvelet Transform, *Journal of Pattern Recognition Research*, Vol(1)17-26

Angshul Majumdar (2007). Bangla Basic Character Recognition Using Digital Curvelete Transform , *Journal Of Pattern Recognition Research*, Vol (1) 17-26

Angshul Majumdar (2008). Multi Font Bangla Character Recognition Via Multiresolution Transforms,PP.1-14

Atallah Mahmoud Al-Shatnawi & Khairuddin Omar (2009). Skew Detection And Correction Technique For Arabic Document Images Based On Cemtre Of Gravity, *Journal Of Computer Science*, Vol(5)(363-368)

B.B. Chaudhuri & U. Pal (1997). Skew Angel Detection Of Digitized Indian Scripts Documents, *Transactions On Pattern Analysis And Machine Intelligence*, IEEE, PP. 182-186

B.B. Chaudhuri & U. Pal (1998). Complete Printed Bangla OCR System, Elsevier Science Ltd. *Pattern Recognition*, Vol(31): 531-549

B. Yegananarayana (2008) "Artificial Neural Network". Prentice-Hall India

Barbara F. Grimes (1997). *Ethnologue: Languages of the World*, 11th edition.

Carlos A.B. de Mello & Rafael D.Lins (1921). A Comparative Study on OCR Tools, Vision Interface'99, Toris-Riviers, Canada, PP.224-232

Dipit Deodhare, NNR Ranga Suri & R.Amit (2005). Preprocessing And Image Enhancement Algorithms For A Form-Based Intelligent Character Recognition System, *International Journal Pf Computer Science & Applications*, Vol(2):131-144

Faruq A. Al-Omari & Omar Al-Jarrah (2004). Handwritten Andian Numerals Recognition System Using Probabilistic Neural Network, *Advanced Engineering Informatics*, Vol(18):9-16

Golam Sarowar, M.A. Naser, S.M. Nizamuddin, Nafiz I.B. Hamid, Adnan Mahmud (2009). Enhancing Bengali Character Recognition Process Applying Heuristics On Neural Network, *International Journal Of Computer Science And Network Security*, Vol(9):154-158

J. N. Kapur, P. K. Sahoo and A. K. C. Wong, A new method for gray-level picture thresholding using the entropy of the histogram, *Comput. »ision Graphics Image Process*. 29, 273Ð285 (1985)

Jalal Uddin Mahmud, Mohammed Feroz Raihan & Chowdhury Mofizur Rahman (2003). A Complete OCR System For Continuous Bangali Characters, IEEE,PP. 1372-1376

Kaustubh Bhattacharyya & Kandarpa Kumar Sarma (2009). ANN-Based Innovative Segmentation Method For Handwritten Text In Assamese, *International Journal Of Computer Science Issues*, Vol.(5):9-16

Laurence Likforman-Sulem, Abderrazak Zahour & Bruno Taconet (2006). Text Line Segmentation Of Historical Documents: a survey, *International Journal On Document Analysis And Recognition*, PP. 1-25

Li Zhuang & Xiaoyan Zhu (2005). An OCR Post-Processing Approach Based On Multi-Knowledge, R.Khosla et al.(EDs):KES , LNAI 3681,PP. 346-352

M.Cheriet, N.Kharma, C.L.Liu & C.Y.Suen (2007). Introduction: Character Recognition, Evolution And Development, Character Recognition Systems: A Guide For Students And Practitioner, PP.1-4

M.S. Alam (2009). Research on Bangla Language Processing In Bangladesh: Progress And Challenges, International Language & Development Conference, Dhaka, Bangladesh, PP.527-533

Md. Abdus Sattar, Khaled Mahmud, Humayun Arafat and A F M Noor Uz Zaman. Segmenting Bangla Text For Optical Recognition, ICCIT 2007, Dhaka, Bangladesh PP. 27-29

Md. Abul Hasnat Mumit Khan (2009). Elimination of Spliting Errors In Printed Bangla Scripts

Md. Abul Hasnat Mumit Khan (2009). Rule Based Segmentation of Lower Modifies In Complex Bangla Script

Md. Abul Hasnat, Muttakinur Rahman Chowdhury & Mumit khan (2009). Integrating Bangla Script Recognition Support in Tesseract OCR

Md. Abul Hasnat, S.M. Murtoza Habib, Mumit Khan (2007). A High Performance Domain Specific OCR for Bangla Script

Md. Al Mehedi Hasan, Md. Abdul Alim & Md. Wahedul Islam , A New Approach To Bangla Text Extraction And Recognition From Textual Image

Md. Al Mehedi Hasan, Md. Abdul Alim, Md. Wahedul Islam & M. Ganger Ali (2005). Bangla Text Extraction and Recognition from Textual Image, NCCPB, Bangladesh, PP.171-176

Md. Wahedul Islam, MD Al Mehedi Hasan & Ramesh Chandra Debnath (2005). Handwritten Bangla Numerical Recognition Using Back-Propagation Algorithm With and Without Momentum Factor, NCCPB, Bangladesh, PP. 177-182

Md. Waliullah Khan Nomani, Syed Mustafa Khelat Bari, Tanwir Zubayer Islam & Mohammed Nazrul Islam (2007). Invariant Bangla Character Recognition Using A Projection-Slice Synthetic-Discriminant-Function-Based Algorithm, *Journal Of Electrical & Electronics Enginering*, Vol(7): 403-409

Mohammad Badiul Islam, Mollah Masum Billah Azadi & Dr, M. M. A. Hashem (2005). Bengali Handwritten Character Recognition Using Modified Syntactic Method, NCCPB, Bangladesh, PP. 264-275

Mohammad Masud Al Hossain Khan, Uzzal K. Acharjee & Bipul K. Sen (2005). Detection Of Bengali Text in Digital Images Using Connected Component Analysis, NCCPB, Bangladesh, PP.292-298

Mohammad Monjur Alam & Mohammad Anwer (2005). Feature Subset Selection Using Genetic Algorithm For Bangali Handwritten Digit Recognition, NCCPB, Bangladesh, PP. 258-263

Mohammad Osiur Rahman, Fouzia Ashraf Mousumi, Edgar Scavino, Aini Hussain & Hassan Basri (2009). Real Time Road sign Recognition System Using Artificial Neural Networks For Bengali Textual Information Box, *European Journal Of Scintific Research*, Vol(25): 478-487

Mohammed Moshiul Hoque & S.M. Faizur Rahman (2007). Fuzzy Features Extraction From Bangla Handwritten Character, ICCIT, Dhaka,Bangladesh, PP.72-75

Munirul Mansur, Naushad Uzzaman and Mumit Khan (2006). Analysis of n-gram Based Text Categorization for Bangla in a Newspaper Corpus, *ICCIT*, Dhaka, Bangladesh, pp.1-24

N. Otsu (1979). A threshold selection method from gray level histograms, *IEEE [1]rans. Systems Man Cybernet.* 9,62-66

Nasreen Akter, Saima Hossain, Md. Tajul Islam & Hasan Sarwar (2008). An Algorithm For Segmenting Modifies From Bangla Text, *ICCIT*, IEEE, Khulna,Bangladesh, PP.177-182

Nirmalya Chowdhury & Diganta Shaha (2005). Bengali Text Classification Using Cohonen's Self Organizing Network, NCCPB, Bangladesh, PP. 196-200

Nirmalya Chowdhury & Diganta Shaha (2005). A Neural Network Based Text Classification Method: A Possible Application for Bengali Text Classification, NCCPB, Bangladesh, PP. 183-188

R Sanjeev Kunte & R D Sudhaker Samuel (2007). A Simple And Efficient Optical Character Recognition System For Basic Symbols In Printed kannada Text, Sadhana, Vol(32), PP.521-533

Rajiv Kapoor, Deepak Bagai & T.S.Kamal (2004). A New Algorithm For Skew Detection And Correction, *Pattern Recognition Letters*, Vol(25): 1215-1229

R. M. Bozinovic and S. N. Shihari (1989). Off line cursive script word recognition, *IEEE trans. Pattern Anal. Mach. Intell.* 11, 68-83.

S. Abirami, Dr. D. Manjula (2009). A Survey Of Script Identification Techniques For Multi-Script Document Images, *International Journal Of Recent Trends In Engineering*, Vol(1):246-249

S.K. Parui, K.Guin, U.Bhattacharya & B.B. Chaudhuri (2008). Online Handwritten Bangla Character Recognition Using HMM, IEEE

S.M. Milky Mahmud, Nazib Shahrier, A.S.M Delowar Hossain, Md. Tareque Mohmud Chowdhury & Md. Abdus Sattar (2004). An Efficient Segmentation Scheme For The Recognition Of Printed Bangla Characters, *ICCIT*

Subhadip Basu, Nibaran Das, Ram Sarkar, Mahantapas Kundu, Mita Nasipuri & Dipak Kumar Basu (2005). Handwritten 'Bangla ' Alphabet Recognition Using an MLP Based Classifier, NCCPB, Bangladesh, PP. 285-291

T.K. Bhowmik, A.Roy and U.Roy (2003). Character Segmentation For Handwritten Bangla Words Using Artificial Neural Network

Tinku Acharya and Ajoy K. Ray (2005). "Image Processing Principles and Applications", John Wiley & Sons, Inc., Hoboken, New Jersey

U. Garain & B.B Chaudhuri (2001). Segmentation Of Touching Characters In Printed Devnagari And Bangla Scripts Using Fuzzy Multifactorial Analysis, IEEE, PP.805-809

U.Pal & B.B Chaudhuri (1995). Computer Recognition Of Printed Bangla Script, *International Journal Of Systems Science*, Vol(26): PP. 2107-2123

U.Pal & B.B. Chaudhuri (2001). Automatic Identification of English, Chinese, Arabic, Devnagari And Bangla Script Line, IEEE,PP.790-794
W.K. Taylor (1964). Character Recognition, Electronics & Power, PP.6-9
Wikipedia, http://en.wikipedia.org/wiki/Optical_character_recognition
Yungang Zhang & Changshui Zhang. A New Algorithm For Character Segmentation Of License Plate
Zhang Ruilin, Hu yan, Fang Zhijian & Zhang Lei (2009). Skew Detection and Correction Method of Fabric Images Based On Hough Transform, *ICICTA*, IEEE, PP. 340-343

The assessment of spatial features and kinematics of characters: an analysis of subjective and objective measures

Anne Hillairet de Boisferon, Jeremy Bluteau and Edouard Gentaz
Laboratoire de Psychologie et NeuroCognition, Grenoble Université
France

1. Introduction

Handwriting is a complex daily activity that involves attention, memory, linguistic, cognitive and perceptual-motor skills. As motor act, writing a letter requires to retrieve the letter storing in memory, to access the corresponding motor program (letter global shape, relative size of letter strokes), to set the parameters for the program (absolute size of letters and writing speed) and to execute the program (muscles recruitment) (Ellis, 1988; Van Galen, 1991). The letter to be traced and the corresponding graphic motion are intimately related in handwriting activity. Because both reading and writing are learned simultaneously in school, it may be assumed that letters are both coded visually and under a sensorimotor form (Hulme, 1981). From this point of view, the most notable example is probably Chinese or Japanese ideograms, which are composed of a number of strokes that must be written in a precise order when learning to read and write. The metaphor "grammar of action" was proposed by Goodnow & Levine (1973) to define stroke composition rules. Subsequently, this order is used as a cue to retrieve the ideograms from memory (Flores d'Arcais, 1994), suggesting that the motor schema specific to each ideogram may be an essential component of their representation. Many others arguments in favour of the tight coupling between the visual and sensorimotor representations of letter shapes can be advanced. First, Anderson et al., (1990) describe the case of a patient whose inability to write letters can be associated with deficits in the visual identification of letters. By contrast, she could easily read all numbers and nonverbal symbols, and she was equally able to write numbers and perform written calculations without difficulty. In a same way, writing movements can help alexic patients whose reading abilities are impaired. When they were asked to trace the outline of the letters with their fingers, they sometimes succeeded in recognizing letters they were not able to recognize only visually (Bartolomeo et al., 2002; Seki et al., 1995). To go further on, some researchers investigated the question of the presence of a global cerebral network including visual and sensorimotor components and mediating a multimodal representation of letters. Longcamp and colleagues (2003) showed activations of a part of the left premotor area during passive observation of isolated letters although no motor response was required. The same zone was also activated when the participants were writing the letters. They suggested that handwriting motions might therefore be activated in memory by the visual presentation of letters. Moreover, this multicomponent neural network could be built up while learning concomitantly to read and write.

In this framework, handwriting acquisition consists in learning the visual representations of letters, which are used to guide their production, and the motor representations (motor programs) specific to each one. Longcamp, et al. (2005) have studied two groups of preschool children (aged 3-5 years) who were learning letters either by handwriting or by typing, and compared letter recognition performances one week later. Results showed that in the older children, handwriting training gave rise to a better letter recognition performance than typing training. Further research in multisensory-training protocols, as opposed to unisensory protocols, produce greater and more efficient learning. These results indicate that multisensory training promotes more effective learning of the information than unisensory training (Ernst & Bülthoff, 2004; Bluteau et al., 2008; Fredembach et al., 2009). The benefit of multisensory exposure is persistent even when information is gathered from unisensory condition (Shams & Seitz, 2008). Theses previous results suggest that character recognition abilities are somehow dependent on the way we learn to write and to read. To acquire proficient handwriting is required to produce legible texts to be read, and to a large extent, to communicate. Indeed, we write words manually to be read, character production is mainly guided by this implicit subjective recognition goal. However, handwriting acquisition is neither trivial nor effortless, and it takes many years of instructions to master this skill. Difficulties are also observed in adults involved in learning new handwriting systems. At the beginning of learning, movements are slow and guided by visual and kinaesthetic feedback resulting in letter forms not yet mastered. With practice, writing becomes more automatic and the control of movement is mostly proactive, that is to say, based on an internal representation of motor acts. The developmental changes in the product and the process of handwriting could be the consequence of a change from retroactive control of movement (based on sensorial, visual and kinaesthetic feedback) to proactive control (Zesiger, 1995; Bara & Gentaz, 2010; Hillairet et al., 2007).

Considering this whole framework, one can understand that handwriting recognition presents a challenge for most researchers working on letter perception. Indeed, how can people accurately discriminate letters given the important variability in handwritten forms? Classically it is assuming that to recognize handwritten letters people must be able to accept distortions on the standard letter. Freyd (1983) proposed an alternative to classical view, and demonstrates that handwriting recognition makes use of information about how the letters are formed. Specifically, perceivers could spontaneously infer the underlying dynamics pattern of motor movements used for a particular handwritten letter by applying their own knowledge of the production processes to its static trace.

To sum up, subjective handwriting recognition evaluation is accurate and relevant for character recognition analysis. A better understanding of the types of information (shape, kinematics, motor internal simulation) used by the perceiver could enhance the development of almost essential computerized character recognition methods. The finding that readers spontaneously extract production information from static handwritten characters may have implications beyond handwriting recognition. Essentially, in developing a handwriting recognition interface one should take into account static input as well as dynamic characteristics of handwriting. As we have seen, character production and recognition both deal with static and dynamic features of letters, because spatial shape and kinematics of production are intimately related in handwriting activity. Finally, the question of "how quantifying handwriting and its static and dynamic characteristics?" despite a large extend of researches is not trivial and remains crucial. The choice and relation between subjective/objective, static/dynamic evaluation criteria is a decisive factor for character recognition.

2. Measure of writing performance

2.1 Historical approach

Over the years, many methods were developed for the evaluation of handwriting proficiency. Since academic instruction aims to write legibly and rapidly, quality and rapidity criteria seemed sufficient to evaluate handwriting. Thus, most of evaluations are based on analyzing the handwritten product and speed. Nevertheless, authors who work on handwriting acquisition run up against the problem of assessment. Since decades, researchers continuously tried to develop and improve standardized evaluations and proposed numerous tools, which can be classified according to whether they involve qualitative or quantitative measures, global or analytic scales, or measures of the handwriting product or process (for a review, see Rosenblum et al. 2003).

Historically, first evaluations were dedicated to an overall judgment of readability of written products. Handwriting production was first evaluated for its "global quality" or "legibility" before researchers developed more analytic evaluations based on predetermined criteria considered as important factors in written products quality. One of the first scales devoted to assess global quality of written product was the Thorndike Scale for Handwriting of Children (1910) (from fifth to eighth grade) based on the rating of "general merit". After handwriting was evaluated for its "general merit", authors proposed scales based on the attribution of an average score assigned by a group of judges who compared written texts to handwriting samples previously graded from "readable" to "unreadable".

In the aim to provide less subjective judgments, some authors proposed to replace global scales by using clearly defined criteria to grade handwriting samples. Analytic scales then gradually replaced the earlier global evaluations. With analytic scales, the various characteristics of handwriting considered as playing a role in the overall quality of written product are rated individually. The most common criteria used to judge writing legibility are letter form, size, slant, spacing, and line straightness. For example, Freeman (1959) scale included the following five criteria: tilt, height, shaping of letters, line quality and an overall score representing the general merit. These parameters still lead to recent development of character production analysis software (Guinet & Kandel, 2010). One of the more used analytic scales is The Concise Evaluation Scale for Children's Handwriting (Dutch abbreviation BHK; Hamstra-Bletz et al., 1987) first developed to examine the readability and speed of writing performance in young dysgraphic children. It should be noted that quantitative measures are sometimes preferred over qualitative ones because it is easier to quantify fluency (e.g., the number of characters a child is able to write in one minute or the total time taken by a child to complete a given text of a predefined number of characters) than legibility (scoring readability of handwriting products requires judges expertise and laborious comparison to numerous standards). For the BHK evaluation, children are asked to copy a standard text that is presented to them on a card for five minutes. The first five sentences (grade 3 level of reading) are evaluated by judging deviations of the child's writing from the standard handwriting text according to 13 criteria (e.g. global size, line straightness, spacing, letters joins, letters distortions, ambiguous shapes, overlaps between letters, wavering and trembling). A total score on all 13 criteria items is calculated to determine writing quality which is subsequently used to categorize the child as a poor or proficient writer). Copying speed is calculated according to the number of letters written in five minutes. The BHK diagnostic sensitivity, the development of norms and use among children in various populations explain the extensive use of the BHK in studies and clinical practice (Blöte & Hamstra-Bletz, 1991).

Although most researchers agree upon criteria used in analytic scales (Bruinsma & Nieuwenhuis, 1991), approaches used to collect handwriting products vary across studies and factors such as the nature of the handwriting task (e.g. copying or writing from memory tasks), given instructions (e.g. fast or slow handwriting) and graphic workspace (e.g. school writing paper or not) can influence written products quality. Moreover, scales are also designed in different aims, including handwriting difficulties assessment, detection of children being at risk to develop handwriting difficulties, developmental changes assessment, etc. Methodological variations hinder direct comparisons between analytic scales and limit the development of optimally effective handwriting assessment. Nevertheless, global and analytic scales permit an analysis of the handwriting final product. Considering the fact that handwriting is a highly dynamical process; it appears that evaluation of handwriting products do not provide many information about the underlying handwriting process. With the development of computerized measures, it is possible to assess the handwriting process while children are writing. Because handwriting movements require a precise organization in time and space, and proper control over pressure, spatial, and temporal measures during writing supply information about the degree of handwriting proficiency. In literature, we face an increasing number of measures dedicated to the analysis of specific aspects of the handwriting process (e.g. average velocity, production time, movement fluency) and dedicated to more static or global criteria (e.g. recognition rates, height, strokes number).

In conclusion, both approaches which assess the product or the process of handwriting have their advantages and inconveniences. Subjective evaluations (when someone has to judge the quality of the handwriting product) suffer from limited accuracy, sensitivity, and reliability, but are simple to implement and nearer to the natural situation of handwriting in the classroom. Moreover, in many cases, for example in presence of motor production noise in learning process or in handwriting troubles which deteriorated presentation conditions, experts still give their preference to subjective judgments of the quality even if human expert can also make mistakes. "In most applications, the machine performances are far from being acceptable, although potential users often forget that human subjects generally make reading mistakes" (Barrière & Plamadon, 1998). The more objective, computerized analyses make possible to evaluate handwriting dynamics by providing more accurate and more reliable data by means of rapid, automated procedures, but, the practical applications (clinical or educational issues) are still limited because the lack of global decisions about the legibility of a written product. In mainly cases of character recognition, subjective judgments remain more accurate than their computerized corresponding scores.

2.2 Human performance

The measure of performance in the execution of a task raises a number of issues, largely present in the literature under the term "motor learning and human performance" (Schmidt & Wrisberg, 2000). This measure depends on three main factors: the subject, the task and the environment.

First of all, the subject which is the fundamental element of any condition of motor performance comes with a number of characteristics: inherent abilities, cognitivo-motor knowledge, sociocultural context and level of motivation. These characteristics can influence the way of carrying out the task and the performance. The estimation of these capabilities such as the level of subject expertise and the nature of the population to be tested may help up in the understanding of this influence. As an example, several normalized tests are applied to a limited population (child, in remedial persons, etc.).

The second factor in motor learning and human performance is the environment. It can affect the production of a task by the application of temporal constraints (limited time to complete a task), or spatial constraints. In the area of character recognition, the limitation by writing templates lines is an example of these environmental spatial constraints.

The last factor influencing the measure of performance is the task. The nature of the task directly affects the demand for performance and achievement. Certain tasks have high sensory demands, such as detection of an approaching ball to return to tennis. Others have high cognitive demands for action, planning and implementation of action. Finally, we can consider the competence necessary to execute the task, that is to say, the ability of the person to make the right move. In some tasks, only one of these factors will determine the performance of the person, but it is more often a succession of analysis, planning, decision and implementation of a gesture that is indicative of the degree of success or failure of the task. A first answer is to classify the task according to the progress of the task: discrete action, actions in series or ongoing activities. Discrete actions are generally fast and well defined from the beginning to the end. A pointing task belongs to this category. Actions in series are a succession of several discrete actions, connected in sequence and whose order is crucial in the successful accomplishment of the task. Some writing of characters (especially composed by several strokes like Chinese characters) obeys to this classification. Finally, the continuous actions are defined by the absence of precise start and end, and are generally repetitive. At a certain level of handwriting expertise, when subject has internalized and automated the motor act, handwriting can be classified as continuous action. Another classification of the tasks is to determine the sensorimotor load and cognitive load. For a beginner writer, drawing a character is mainly interfered with the control of its movements. Gestures are slow and guided by visual and kinaesthetic feedbacks. Children have to constantly check on their handwriting trace in order to guide their fingers in the right way. Then, with fluency, writing access the stage of cognitive treatments, by concatening letters to make words, and then sentences with meaning. As an example, we can also cite the learning of Japanese or Chinese characters. At the end of the first elementary cycle, the students have to know a small set of 1006 kanji (denoted as gakushuu kanji) ordered by increasing level of difficulty. Finally, tasks can also be classified according to the degree of predictability of the environment. A task performed in a changing, unpredictable and open environment, requires an adaptation of the person. Writing a phone number while someone is driving on a bumpy road is a quite unpredictable environment. A closed task will be realized in a stationary environment and predictive. The person could then plan ahead the completion of the task. That fact explains the needs of closed tasks for most of the normalized test or objective measure of character recognition to be effective. Gentile (Gentile, 1987) proposed a classification in two dimensions, depending on the predictability of the environment and the sensorimotor and cognitive load of the task. The change of type of task highly influences the intra individual performance of the task (Higgins & Spaeth, 1972; Franks et al., 1982), as illustrated in figure 1.

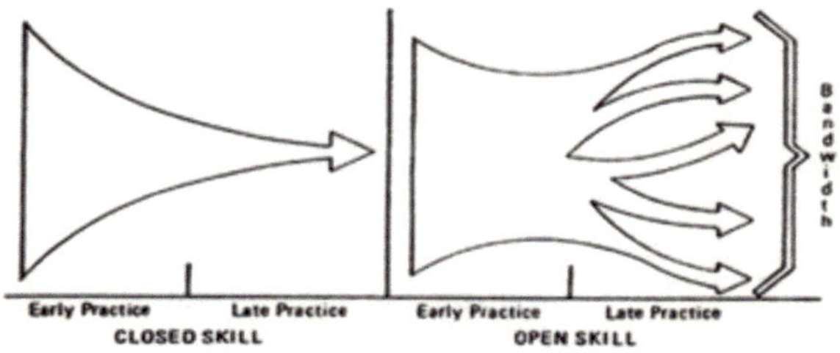

Fig. 1. Change of intra individual performance variability during closed or open skill environment. From Higgins & Spaeth (1972).

In this context, the question of which measure criteria should be used to evaluate motor performance remains. To clarify the multitude of possible measures, authors working in the field of human performance list three main types of measures (Guthrie, 1952):
1) **the maximum certainty of achieving the goal**;
2) **the minimum energy expenditure**, and
3) **the minimum completion time**.
Their variation is seen as a variation of the degree of achievement of performance, from performance considered as beginner level to expert level (see figure 2). Performers who are more proficient in movements designed to achieve a particular goal usually demonstrate one or more of the qualities mentioned previously.

Reference	**Early stage of learning** →	**Later stage of learning**
Fitts and Posner (1967)	Cognitive (trial and error), associative (homing in)	Autonomous (free and easy)
Adams (1971)	Verbal motor (more talk)	Motor (more action)
Gentile (1972)	Getting the idea of the movement	Fixation and diversification (closed or open skill)
Newell (1985)	Coordination (acquire the pattern)	Control (adapt the pattern as needed)
Associated Motor Performance Characteristics		
Early learning →		Later learning
Stiff-looking	More relaxed	Automatic
Inaccurate	More accurate	Accurate
Inconsistent	More consistent	Consistent
Slow, halting	More fluid	Fluid
Timid	More confident	Confident
Indecisive	More decisive	Certain
Rigid	More adaptable	Adaptable
Inefficient	More efficient	Efficient
Many errors	Fewer errors	Performer recognizes errors

Fig. 2. Theoretical depictions of the stages of motor learning and associated motor performance characteristics. From Schimdt & Lee (1987).

The maximum certainty of goal achievement implies that a person is able to meet a performance goal regardless to the situation, on demand and without luck. This criterion can often be seen as a combination of low variability in task performance regarding to a predefined performance level. We can notice that variability in the required movements may help acquiring a maximum certainty of goal achievement as demonstrated in other motor learning fields such as sports (Barlett et al., 2007). The minimum energy expenditure is a consequence of a low noise action, realized without unwanted and unnecessary movements. Finally, the minimum completion time supposes that a skilled movement has a higher level if its duration is shorter than another movement, with the same level of precision. A contradiction remains with the certainty of goal achievement criterions while speed and accuracy are antinomic. Fortunately, humans seem to have the capability to swap speed for accuracy, depending on the task requirements.

The way to access to the three main types of measure of performance is founded on two types of information. The first class of information is directly accessed by internal states of sensorimotor system. Observations such as physiological parameters (ECG, EMG, etc.) or subjective evaluations about the performance belong to this group. These parameters are rich but often suffer from a complex analysis mainly due to the motor noise and complexity of the system. Furthermore, external states such as traces, on-line recording (cf. figure 3.a) or off-line recording (cf. figure 3.b) and observer evaluations can be seen as a second group of measurements. These former parameters suffer also from computation noise and/or subjectivity of observers, but are quite easier to analyse due to the recording of only a part of the system. In lots of performance evaluations, these criterions are preferred and proved their efficiency in constrained domains such as postal addresses (Cohen, 1991), bank check or census forms reading. In character recognition and performance measurement, both internal and external states information can be used simultaneously: for the writing task, EMG would be valuable for the estimation of minimum muscle energy expenditure and off-line record of several paper trails would be valuable for maximum certainty of achieving the goal. The two ways to access information have both complementary meanings. The special case of on-line recording allows access to the internal states of the system (pressure, forces, velocity, angles...) through the development of new sensors, and can be seen as belonging to both groups. For a detailed survey on off-line and on-line character recognition, see Plamadon (Plamadon, 2000).

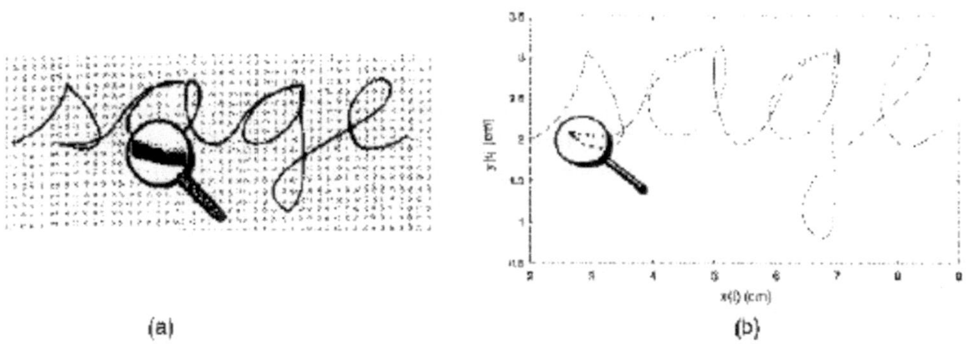

Fig. 3. a) Off-line word. The image of the word is converted into grey-level pixels using a scanner. b). On-line word. The *x,y* coordinated of the pen tip are recorded as a function of time by a digitizer (haptic device, tablet,...). From Plamadon, 2000.

3. Challenges: Which criteria do I have to choose for what?

Regarding human performance knowledge, a set of criteria chosen in the three main types (maximum certainty of achieving the goal; minimum energy expenditure, and minimum completion time) correctly depict the analysis of human performance. Nevertheless, the authors working on the acquisition of handwriting still face the problem of evaluation of character recognition. What class of criteria should we adopt in assessing the performance of manual gestures such as writing? Another way to classify character recognition performance criteria is based on the separation between objective and subjective measures. Subjective (qualitative) criteria result from a judgment, and objective (quantitative) criteria refer to a computerized numerical analysis. Creating tools to assess the quality of writing (i.e. character recognition) remains difficult despite the presence of many standardized assessments, and many measures that can be classified according to their consideration of qualitative or quantitative parameters. Historically, the production of writing was first evaluated on subjective criterions. Technological advances in computation and preference for objective scientific method has reversed the trend. However, the use of subjective criteria is still relevant for character recognition performance analysis and stay the final goal of character production. Indeed, we write words manually with the final objective to be read (i.e. give a trace to be visually evaluated). The character production is mainly guided by this implicit subjective recognition goal. In addition, two levels are accessible for such manual gesture and are offering to evaluate the performance: the writing process (gesture) and production (static trace) (Rosenblum et al., 2003). Each level includes different information respectively kinematics of gesture and static final quality of character. The fact that writing is a highly dynamic process with the support of strong relations between action and perception, allow us to study the process of production (gesture) to enrich the product evaluation (static trace). Technological advances made possible to study and quantify the links between spatial accuracy and kinematics of handwriting. But we face with a plethora of measures in the literature dedicated to the analysis of specific aspects of the writing process (average speed, production time, fluidity of movement...) and static global criteria based on the production (recognition rate, size of letters, number of strokes,...) with few links among them.

To clarify criteria choice for both gesture and handwriting products evaluation and quantification, we propose to identify the relation between static (product) and dynamic (handwriting process) measures in an objective and subjective evaluation of on-line acquisition of writing.

As suggested by several researches presented in §1, many connections between perception and action can be observed in humans. As the judgment of product and process involve human perception, correlation amongst static subjective criteria (mainly related to shape) and dynamic subjective criteria (related to kinematics) should appear (Hypothesis 1). Literature tends to distinguish in one hand static objective criteria related to shape and in the other hand, dynamic objective criteria, related to kinematics of production. Then, we should observe some strong links between static measures, and strong links between dynamics criteria. However, this hypothesis has to be contrasted in regards to existing tight coupling between spatial shape and kinematics in handwriting production. So, we also assume some correlation between static and dynamic objective measures (Hypothesis 2). The obvious example of mean velocity computation (distance divided by time) tends to suggest a relation between static objective measure (distance) and dynamic objective measure (time). At last, comparison between subjective judgments and objective measures should be somehow related, justifying the current use of objective criteria instead of the classically performed subjective character recognition and evaluation (Hypothesis 3).

4. Experimental evaluation of kinematics and spatial features: an analysis of subjective and objective measures

To access relations between spatial criteria and kinematics of handwriting and relations between subjective and objective judgments, we designed a two step experiment. The first phase consisted in the acquisition of children and adults handwriting. The second phase consisted in an evaluation of handwriting with an objective computation of criteria and subjective judgments.

4.1 Acquisition of handwriting

The acquisition phase differs in children and adults. By choosing two different populations, we wanted to access whether traditional handwriting evaluations could be generalized to pre-scripter children, who present more variable handwriting and are more susceptible to noise generated by the establishment of fine motor control. In addition, we wanted to generalize this evaluation with the learning of novel trajectories with adults. In traditional handwriting of cursive Latin characters, adults are considered as expert-scripter and a clear ceiling effect would have occurred on each evaluation criteria. Indeed, to avoid this effect, unknown trajectories were proposed to the participants. This choice is also related to the characteristics of subjects (developmental difference in sensory motor control) which have to be considered as proposed by human performance researches (cf. §2).

4.1.1 Participants

Forty-four children between the ages of 4.9 and 5.9 months (21 boys and 23 girls, mean age: 5.3) from two senior kindergarten classes in Grenoble participated in this study. All participants spoke French as their first language and no child had a statement of special educational needs. Permission for recruitment was gained from the head teacher of the school, and written informed consent for the participation of the children was obtained from their parents. At the same time, we asked 23 adults participants aged between 18 and 26 (including 13 girls, mean age: 21.3± 2.5) to participate in this study. All adult participants were unfamiliar with Arab or Japanese languages, and none of them had known motor trouble or neurological dysfunction. Their participation was done after their informed written consent, in respect with Helsinki declaration.

4.1.2 Method

The acquisition methodology differs in children and adults in order to take these two population specific needs.

On the one hand, children were seated comfortably in front of a table, upon which a digital tablet (Wacom®) was placed. In this measuring system, the positions of the pen were sampled at a frequency of 100 Hz and at a spatial resolution of .008 cm. The pen used in order to write on the tablet was a ball-point pen (Intuos Ink Pen, Wacom®) allowed to receive feedback of the written samples. A white paper was placed on the digital tablet. We asked children to copy on the paper the 26 cursive letters of the alphabet. Each letter was presented separately on a paper placed in front of the child (for example see fig 4). There were no time and size constraints. The order of letter presentation was counterbalanced across participants. The test lasted approximately 10 min by participants. We randomly chose 250 trajectories over the 1144 collected for the incoming subjective judgments and objective analysis.

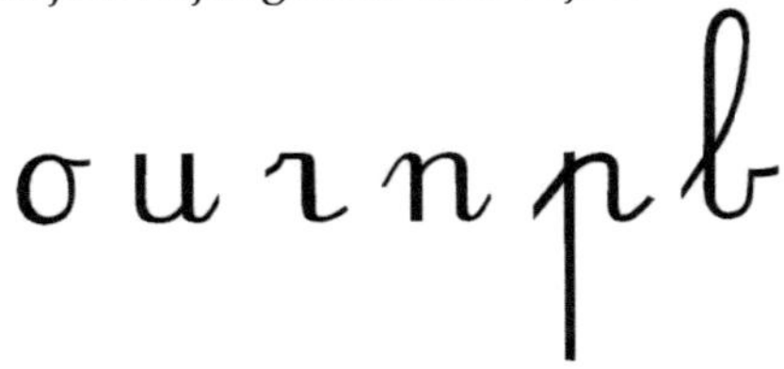

Fig. 4. Examples of standard cursive letters proposed to children participants

On the other hand, adult participants were asked to produce four foreign characters (Japanese inspired and Arabic letters - cf. figure 5). The choice of novel trajectories was a way of experimenting participants with a lower motor skill level, in order to avoid ceiling effect in both handwriting performance and character recognition. The digitalization of their traces was performed using a haptic device (PHANToM Omni® from SensAble). The desired trajectory was displayed on a horizontal screen and the participant's pen trajectory was recorded from the haptic device, placed over the screen (Bluteau et al., 2008). Ergonomics efforts have been made to achieve this virtual co-located configuration, close to the real writing task, allowing standardize protocol of trajectories presentation and recording (Bluteau et al., 2008). As a result, we recorded at 1000 Hz the positions and forces applied during the drawing of characters. Each adult participants has to draw 20 trajectories, given in a pseudo random order (two consecutive and identical letters were not allowed). We kept only 250 of the 460 trajectories, randomly chosen for our analysis.

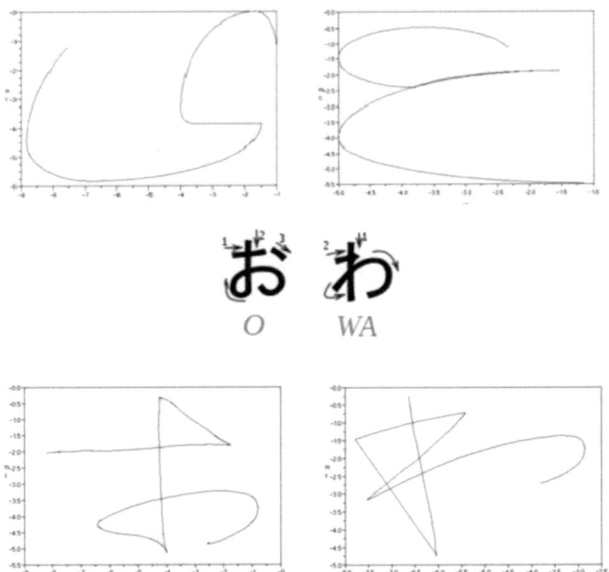

Fig. 5. Trajectories proposed to adult participants. The two upper letters were issued from Arabic alphabet. The two lower letters were issued from Japanese hiragana alphabet, with the order of drawing indicated above.

4.2 Evaluation of handwriting

In this second phase, subjective judgments and objective evaluations were performed. As we wanted to study the relationship between human evaluations and objective measures, the recordings from children and adults productions went through these two evaluations.

4.2.1 Subjective evaluation

Method

First of all, a "judgments" software (NoteSub) was developed to normalize the presentation of trajectories and gather the judgments. Two different display methods were proposed to get static (accuracy of the trace mainly based on spatial characteristics) and dynamic judgments (kinematics of the motor production) (cf. figure 6). The static display in which each of the shapes appear simultaneously on a computer screen was used to assess the quality of the product. The dynamic display, in which letters were printed on a computer screen, according to the cinematic of production of the writer, was used to evaluate the process of writing (kinematics). Two orders were given for either static presentation: "judge the graphical quality"; and dynamic presentation: "judge the quality of movements" of the presented letters. The letters were presented randomly in blocks of 50 letters for a static or dynamic judgment, in order to avoid a fatigue effect. The order of these blocks was balanced using a standard Latin square protocol. In total, judges rated two times each of the 250 letters (a static judgement and a dynamic judgment). Each judge had to recognize the character before evaluating the quality (rate from 1 - lowest quality, to 10 - highest quality) and were asked to describe the underlying criteria on which they based their judgment. In addition, a judgment was considered by the software as valid only when an "active" displacement of the rating cursor was performed (in order to avoid by default judgment). Finally, we obtained two subjective ratings for each trace: a score based on the product of handwriting, closely related to the shape or spatial criteria and a score of production process, closely linked to kinematics.

Fig. 6. Screen capture of NoteSub, the subjective evaluation software. (Left) Static Presentation of letters. (Center) Dynamic presentation of letters. (Right) Example of dynamic presentation, the letter appears gradually, in respect with subject movement velocity, pauses and pen lift up.

Participants/Judges

Ten judges evaluated the quality of character and writing process. Four of them were asked to judge the 250 children productions and six were asked to judge the 250 adult productions. Concerning adults production judgments, evaluators mean age was 32.6 years (± 9.6); concerning children production judgments, evaluators mean age was 28.2 years (± 2.8).

Subjective criteria

As previously describe, we asked judges to rate the "graphical quality" of the handwriting product (static trace) and the "movement quality" of the handwriting process (dynamic). In addition, for each set of letters, judges were asked to report underlying criteria of their judgments

a. Static presentation

Basing their assessment on a static presentation (called "static judgment" later in this chapter) judges had access to traditional presentation of character. Their character recognition performance and evaluation should include several spatial criteria such as tilt, orientation and shaping of letters encountered in literature. However, we can hypothesize that judges could also access to cinematic characteristics of the production given its subtle link to the written shape. For example, static clues such as curvature of letters could call to judge corresponding knowledge of rule production, the well known "two-third power law" (Viviani & Terzuolo, 1982) and allow access to cinematic parameters such as velocity. But we believe that their static judgment will be mainly based on spatial shape information.

b. Dynamic presentation

In the dynamic presentation, the judge had access to kinematics of production. This evaluation (called "dynamic judgment" later in this chapter) allows the extraction of cinematic parameters induced by pauses, accelerations and order of strokes. In order to avoid judgment based on shape's features, the character immediately disappears after dynamic presentation. We make the assumption that their dynamic judgment will be mainly based on kinematics of production. To our knowledge, this kind of kinematics judgments has not been implemented in literature but appears to be a substantial source of information.

4.2.2. Objective evaluation

Method

In parallels with subjective evaluation, the computation of objective measures was done using a normalized Matlab script. For each of the 250 adults and children trajectories, we calculated a number of objective measures, inspired by the literature. Quantitative spatial measurement considered were the number of strokes, the distance and a score of similarity between the "experimental trajectory" and "theoretical trajectory". This score (Dynamic Time Warping - DTW) provides access to a criterion of similarity of form. The quantitative cinematic measures considered include the duration of movement, duration of pauses, average speed and the number of velocity peaks. Their calculation was performed by a Matlab™ script, from the acquisition of positions at 1000 Hz for the adult production and 100 Hz for the children productions. In addition for further analysis, we computed predictors (or control variables) by taking in account the total distance of the track, standing for the difficulty of trajectories and the level of initial motor skills for children by a figure copy task. These various objective criteria are described in details below.

Objective criteria

a. Spatial shape

Number of Strokes and Number of pen up/pen down

We defined a stroke as a continuous drawing of trajectory according to pen up/pen down actions. These measures are linked and are both indicators of the difficulty of the letter and the global formation of the shape of the letter. By counting the number of strokes, we are able to extrapolate the degree of fluency of writing for a specific letter. For example, in children above 7-years-old, the number of pen up/pen down (or number of strokes) is usually larger than the theoretical number of strokes required to trace the letter. This is due to absence of achieved motor program and efficient control of the trajectory (in charge of topokinesis and morphokinesis). Due to one-stroke design of adult trajectories, these criteria were only computed for children.

Distance of trajectories

We computed the total distance of the trajectories of our participants. Distance criterion could be considered as size information, one of the most common criteria used to judge writing legibility. This criterion is particularly used in children evaluation of written letters because size variations are important during handwriting acquisition. Young children's handwriting is often characterized by the production of large letters. When children better master fine movements required in writing, letters size decrease (Blöte & Hamstra-Bletz, 1991).

Dynamic Time Warping (DTW)

The computation of a distance score between two curves is a usual way of quantifying the differences or to put a figure on likeness. Classical distance measures include point-to-point distance quantification (also known as Euclidean distance), point-to-closest point or even unidimensionnal distance (known as Manhattan distance or nearest prototype). In 1983, Joseph Kruskal and Mark Liberman introduced a new technique to calculate the distance between two curves. This technique, called time warping, proposes to match the two curves by distorting time axis (or "warping"as called by its authors). This means that variation in writing speed is considered as noise and then will be deleted (or at least decreased) by the algorithm. This algorithm has been applied to many fields, including speech recognition, handwriting pattern recognition, video analysis, quality of cursive character in reference to a standard (Niels, 2004) and also sequence alignment. We will take this last example to detail the algorithm. In genetics, sequence alignment consists in transforming one sequence into another using edit operation that replaces, inserts or removes an element. Each operation has an associated cost, and the final alignment will be given by the lowest cost standing the sequence of editing operations. Note that the lengths of the two sequences do not have to be equal. The Dynamic Time Warping (DTW) belongs to dynamic programming methods, that solve complex problem by breaking it into simpler steps, and provides solutions to such genetic questions. The problem can be stated naturally as a recursion, a sequence A is optimally edited into a sequence B by either:

1. inserting the first character of B, and performing an optimal alignment of A and the tail of B
2. deleting the first character of A, and performing the optimal alignment of the tail of A and B
3. replacing the first character of A with the first character of B, and performing optimal alignments of the tails of A and B.

The same reasoning is valuable for comparison of distance between two sequences of points (*P1* and *P2*), where step 1 stands for the computation of distance between *P1(i)* and *P2(i+1)*, step 2 stands for the computation of distance between *P1(i+1)* and *P2(i)* and finally, step 3 stands for the distance computation between *P1(i)* and *P2(i)*. The partial alignment of the two sequences (or curves) can be tabulated in a matrix, where *cell(n,m)* contains the cost of the optimal alignment of $A[1..n]$ to $B[1..m]$ (or *P1(1..n)* to *P2(1..m)*). The cost in *cell(i,j)* can be calculated by adding the cost of the relevant operations to the cost of its neighbouring cells, and selecting the optimum. In other words, the global DTW cost is given by "finding the way of the valley of minimum cost into the cost matrix"(cf. Figure 7).

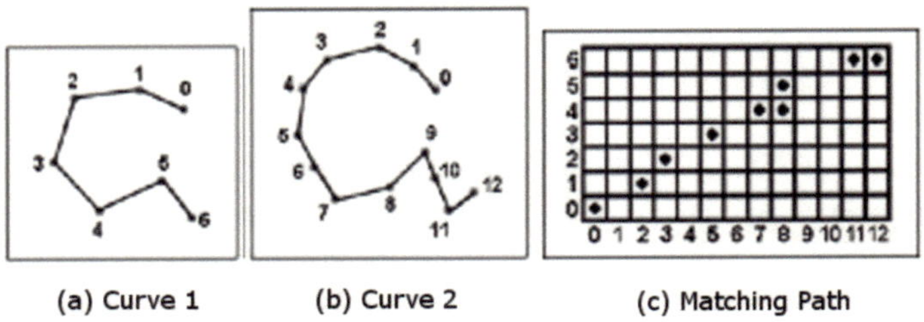

Fig. 7. Example of Matching path. (c) shows a possible matching path of the curves shown in (a) and in (b). Curve 1 is on the vertical axis and curve 2 is on the horizontal axis of the matching path. If we had filled the matching matrix with distances between points, this matching path would have been the visualisation of the way of the valley of minimum costs.

After the definition of the matching path, a backtracking algorithm allows visual checking of the alignment of the two sequences (cf. figure 8).

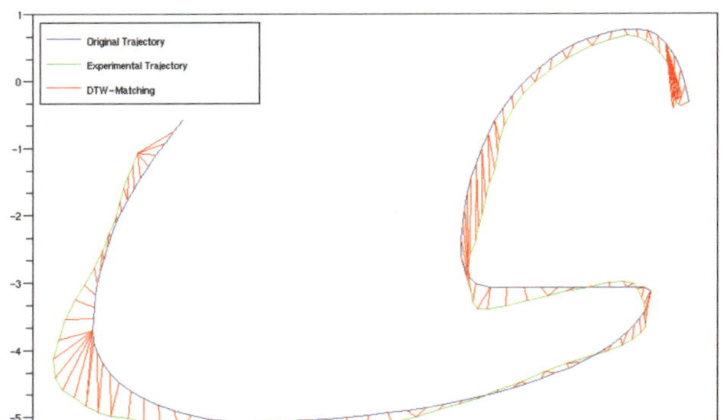

Fig. 8. Application of Dynamic Time Warping algorithm on a trajectory used in our experiment with adults and visualisation of the alignment using a backtracking algorithm. Optimal alignment (red) computed between theoretical trajectory (blue) and experimental trajectory (green) by a temporal distortion corresponding to a delay or advance between the two traces.

DTW allows comparison of sequences without re-sampling and has been demonstrated to be successful for comparison of discrete and online handwriting acquisitions (Niels, 2004;

Di Brina, 2008; Bluteau et al., 2008). This algorithm has a real application in character recognition as shown by this citation from Di Brina and colleagues (2008): "By objectively analyzing the spatial-temporal patterns, DTW captures the essential character of writing, i.e., the overall shape of its graphic output".

b. Cinematic criteria

Number of velocity peaks

This measure is classically seen as an indicator of writing fluidity and is related to the number of accelerations and decelerations during production. A movement is seen as jerky as soon as the number of velocity peaks is high. The number of velocity peaks is given by counting the number of zero crossing of the acceleration ($\partial v = 0$). The velocity profile has to be filtered to reduce acquisition noise. The filtering process implies different values in adults and children to access the number of velocity peaks. In our experiment, we used a third order Butterworth filter with a cut-off frequency of 12Hz to filter the adult productions (down-sampled at 100Hz); and we used a third order Butterworth filter with a cut-off frequency of 6Hz to filter the children productions (sampled at 100Hz). We chose Butterworth filter for its large use in literature and its intrinsic parameters (slow roll offs around cut-off frequency and no ripples) compare to other quicker roll offs cutting filters (Chebishev filter, Elliptic filter, etc.).

Mean Velocity

This measure is also a traditional criterion to evaluate the fluidity of writing. Normalized tests have integrated it by counting the number of words or characters copied in a certain amount of time (i.e,. fluency); Other researchers have used it to assess the level of expertise and writing performance with adults (Bluteau et al., 2008) or with children (Palluel-Germain et al., 2007). Many researchers claim that children's competence in writing depends, in part, on their mastery of handwriting. They found that handwriting skills, particularly handwriting fluency, improve with age and schooling (Graham et al., 1998; Hamstra-Bletz & Blote, 1990) and these individual differences in handwriting fluency predict how much and how well children write (Graham et al., 1997). This measure enters in the minimum completion time class of human performance classification of criteria as soon as the required trajectory has a fixed length (distance).

Duration measures

Total duration of the trajectory

We computed the total duration to draw a character. This criterion gives an indication of the temporal performance on the path. It is linked to the average velocity and belongs to the same class (minimum completion time) of human performance classification.

Pen up duration

This criterion corresponds to the duration when the pen was up during the production of the character. An increase of this last measure indicates augmentation of breaks, and thus would reveals lacks in motor production of the character.

Number of pauses in character production

We defined a pause as a minimum of 150 ms period while the pen was down on the paper but no active movement was performed. This measure is an important indicator especially for children who often make pause while writing to visually check the model or their production in case of substantial breaks (i.e., allowing retroactive control based on visual and sensory motor feedbacks). This measure can also be an indicator of jerky handwriting in case of shorter breaks. This criterion is correlated with the level of expertise of the task.

Number of Strokes and Number of pen up/pen down
These criteria were already presented as shape specific criteria but they implicitly belong to dynamic criteria category. Indeed, the number of strokes of a writing production is intuitively correlated to cinematic criteria. A very high number of strokes reveal a quite bad cinematic of writing, thus referring to cinematic criteria. The same remark is valuable for the number of pen up/pen down criterion. This dual membership is also linked to the relation between action and perception. By the perception of some characteristics (such as the number of strokes), humans are able to deduce the actions performed to generate this product, and thus, to access the cinematic of production.
c. Predictors or Control variables
Distance of trajectories
This measure, previously classified as static, appears in the computation of the mean velocity and is implicitly linked to the difficulty of the trajectory. In a way, this criterion can be taken as a normalization index that could explain relations between kinematics and shape characteristics, especially in adults' productions.
Designs copying task (NEPSY)
We evaluate children motor and visuospatial skills using the designs copying subtest of the NEPSY – A Developmental Neuropsychological Assessment (Korkman et al., 1998). This subtest is an untimed two-dimensional constructional task that requires the integration of visuospatial analysis and graphomotor skills. Children have to reproduce paper-and-pencil copies of geometric designs of increasing complexity. These copies are then rated according to a set of indicators. Final normalized scores are comprised between 1 and 19. This measure does not count for character production evaluation but can be seen as a predictor variable of handwriting abilities.

4.3 Results

4.3.1 Preliminary analysis

After the second step of subjective judgment, we retrieved a static and a dynamic score for each of 250 letters from children or adults, associated to the character actually recognized. We kept the recording if the required character matches the recognized one, and only if all judges recognized the letter. This work has to be done to avoid nonsense statistical means. This cleaning process leads to 204 trajectories for the children set and 221 trajectories for the adult set. We performed inter-judges correlation using reliability test (calculating Cronbach's alpha) that informed us about the homogeneity of scores through judges (α = .797 for static judgments and α = .772 for dynamic judgments of adults characters; α= .824 for static judgments and α = .851 for dynamic judgments of children characters). Regarding this preliminary analysis, we averaged static scores of judges for each character in a new variable, called *mean static* later in this chapter. The same operation was done for dynamic judgments in a new variable called *mean dynamic*.

4.3.2 Criteria's descriptive data

The Table 1 represents mean results and standard deviations obtained for each subjective and objective criteria collected for both children and adults handwriting products and process.

Criteria	Children Mean	Children SD	Adults Mean	Adults SD
Mean static	5.34	1.80	4.22	1.36
Mean dynamic	5.80	1.90	4.84	1.20
Total duration (s)	6.24	3.75	18.63	11.19
Pen up duration (s)	1.56	2.28	-	-
Mean velocity (cm/s)	1.84	1.02	1.37	0.66
Number of velocity peaks	12.14	7.53	5.44	2.49
Number of pauses	1.48	2.99	-	-
Number of strokes	1.96	1.45	-	-
Number of pen up	0.96	1.45	-	-
Distance (cm)	9.57	4.88	20.23	5.36
DTW	3.27	2.43	7.26	4.41
Designs copying	12.23	2.51	-	-

Table 1. Means and standard deviations (SD) of each static and dynamic criteria in children and adults.

Descriptive data reveal that despite mean distance, mean total duration and DTW score are more important and mean velocity is lower in adults trajectories, adults produced less acceleration and deceleration (i.e., number of velocity peaks) while they traced letters. These findings have to be related to the size of required trajectories in adults (cf. figure 5).

4.3.3 Correlation between static and dynamic subjective scores

We performed for each subjective judgment, correlations (Bravais-Pearson *r*) between static score and dynamic score attributed to children and adults handwriting products and process. Results showed a mean correlation coefficient of $r = .56$ (.55 to .60) in the judgment of children characters and a mean correlation coefficient of $r = .51$ (.35 to .61) in the judgment of adults characters.

4.3.4 Inter-correlation of static objective scores

We performed for each static objective measures inter-correlations (Bravais-Pearson *r*). Results are presented in table 2.

	Criteria	Children (1)	Children (2)	Children (3)	Adults (1)	Adults (2)
(1)	Distance (cm)	-	.42**	.17*	-	-.33**
(2)	DTW	-	-	.27**	-	-
(3)	Number of strokes	-	-	-	-	-

*p<.05 significance, **p<.01 significance

Table 2. Correlations between objective static criteria in children and adults

Table 2 indicates mean levels of correlation between the three objective static criteria scores in children. The closest link is between distance measures and dynamic time warping (DTW) scores (.42). The relations between DTW and number of strokes scores and between distance and number of strokes scores (respectively .27 and .17) are weaker. All correlations are significant and positive. The longer the trajectories are, the more the number of strokes is susceptible to increase, and the more the gap between the theoretical trajectory and the effective trajectory is susceptible to increase. In adults, as letters were always produced within one stroke, only two criteria were taken into account. The longer trajectories are, the smaller the gap between the theoretical trajectory and the effective trajectory tends to be.

4.3.5 Inter-correlation of dynamic objective scores

We performed for each dynamic objective measures inter-correlations (Bravais-Pearson *r*). Results are presented in table 3. This table indicates strong to weak levels of correlation between the six objective dynamic criteria scores in children and the three dynamic criteria scores in adults. Number of velocity peaks, total duration and mean velocity scores are correlated with most of objective criteria in children as well as in adults. Compare to previous criteria, pen up duration and number of pauses show less significant correlations with other objectives measures. Finally, number of pen up shows almost no correlation with other measures. More precisely in children, the closest links are between total duration and the number of velocity peaks (.89) and between number of pen up and the total duration (.77). Weaker correlations can be observed in this population between the number of velocity peaks and number of pauses (.50), the number of velocity peaks and mean velocity are negatively correlated (-.47) and finally low correlation appears between the number of velocity peaks and the pen up duration (.14). We can notice that mean velocity score is negatively correlated with the majority of dynamic criteria (total duration, pen up duration and number of pauses).

In adults, the closest links are found between total duration and the number of velocity peaks (.70), and between total duration and the mean velocity (-.71) which are negatively correlated. Moderate negative correlation also appears between the number of velocity peaks and the mean velocity (-.35).

	Children						Adults		
Criteria	(1)	(2)	(3)	(4)	(5)	(6)	(1)	(2)	(3)
(1) Number of velocity peaks	-	-.47**	.89**	.14*	.50**	.08	-	-.35**	.70**
(2) Mean velocity (cm/s)	-	-	-.49**	-.002	-.33**	.08	-	-	-.71**
(3) Total Duration (s)	-	-	-	.09	.77**	.04	-	-	-
(4) Pen up duration (s)	-	-	-	-	-.02	.64**	-	-	-
(5) Number of pauses	-	-	-	-	-	.04	-	-	-
(6) Number of pen up	-	-	-	-	-	-	-	-	-

*p<.05 significance **p<.01 significance

Table 3. Correlations between objective dynamic criteria in children and adults

4.3.6 Correlation between static and dynamic objective scores

We performed for each objective measures, correlations (Bravais-Pearson *r*) between static score and dynamic score attributed to children (table 4) and adults (table 5) handwriting products and process.

Static/Dynamic	Number of velocity peaks	Mean velocity (cm/s)	Total Duration (s)	Pen up duration (s)	Number of pauses	Number of pen up
Distance (cm)	.47**	.32**	.51**	.12	.28**	.17*
DTW	.29**	.003	.33**	.25**	.23**	.27**
Number of strokes	.08	.08	.04	.64**	.04	-

*p<.05 significance, **p<.01 significance

Table 4. Correlations between static and dynamic criteria in children

In children, some moderate positive correlations can be observed amongst static and dynamic criteria. The closest link is observed between the number of strokes and the pen up duration (.64). It is interesting to note that the number of strokes is only correlated with this dynamic measure. Medium positive correlations are observed between distance and total duration (.51), between distance and the number of velocity peaks (.47). Weaker correlations implying distance are observed with mean velocity (.32), the number of pauses (.28) and the number of pen up (.17). We observed that the DTW (considered as a static indicator in literature) is correlated to most of dynamic scores (except mean velocity).
Should be noticed that despite inter-correlation between all static measure (table 2) and a majority of inter-correlation between dynamic measures (table 3), some correlation between static and objective measure seem important. For example, the number of pen up only correlated with the corresponding dynamic measure of pen up duration (.64) but correlated with two static criteria, the distance (.17) and the DTW (.27) scores

Static/Dynamic	Number of velocity peaks	Mean velocity (cm/s)	Total Duration (s)
Distance (cm)	.37**	.40**	.10
DTW	-.27**	.04	-.24**

*p<.05 significance, **p<.01 significance

Table 5. Correlations between static and dynamic criteria in adults

Concerning adults characters analysis, we also observed strong correlations between static and dynamic scores. Medium and positive correlations are observed between distance and the number of velocity peaks (.37), and between distance and mean velocity (.40). The DTW measure is found to be negatively correlated with the number of velocity peaks (-.27) and with the total duration (-.24). These correlations remain moderates. As in children, some correlation between static and objective measure seem important but results also show that strongest links are found in adults between dynamic criteria (table 3), the total duration and the number of velocity peaks (.70) and the mean velocity along the path (-.71)

4.3.7 Correlation between objective and subjective evaluations in each population

To analyse the possible existing relation between subjective and objective evaluations, we performed forward stepwise regressions using subjective judgments as references. This analysis computes step by step linear regression, by including in each step predictor variable (objective criterion) with the highest shared amount of variance with the predicted variable (subjective criterion). At each stage in the process, after a new variable is added, a F-test (Fisher-Snedecor) is made to check if some variables can be deleted without appreciably increasing the residual sum of squares (RSS). The procedure terminates when the measure is maximized, or when the available improvement of the model falls below some critical value.

Regarding static criteria in children, the stepwise regression analysis reveals that number of strokes, distance and designs copying taken together explain 11% of the mean static judgment score [F(2.200)=9.33;p=.034]. Analysis of partial correlations indicates that number of strokes explain a unique amount of mean static judgment's variance [5%,t(200)=-3.36,p<.001], designs copying explain also a unique amount of variance [2.5%,t(200)=2.24,p<.05] and finally, distance criteria explains a unique amount of variance too at a level of 2.3%[t(200)=-2.19,p<.05]. On the dynamic criteria side, the analysis reveals that pen up duration, DTW and number of pauses taken together explain 38% of the mean dynamic judgment score [F(3,200)=43.19,p<.01]. Analysis of partial correlations indicates that the pen up duration explains a unique amount of mean dynamic judgment's variance [22%,t(200)=-7.49,p<.001], DTW explains a unique amount of variance [12%,t(200)=-5.24,p<.001] and finally, the number of pauses explain a unique amount of variance too [4.2%,t(200)=-2.96,p<.01].

Concerning static criteria in adults, the analysis reveals that DTW and mean velocity taken together explain 13% of the mean static judgment score [F(2,218)=3.91,p<.05]. Further partial correlations analysis reveals that the DTW [12%,t(218)=-5.51,p<.001] and mean velocity [1.8%,t(218)=-1.98,p<.05] both explain a unique amount of variance of the mean static judgment. The analysis of the dynamic judgment score in adults reveals that the number of velocity peaks, DTW, mean velocity and total duration taken together explain 16% of the mean dynamic judgment scores [F(4,216)=4.14,p<.05]. Partial correlations analysis reveal that the number of velocity peaks [3.9% ,t(216)=-2.97,p<.01], the DTW [10.2%,t(216)=-4.95,p<.001], the mean velocity [4.5%,t(216)=-3.18,p<.01] and the total duration [1.9%,t(216)=-2.03,p<.05] explain each a unique amount of variance of the dynamic judgment score.

5. Discussion and Conclusion

This study was designed to identify the relationship between spatial features and kinematics of handwriting process through static and dynamic criteria in an objective and subjective evaluation of handwriting. The underlying purpose was to clarify and help criteria choice for both gesture and handwriting products evaluation and quantification.

First, statistical analysis of inter-correlation of subjective judgements puts forward the existence of a link between the static and dynamic judgments. High scores based on a dynamic presentation (and thus involving kinematics) correspond to high scores based on static one (involving characteristics related to accuracy of trace) and inversely. This result supports our first hypothesis (cf. §3) based on the action/perception and product/process links described in literature. As suggested by Freyd (1983), human could extract dynamic information in the perception of static forms. For recall, the author asked subjects to learn some artificial characters, drawn in real time, and then to recognize distorted versions of these characters presented statically. In accordance with her theory, subjects were faster on static character recognition when the distortion was consistent with the drawing method (Badcock & Freyd, 1988; Freyd, 1983). Our results showed the same underlying process and extended it to the measure of the product quality. Characters subjectively considered as well produced leads to a good rate of the character product. In other words, when we perform character evaluation of the quality in a static manner, we could also access to kinematics information and take it into account in our final judgment. The analysis of judges' comments on criteria they used during the subjective evaluation emphasizes the supposed combination between static and dynamic components for both static and dynamic presentations. As example in static judgments, the underlying criteria are mainly related to the shape ("a space between the center loop and the end is too big","Dissymmetry between top and bottom") and aesthetic ("precise, nice character", "clear and precise") but are also present some dynamic components ("jerky writing", "several breaks in the letter"). In dynamic judgments, same dual process exists, the underlying criteria are mainly related to kinematics ("correct movement", "regular motion", "too quick/slow", "wrong strokes order") but also related to shape criteria ("too titled", "an additional stroke") and aesthetics ("nice realisation"). Same confusing frontier exists in normalized test such as BHK, where shape criteria (size, tilt, orientation) are combined with kinematics criteria (jerkiness, speed indicators, hesitance, etc.). To conclude, in accordance with our first hypothesis, a significant overlap between criteria initially considered as purely static and purely dynamic judgments exists.

Secondly, we tried to verify the feasibility of the classic distinction proposed in literature between static objective criteria related to shape and dynamic objective criteria related to kinematics of production (hypothesis 2, cf. §3). Our second set of results reveals that in majority, dynamic criteria are correlated together (e.g. number of velocity peaks, mean velocity, duration and number of pen up) the mean correlation coefficient is r=.53 in children and r=.59 in adults. Static criteria are also correlated together (Number of strokes, distance and DTW) the mean coefficient is r=.29 in children and r=.33 in adults. Due to the influence of gesture production on the product, correlation showed that several static criteria are linked to dynamic measures (e.g. distance with number of velocity peaks, DTW and total duration of the trajectory, etc.). The mean coefficient of correlation between static and dynamic objective criteria is about r=.32 in children and about r=.34 in adults. These second set of results emphasize the difficulty to classify criteria in the two main category used in literature (static or dynamic; product and process). Moreover, interesting difference in correlations between criteria is observed in children and adults. The correlation between distance and total duration disappears in adults production. We can suggest that this effect is mainly due to absence of isochrony in children production. The isochrony law was formulated for the first time by Binet & Courtier (1893). They found that the speed of movement remains constant regardless of size variations of trace to be produced. In adults, we observed behaviour in accordance with isochrony law: the more letter size is important, the more velocity increases to remain constant in gesture duration. In children, even if we observed an increase of the velocity to preserve duration of the production on larger letter, we still notice a correlation between distance of the path and the corresponding duration. This specific correlation suggests that children do not master all fine motor control mechanisms and cannot already respect all handwriting motor rules. In regard with this result, one should understand that scripter expertise has to be carefully taken into account in character recognition and evaluation.

Then, we evaluated the link between subjective judgments and objective measures. We used the subjective judgments, traditionally considered as more accurate than their computerized corresponding scores, as criterion to be predicted in stepwise regression analysis. In adults, the resulting model for static judgments (mean static) reveals two predictive criteria: the DTW, classically considered as static information, and the mean velocity along the path, considered as dynamic information. The model for subjective dynamic judgment (mean dynamic) reveals three objective dynamic criterion as predictors, the number of velocity peaks, the mean velocity and the total duration of the path, and one static criteria as predictor, the DTW score. These models raise a number of issues. First of all, the mean velocity, often used in the literature for cinematic analysis, can explain the static judgment. Partial correlation reveals that the more the mean velocity of the production was important, the more the static judgment was low. Several assumptions can be made. (1) The judges have access to the dynamic component of the course by analyzing visual cues present in the trace. This hypothesis is supported by studies which showed activations of motor areas during observation of human movements (Saygin et al., 2004) or during observation of static pattern previously learned to be traced (Longcamp et al., 2003). Theories of motor simulation (Jeannerod, 2009) could also follow our direction. At last, Viviani (2002) assert that access to dynamic properties could occur through a motor representation of the act of writing. (2) In the static presentation modality, the judges have access to the size of the letter; they could deduce the calculation of mean velocity (by divided the distance by the duration). Nevertheless, participants had no access to duration information and the involvement of the distance was not notice in regression model. (3) This third assumption, referred to the close link between the spatial shape and the kinematics of production. In adults writing news characters, higher velocity production could mean poor letter shape. In this case, an obvious correlation would appear between dynamic and static criteria with no need of simulation or knowledge of handwriting motor rules.

Another significant result concerns the link between DTW and both static judgment and dynamic judgement. It seems that this objective measure, generally regarded as a method of static analysis of production, could also be taken into account for kinematics assessments of characters. Partial correlation reveals that the less the distance is important between the standard trajectory and the effective trajectory, the more important are the static or dynamic judgment scores. The link between DTW score and dynamic judgment score is not surprising. Indeed, the application of this algorithm is limited by computational initial condition such as the matching of the starting point and pen-up/pen down sub sequence computation. Thus, order of strokes production (not always respected in children handwriting, seen as a dynamic characteristic, is taken into account in the DTW computation. Same kind of relation between DTW methods and kinematics has been found by Di Brina (2008). We make the assumption that this index could be used as an overall indicator of the quality of handwriting production in is double assessment of spatial characteristics and kinematics features, as already suggested by several researches (Niels, 2004; Di Brina, 2008).

As introduced previously, developmental differences could also influence the choice of character recognition and evaluation criteria. In children, the resulting model for static judgments (mean static) reveals two predictive criteria: the number of strokes and the distance classically considered as static information, and the designs copying scores used as an indication of children visuospatial and motor skills. Prediction from DTW on static judgment is not shown in children. This could be due to the fact that children do not always produce characters in the correct order. Indeed, DTW score is quite sensible to the order of strokes production but in static presentation this information is not available and could not be used by judges. The model for subjective dynamic judgment (mean dynamic) reveals two objective dynamic criteria as predictors, the number of pauses and the number of pen up, and one static criterion as predictor, the DTW score. As children movements are classically slower than movement that would have been performed by expert scripter, we suggest that pen up duration and number of pauses are probably the more prominent criteria for perceptual judgements In contrast, in adults, the following objective dynamic predictors, the number of velocity peaks, mean velocity and duration seem to be more distinct indicators for handwriting fluency.

In conclusion, this research highlights the difficulty to classify criteria as clearly static or dynamic. Correlations amongst and between static and dynamic criteria, objective and subjective, are observed in both children and adult populations. These results moderate existing classifications considering criteria as more related to static or more related to dynamic information. Moreover, dynamics criteria considered in children and adults production are not the same and do not have the same meaning, probably due to the differences in motor production skills. Finally, subjective evaluation which can be seen as more relevant in character recognition and evaluation tasks is linked with objective criteria but differs amongst tested populations. In definitive, the best way to perform handwriting character recognition and evaluation would be an evaluation including a large sample of both spatial and dynamic criteria as suggested by human performance classification (taking into account each type of performance criterion of maximum certainty of achieving the goal type, minimum energy expenditure type, and minimum completion time type) in either objective or subjective evaluations.

6. Acknowledgments

The authors gratefully thank all participants (scripters and judges) for their implication in this research. We also thank Sébastien Boisard for the development of the subjective data collection software and his help in data analysis, and Francois Branchon and Heather Larin for their english review.

7. References

Anderson, S. W., Damasio, A. R. & Damasio, H. (1990). Troubled letters but not numbers: Domain specific cognitive impairments following focal damage in frontal cortex. *Brain, 113*, 749-766.

Babcock, M. K. & Freyd, J. J. (1988). Perception of Dynamic Information in Static Handwritten Forms. *The American Journal of Psychology, 101*(1), 111-130.

Bara F. & Gentaz, E. (2010) Apprendre à tracer les lettres : une revue critique. Psychologie Française, 55 (2), 129-144

Barriere, C. & Plamondon, R. (1998). Human identification of letters in mixed-script handwriting: anupper bound on recognition rates, *IEEE Transactions on Systems, Man, and Cybernetics, Part B, 28*(1), 78--81.

Bartlett R., Wheat J. & Robins M. (2007). Is movement variability important for sports biomechanists? *Sports Biomechanics, 6*(2), 224–243.

Bartolomeo, P., Bachoud-Lévi, A.-C., Chokron, S. & Degos, J.-D. (2002). Visually- and motor-based knowledge of letters: Evidence from a pure alexic patient. *Neuropsychologia, 40*, 1363-1371.

Binet, A. & Courtier, J. (1893). Sur la vitesse des gestes graphiques [On the speed of voluntary movements]. *Revue Philosophique, 35*, 664-671.

Blöte, A. & Hamstra-Bletz, L. (1991). A longitudinal study on the structure of handwriting. *Perceptual and Motor Skills, 72*, 983-994.

Bluteau, J., Coquillart, S.; Payan, Y. & Gentaz, E. (2008). Haptic guidance improves the visuo-manual tracking of trajectories. *PLoS ONE, 3*(3), e1775.

Bruinsma, C. & Nieuwenhuis, C. (1991). A new method for the evaluation of handwriting material. In A. M. Wann, Wing & N. Sovik (Eds.), *Development of Graphic Skills* (pp. 41-51). New york: Academic Press.

Cohen, E. (1991). Understanding handwritten text in a structured environment: determining zip codes from addresses', *International journal of pattern recognition and artificial intelligence*, 1(2), 221--264.

Di Brina, C. D., Niels, R., Overvelde, A., Levi, G. & Hulstijn, W. (2008). Dynamic time warping: A new method in the study of poor handwriting. *Human Movement Science*, 27(2), 242 - 255.

Ellis, A. W. & Young, W. (1988). *Human Cognitive Neuropsychologie*. London: Lawrence Erlbaum Associates Publishers.

Ernst, M. O. & Bülthoff, H. H. (2004). Merging the senses into a robust percept. *Trends in Cognitive Sciences, 8*(4), 162-169.

Flores d'Arcais, G. B. (1994). Order of strokes writing as a cue for retrieval in reading Chinese characters. *European Journal of Cognitive Psychology, 6*, 337-355.

Franks, I. M., Wilberg, R. B. & Fishburne, G. J. (1982). Consistency and error in motor performance. *Human Movement Science*, 1(2), 109 - 123.

Fredembach B., Hillairet de Boisferon A., Gentaz E. (2009) Learning of Arbitrary Association between Visual and Auditory Novel Stimuli in Adults: The "Bond Effect" of Haptic Exploration. PLoS ONE 4(3): e4844. *doi:10.1371/journal.pone.0004844*

Freeman, F. N. (1959). A new handwriting scale. *Elementary School Journal, 59*, 218-221.

Freyd, J. J. (1983). Representing the dynamics of a static form. *Memory and Cognition, 11*, 342-346.

Gentile AM. Skill acquisition: action, movement, and neuromotor processes. In: Carr JH, Shepherd RB, editors. *Movement science foundations for physical therapy in Rehabilitation*. 2nd ed. Gaithersburg: Aspen, MD; 2000. p.111-187.

Goodnow, J. J. & Levine, R. A. (1973). "The grammar of action ": Sequence and syntax in children's copying. *Cognitive Psychology, 4*, 82-98.

Graham, S., Berninger, V., Abbott, R., Abbott, S. & Whitaker, D. (1997). Role of mechanics in composing of elementary school students: A new methodological approach. *Journal of Educational Psychology, 89*, 170-182.

Graham, S., Berninger, V. W. & Weintraub, N. (1998). The relationships between handwriting style and speed and legibility. *Journal of Educational Research, 5*, 290-296.

Guinet, E. & Kandel, S. (2010). Ductus: A software package for the study of handwriting production. *Behavior Research Methods, 42*, 326-332.

Guthrie, E. (1952). *The psychology of learning*. Peter Smith Publication Inc.

Hamstra- Bletz, L., DeBie, J. & Den Brinker, B. (1987). *Concise Evaluation Scale for children's handwriting*. Lisse, Swets & Zeitlinger.

Hamstra-Bletz, L. & Blöte, A. W. (1990). Development of handwriting in primary school: A longitudinal study. *Perceptual and Motor Skills, 70*, 759-770.

Higgins, J. & Spaeth, R. (1972). The relationship between consistency of movement and environmental conditions. *Quest, 17*, 61-69.

Hillairet de Boisferon, A., Bara, F., Gentaz, E., & Colé, P. (2007). Préparation à la lecture des jeunes enfants: Effets de l'exploration visuo-haptique des lettres et de la perception visuelle des mouvements d'écriture. L'Année Psychologique, 107, 537-564

Hulme, C. (1981). *Reading retardation and multisensory teaching*. Londres: Routledge & Kegan Paul.

Jeannerod, M. (2009). *Le cerveau volontaire*. Odile Jacob.

Korkman, M., Kirk, U. & Kemp, S. A. (1998). *Developmental Neuropsychological Assessment*. The Psychological Corporation: San Antonio.

Kruskall, J. & Liberman, M. (1983). The symmetric time warping problem: From continuous to discrete. In *Time Warps, String Edits and Macromolecules: The Theory and Practice of Sequence Comparison*, 125--161, Addison- Wesley.

Longcamp, M., Anton, J. L., Roth, M. & Velay, J. L. (2003). Visual presentation of single letters activates a premotor area involved in writing. *Neuroimage, 19*, 1492-1500.

Longcamp, M., Zerbato-Poudou, M. T. & Velay, J. L. (2005). The influence of writing practice on letter recognition in preschool children: A comparison between handwriting and typing. *Acta Psychologica, 119*, 67–79.

Niels, R. (2004). Dynamic Time Warping: An Intuitive Way of Handwriting Recognition? Master's thesis, Radboud University Nijmegen.

Palluel-Germain, R., Bara, F., Hillairet de Boisferon, A., Hennion, B., Gouagout, P. & Gentaz, E. (2007). A visuo-haptic device - Telemaque - increases the kindergarten children's handwriting acquisition. *IEEE WorldHaptics*, 72-77.

Plamondon, R., Srihari, S., Polytech, E. & Montreal, Q. (2000). Online and off-line handwriting recognition: a comprehensive survey. *IEEE Transactions on Pattern Analysis and Machine Intelligence*, 22(1), 63--84.

Rosenblum, S., Weiss, P. L. & Parush, S. (2003). Product and Process Evaluation of Handwriting Difficulties. *Educational Psychology Review, 15*(1), 41--81.

Saygin, A. P., Wilson, S. M., Hagler, J., Bates, E. & Sereno, M. I. (2004). Point-Light Biological Motion Perception Activates Human Premotor Cortex. *Journal of Neuroscience, 24*(27), 6181-6188.

Schmidt, R. A. & Lee, T. D. (1987). *Motor Control and Learning: A Behavioral Emphasis*. Champaign, IL: Human Kinetics.

Schmidt, R. A. & Wrisberg, C. A. (2000). *Motor Learning and Performance*. Human Kinetics Publishers.

Seki, K., Yajima, M. & Sugishita, M. (1995). The efficacy of kinesthetic reading treatment for pure alexia. *Neuropsychologia, 33*, 595-609.

Shams, L. & Seitz, A. R. (2008). Benefits of multisensory learning. *Trends in Cognitive Sciences, 12*(11), 411-417.

Thorndike, E. L. (1910). Handwriting. *Teacher College Record, 11*, 83-175.

Van Galen, G. (1991). Handwriting: Issues for a psychomotor theory. *Human Movement Science, 10*(2), 165-191.

Viviani, P. & Terzuolo, C. (1982). Trajectory determines movement dynamics. *Neuroscience, 7*(2), 431--437.

Viviani, P. (2002). *Common Mechanisms in Perception and Action: Attention and Performance.* Oxford University Press, New York, chapter Motor competence in the perception of dynamic events: a tutorial, pp. 406-443.

Zesiger, P. (1995). *Ecrire : Approche cognitive, neuropsychologique et développementale*. Paris: Presses universitaires de France.

7

Video based Handwritten Characters Recognition

Chen-Chiung Hsieh
Tatung University
Taiwan

1. Introduction

Video as an input device[1] is becoming a viable method for information products because of its lower cost along with increasing power of computer processor. Its supporting human-computer communication is evident. (Mann, 1996) used video-cam as the input device of a wearable computer system has reported that video becomes a "visual memory prosthetic", a perception enhancer, allowing one to remember faces better, and see things that normally would never have been seen. Some researches in this area are of assistive technology oriented. (Betke et al., 2002) have developed a visual tracking system that interprets visible-light video to provide computer access for people, in particular, children with severe disabilities. Their system “Camera Mouse” was named because it tracked a body feature like the tip of the nose with a video camera and used the detected motion of the feature to directly control the mouse pointer. However, the spelling board was used to control what was typed by selecting the letters with the Camera Mouse. It took more than 20 seconds to input a character.

(Cantzler & Hoile, 2003) proposed a novel form of a pointing device to control the mouse pointer by moving the camera freely in space in a similar fashion to the way a laser pointer controls a laser dot. They locate the computer display in the camera image by finding structured or large regions. The chosen method exploits the fact that there is much structured content in screen. This is sometimes too restrictive for diversity of window applications. Another vision-based pointer device, Gray level VisualGlove, intended for wearable computers, was presented by (Iannizzotto et al., 2001). While previous methods are mainly based on color for image segmentation and human skin detection, their system only relies on gray level gradient to be of low computation cost. Template matching with the highest degree of confidence, the lowest Hausdorff distance, is chosen as a possible detected object. However, it could not deal with scaled or rotated finger motion.

---

[1] http://en.wikipedia.org/wiki/Input_device.

2. Related Works

(Zhou et al., 2007) presented the Visual Mouse (VM) system for interaction with display via hand gestures. The method includes detecting bare hands using the fast SIFT algorithm to save long training time of the Adaboost algorithm, tracking hands based on the CAM-Shift algorithm, recognizing hand gestures in cluttered background via Principle Components Analysis (PCA) without extracting clear-cut hand contour, and defining simple and robustly interpretable vocabularies of hand gestures, which are subsequently used to control a computer mouse. However, bare hands are restricted to move on table and can't be extracted when overlapped with complex background.

The extracted and tracked pointing device can be used to do dynamic gesture recognition (Min &Yoo, 1997; Davis & Shan, 1994). A number of researchers have explored the use of hand gestures as a mean of computer input, using a variety of technologies. (Lin & Tang, 2003) proposed a video based handwritten Chinese character recognition system that combines the advantages of both the online and offline approaches (Munich & Perona, 2003). Since writing on paper is the most natural way for handwriting, the system allows users to write on any regular paper just like using the off-line system. The temporal information of each stroke is extracted based on the comparison and tracking of ink pixels (pen-down motions) (Tang et al., 2000, Tang & Lin, 2002). However, their approaches struggle to accurately extract the dynamic information for every single ink pixel, which is often mixed with the pen, hand, and their shadows.

(Chen et al., 2006) presents the design and implementation of a fingertip writing interface which can recognize the moving trajectory of the user's fingertip into alphabets and numerals. The processes are divided into tracking and recognition. For the fingertip tracking process, it deploys background subtraction, skin-color modelling, finger extraction, fingertip positioning, and Kalman filter prediction. To recognize the fingertip trajectories, four types of features are defined for recognition with Hidden Markov Models. However, finger tips are easily confused with facial color and the tracking results are not so reliable.

In this chapter, we are focused on video based pointing method which could be utilized as a choice for information input. Given people's experiences with currently available technology devices, our goal has been to develop a non-contact, comfortable, reliable, and inexpensive communication device that is easily adaptable to serve different applications. Motion, color, contour, and curvature are all combined to reliably extract the fingertips. Kalman filter (Mahmoudi & Parviz, 2006) is also adopted to speed up the tracking process. Section three gives an overview of the proposed system. Section four describes the detection of the moving forefinger. In Section five, the tip of forefinger is extracted and the corresponding positions in each frame are accumulated as the written strokes. Directional strokes, semi-circle strokes, and loop strokes are defined for 1-D character representation. Here, pen-up and pen-down are not easy to be differentiated with only one camera. In Section six, strokes connection rules are induced for pen-up strokes detection. All possible 1-D extracted strokes sequences are matched with the pre-built 1-D character models by the Dynamic Time Warp matching algorithm for character recognition. Experiments were conducted to verify the effectiveness of the proposed system in Section seven. Finally, conclusions and discussions are given in the last section.

3. System Overview

A webcam attached on top of the screen is deployed to capture the user gesture in front of it. The system can detect the fingertip without any marks and track it continuously. The fingertip serves as the pointing device usually is the highest point of the moving hand. Figure 1 show the system architecture which could be divided into two modules.

- Fingertip tracking module: it extracts the forefinger tip by frame differencing and skin color. Then, contour around that point is used to calculate the curvature for verification.
  - Motion Detection: two consecutive images are compared to get the changed areas. A motion mask is formed if the difference is greater than a given threshold. If no motion mask is produced, the previous image is skipped and continues with the next image.
  - Finger Tip Extraction: by overlapping the skin color image with the motion mask, the moving hand and finger would be the largest region after connected component labeling. The fingertip can be defined as the top point of that region.
  - Finger Tip Tracking: If the fingertip is found, the position is recorded and continues to the next frame. If user stops writing, the fingertip would not be found and the system goes to the character recognition module. The system performance could be greatly improved by utilizing Kalman filter to predict the fingertip.

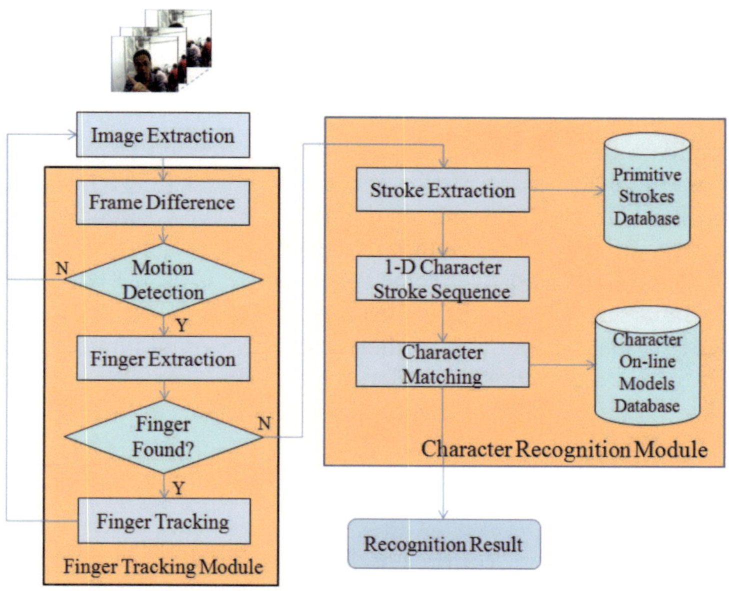

Fig. 1. Functional block diagram of the proposed video-based character recognition system.

- Character Recognition module: it consists of two stages, stroke extraction and character matching. Time warp matching algorithm which could tolerate symbol insertion, deletion, and replacement is used in both of these two stages.
  - Stroke Extraction: from the written character trail, time warp matching algorithm is used to extract all possible strokes defined by the 1-D line segment sequences. In

(Hsieh & Lee, 1992), Hsieh and Lee defined several stroke types for Chinese characters. Here, we defined 3 kinds of stroke types for alphanumeric characters.

- Written Character Representation: all combinations of the extracted strokes are represented as 1-D strings by the temporal information for character matching.
- Character Recognition: time warp matching algorithm is used again to do 1-D strings matching between generated strokes sequence and the stored character on-line model bases. The written trail is recognized as the character model with the minimum distance.

4. Fingertip Detection and Tracking

The tip of forefinger is adopted as the pen tip for writing characters. The forefinger tip has the following properties: skin color, motion region, and of high curvature. Therefore, we design a sequence of functions adaptive skin color detection, temporal frame difference, and connected components labelling to extract it. Adaptive skin color model is developed to produce the skin regions. If the skin regions are of motion regions, those regions would most likely be hand regions. Among the extracted regions, the forefinger tip is usually the highest point and it could be verified by the property of high curvature.

4.1 Adaptive Skin Color Detection

By exploiting information from individual face to create the skin color model for each person will improve the robustness of skin detection because of the reduced amount of color variations within a person's face and hands. In this subsection, we utilize the enhanced adaptive skin color detection method (Hsieh et al., 2010) which is based on individual's face skin color. Firstly, face detection (Viola & Jones, 2001) is applied to find each person's face skin region. By assuming face skin gray levels could be modeled by a Gaussian distribution, non-skin pixels like hair and eyes are of darker gray levels could be excluded by the symmetric property of Gaussian distribution. Remaining pixels most likely to be skin color are transformed into normalized *RGB* color space, say *(r, g, b)*, for building adaptive skin color model. The built skin color model is then used to detect the other skin color pixels such as hands belonging to that person. This method is independent of illumination, ethnic group, shading, and so on. Face detection, face skin region extraction, skin color modeling, ROI setting, and skin color pixels classification are described in detail in the following subsections.

4.1.1 Face Detection

(Viola & Jones, 2001) designed a sequence of classifiers based on a set of haar-like features and combined these increasingly more complex classifiers in a "cascade" which allows background regions of the image to be quickly discarded while spending more computation on promising object like face regions. (Lienhart & Maydt, 2002) then introduced a novel set of rotated haar-like features which significantly enrich the basic set of simple haar-like features and can also be calculated very efficiently. The characteristic of this method is by use of the black-white haar-like patterns to detect eyes that is independent of the skin colors of people. However, it would produce false alarms along with true positives.

Here, false alarm would be filtered out if the number of skin pixels within the detected face region is less than a given threshold. In order to reduce the computational complexity, the size and location of face are used to set the region of interest (ROI) for face detection in the next frame. It is assumed that user would not move around dramatically in the environment and the location of face in the next frame would be confined in the ROI centered at the previous location of face. If no face is detected, then it is necessary to search face in the whole image. An example is given in Fig. 2. The detected face is enclosed by a rectangle as shown in Fig. 2(a) and the ROI as shown in Fig. 2(b) is set 1.5×1.5 times the size of that rectangle.

(a) (b)

Fig. 2 (a) Detected face is enclosed by a red rectangle. (b) The ROI set for face detection in the next frame.

4.1.2 Facial Skin Color Sampling

After extraction of face region, we could sample the representative skin color pixels for that person. By observing the histogram of extracted face region, darker pixels like eyes or hair locate at the extreme left. Assume the skin color pixels are of Gaussian distribution in Y (luminance), the shape should be symmetric around the center peak. Therefore, the peak location of the histogram is the mean value. The longer part of the left hand side of the mean could be trimmed by mirroring the right hand side to avoid selecting those darker pixels. Fig. 3(a) gives an example of detected face and Fig. 3(b) shows the corresponding histogram of the inner region of face. The left hand side is apparently longer than the right hand side. We could trim the darker pixels by the symmetric property of Gaussian distribution. Fig. 3(c) shows that the darker pixels are successfully removed from the inner face region and this demonstrates the mechanism of proposed sampling method.

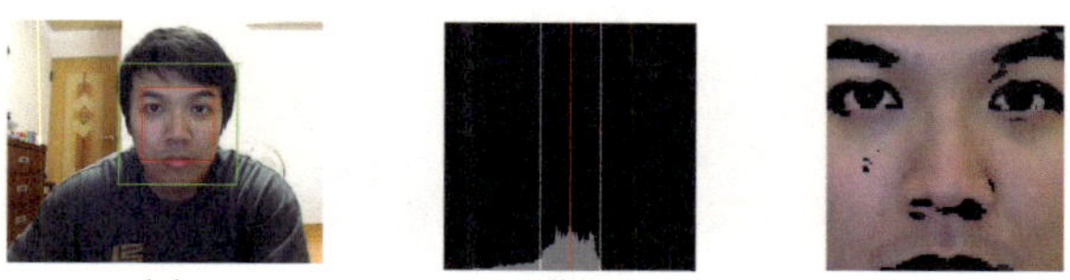

(a) (b) (c)

Fig. 3 (a) Detected face where the inner region is used for sampling. (b) Luminance histogram of the inner region in (a). (c) Resulting inner region after removal of non-skin color pixels. Note that the non-skin color is indicated in black.

The choice to remove darker pixels in the frontal view inner region is apparent. As shown in (Soriano et al., 2000), the skin scope as defined in Eq. (6) would include white pixels in general. White pixels such as highlights due to illumination reflections happened would be kept in the skin region. Similarly, golden or whitish hair looks like skin color may also be considered as skin color.

$$r = \frac{R}{R+G+B} \tag{1}$$

$$g = \frac{G}{R+G+B} \tag{2}$$

$$Q_+ = -1.3767r^2 + 1.0743r + 0.1452 \tag{3}$$

$$Q_- = -0.776r^2 + 0.5601r + 0.1766 \tag{4}$$

$$W = (r-0.33)^2 + (g-0.33)^2 \tag{5}$$

$$skin = \begin{cases} Q_+ > g > Q_- \\ W > 0.0004 \\ 0.6 > r > 0.2 \end{cases} \tag{6}$$

4.1.3 Adaptive Skin Color Model

R color and normalized *RGB* colors *(r, g)* are used to set up the adaptive skin color model for *(r, g, R)* is less sensitive to changes in light source and suitable for real world applications. Fig. 4 shows the *(r, g, R)* histograms of the skin color pixels in Fig. 3(c). They are symmetric and converge tightly. Therefore, we could model the skin color of that person by Gaussian distributions $GM_i(\mu_i, \sigma_i)$, where μ_i is the mean and σ_i is the standard deviation, $i=r, g$, and R. μ_i and σ_i are calculated as in Eq. (7) and (8).

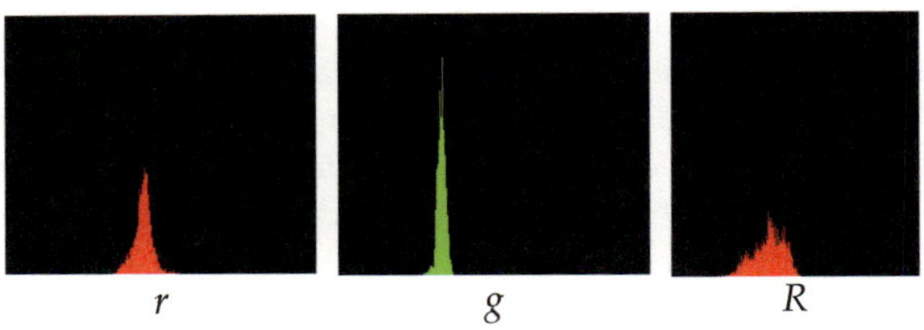

Fig. 4 The skin color distributions of Fig. 3(c) in *(r, g, R)* which could be modeled by three narrow Gaussian distributions.

$$\mu_i = \frac{1}{n} \sum_{(x,y)\in face} I_i(x,y), \quad i = r, g, R \tag{7}$$

$$\sigma_i = \sqrt{\frac{1}{n} \sum_{(x,y)\in face} (I_i(x,y) - \mu_i)^2}, \quad i = r, g, R \tag{8}$$

where n is the number of pixels in the trimmed face region.

4.1.4 ROI setting and skin color detection

ROI setting is designed to speed up the processing time. It can be designed for situations that there are more than one person in the image. Each person has his/her own personal skin color model for hand gesture segmentation. Thus, the accuracy of hand gesture recognition could be increased for occurrence of multiple persons at the same time.

To detect skin color pixels such as the dynamic hand gestures based on the above developed adaptive skin color model, each person has his own ROI as setup in Eq. (9). In most cases, the hand regions fall within the rectangle as shown in Fig. 5. The actual size of ROI can be adjusted according to application requirements. However, in order to objectively compare the proposed skin color detection method with previously mentioned methods, the ROI is set as the whole image in our experiments.

$$ROI_m(x,y,w,h) = (face_m.x - 5\times face_m.r,\\ face_m.y - 5\times face_m.r, 10\times face_m.r, 10\times face_m.r), \tag{9}$$

where m represents the index of detected face, (x, y) is the coordinate of the top left corner point of the m-th ROI and (w, h) is its width and height. $face_m$ is a data structure with data members x, y, and r, where $(face_m.x, face_m.y)$ is the center of circle of detected face with radius r.

Fig. 5. ROI setting for hand gesture detection.

With the built personalized skin color model $GM_i(\mu_i, \sigma_i)$, i=r, g, and R, we can now set the upper and low limits for skin color detection as in Eq. (10) and (11), respectively. Note that there is a scale factor for controlling the color range. It is set as two to cover 95%[2] of the samples in our experiments. For each pixel in the set ROI, it is classified as skin color if it satisfies Eq. (12). Fig. 6 shows the mean and the up and low limits for each color component r, g, and R.

$$UpBound_i = \mu_i + 2\times\sigma_i, \quad i = r, g, R \tag{10}$$

$$LowBound_i = \mu_i - 2\times\sigma_i, \quad i = r, g, R \tag{11}$$

$$skin = \begin{cases} UpBound_r > r > LowBound_r \\ UpBound_g > g > LowBound_g \\ UpBound_R > R > LowBound_R \end{cases} \tag{12}$$

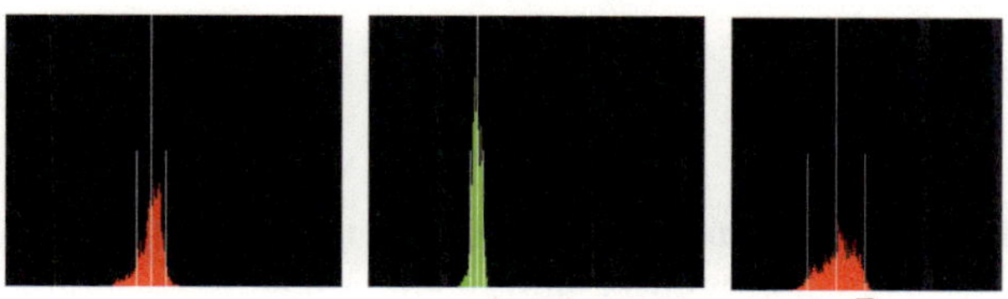

r g R

Fig. 6. The scope for each color component (r, g, R). The center line indicates the mean value and the left/right shorter line is the low/up limit.

[2] http://www.itl.nist.gov/div898/handbook/pmc/section5/pmc51.htm

4.2 Fingertip Extraction

By the proposed adaptive skin color model, we could obtain the hand regions. Frame difference is then performed by subtracting the previous frame from current frame. Fig. 7(a) and (b) are two consecutive frames and Fig. 7(c) is the resulting difference frame with threshold set as 20 according to our experience. The motion of hand is apparent in contrast to the other regions in this case. If we restrict the detection of skin pixels within the motion masks, false regions like face or other stationary skin regions can be eliminated for they have no obvious corresponding motion masks.

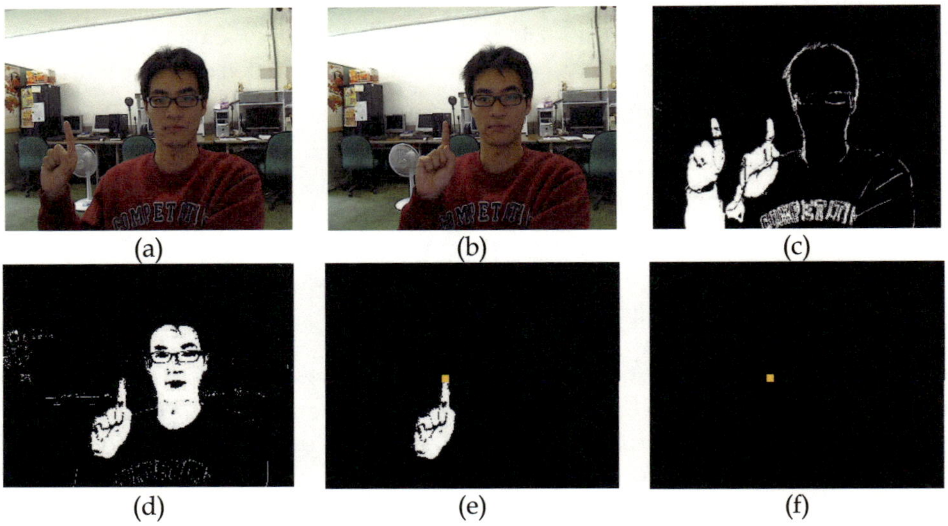

Fig. 7. Finger extraction via adaptive skin color detection and frame differencing. (a) The previous image. (b) The current image. (c) The difference frame with threshold set as *20*. (d) The current skin color image. (e) The extracted current hand region by overlapping motion mask (c) with skin color image (d). Note that the noises were removed. (f) The highest point was extracted as the forefinger tip.

The regions that are both moving regions and skin colors would most likely be hand region. We could define the moving skin color image $H_i(x, y)$ by overlapping motion mask $M_i(x, y)$ with skin color image $S_i(x, y)$ as in Eq. (1).

$$H_i(x, y) = M_i(x, y) \cap S_i(x, y) \tag{13}$$

Through observations and experiments, the fingertip usually is the highest point of moving skin color regions. By connected component labeling, small size regions less than a given threshold are considered as noises and removed. In turn, the moving hand is usually the largest region with size greater than a given threshold, say about 100 pixels. Fig. 7(d) shows the skin color image of Fig. 7(b), and Fig. 7(e) shows the resulting hand region by overlapping Fig. 7(c) and 7(d). The highest end point as shown in Fig. 7(f) was the extracted forefinger tip. It can be further verified by its high curvature.

Kalman filter is adopted to predict the next position of fingertip in the target frame. Because our fingertip is moving in a smooth style, the tracking is based on a dynamic linear system in the time domain. Fig. 8 gives an example for fingertip tracking. The predicted fingertip position is marked by a small yellow triangle and the previous position is marked by a small red circle as shown in Fig. 8(b). Then, the blue rectangle defined as half the size of the image is used for fingertip searching.

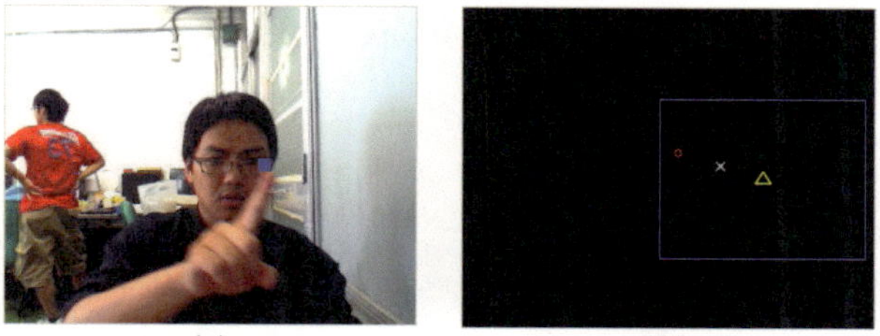

(a) (b)

Fig. 8. Fingertip prediction by Kalman filter. (a) Current fingertip is marked by a blue dot. (b) Previous, current, and predicted fingertip positions are marked by ×, ○, and Δ, respectively. Note that the blue rectangle represents the search range

From experimental results, the average throughput of fingertip extraction is 13.184 frames per second with Kalman filtering which is faster than the processing speed 10.216 frames per second without Kalman filter.

5. Stroke Extraction

The top point of forefinger extracted by the method discussed in the previous section is deployed as pen-tip to write characters. Each tip position of the forefinger in the image sequence is recorded at the speed of 10-15 frames per second. By connecting consecutive positions along the time series, we can get the written trails.

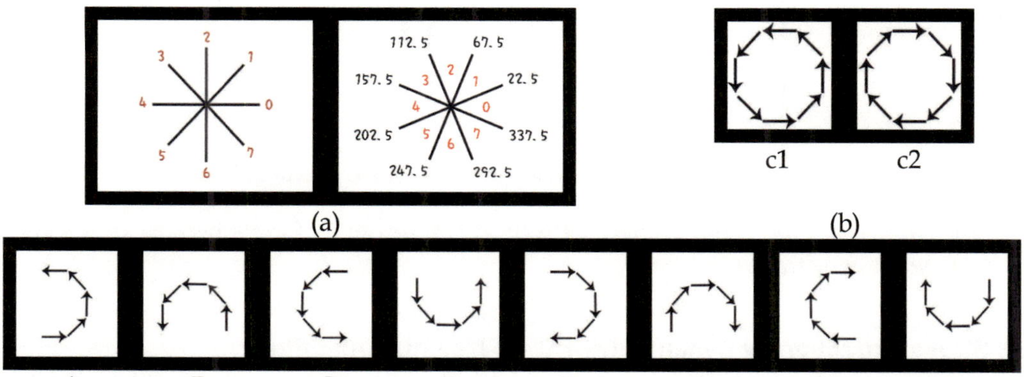

A B C D E F G H

(c)

Fig. 9. The defined stroke types for alphanumerical characters. (a) Primitive directional stroke types and their tolerance. (b). Loop stroke types. (d) Semi-circle stroke types.

5.1 Stroke Types

We defined eight primitive directional strokes types, two loop stroke types, and eight semi-circle stroke types as shown in Fig. 9 for alphanumerical character representation. The primitive stroke types are of straight line segments as shown in Fig. 9(a). To tolerate the writing variety among different users, we allow at most 45 degree variation range. Fig. 9(b) and (c) show the loop stroke types and semi-circle stroke types, respectively, by the consisting short straight line segments. Note that the shapes of A~D are written counter-clockwise and E~F are written clockwise. Similarly, the same shape of the two loop stroke types are written in opposite directions.

5.2 Pen-up Stroke Detection

Due to the lost depth information, we induced some rules to prevent extracting too many possible strokes. In this chapter, alphanumeric characters were analyzed to detect the pen-up strokes which move the pen-tip from the end point of current stroke to the starting point of next stroke. For example, the line segment sequence '→', '↓', '← ', and '→ ' can be analyzed to be a compound stroke '⊃' concatenated with a pen-up stroke '→'. For a written 1-D stroke sequence, there may be several ways to decompose that character. Each corresponds to a possible character. Thus, to reduce the number of possible combinations, we could extract only the possible strokes after removal of pen-up strokes.

According to the writing habit, the successive stroke denoted 2 in Fig. 10 is considered as a pen-up stroke which is impossible to be a written stroke. In case one as shown in Fig. 10(a), it shows that we would not write the second stroke in the opposite direction of the first one. Note that the first stroke may not be horizontal. In case two as shown in Fig. 10(b), it reveals that the second stroke would never go north or northwest given a horizontal line segment from right to left. In case three as shown in Fig. 10(c), it demonstrates that the second stroke would not be written from bottom to top given the first stroke written from left to right. For these cases, the second stroke can be extracted and recognized as a pen-up stroke. Furthermore, the pen-up stroke is in fact the directional relationship between the first and the third pen-down strokes.

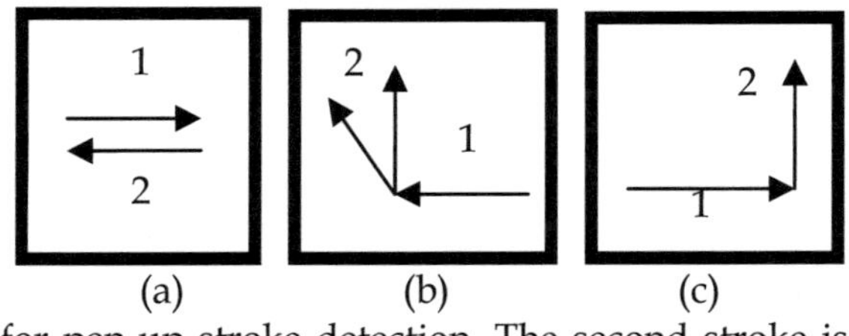

Fig. 10. Three cases for pen-up stroke detection. The second stroke is pen-up stroke given the first pen-down stroke.

5.3 Stroke Extraction by Dynamic Time Warp Matching Algorithm

By connecting tracked fingertip positions in consecutive images, we can obtain the trail which is the written character. The written trail can be parsed to extract the defined stroke types as shown in Fig. 9. Initially, the input trail could be segmented into several connected pen-down strokes by the rules for pen-up strokes detection. Parse each segmented input trail by the finite automata for each defined stroke type, the pen-down strokes could be recognized. Here, the Dynamic Time Warp (DTW) matching algorithm (Weste et al., 1983) is adopted as the finite automata for pen-down stroke recognition. In fact, DTW is an algorithm for measuring the similarity between two 1-D sequences which may vary in time or speed. The algorithm for pen-down stroke extraction is described as follows.

Algorithm: Stroke extraction
Input: 1-D straight line segment sequence.
Output: Possible strokes for each stroke type.
1. Pen-up stroke detection and segmentation of written trail.
2. **For** each segmented input trail x_i
    $k=0;$
    Repeat
        For each stroke type y_j
            DTW initialization;
            Calculate all the partial sum
                $S_{m,,n} = min\{ S_{m-1,n-1}+R(x_{i,m}, y_{j,n}), S_{m-1,n,}+D(x_{i,m}), S_{m,n-1}+I(y_{j,n})\}$
                between x_i and y_j by dynamic programming;
            If y_j matched with x_i **then**
                A stroke y_j' of type y_j in x_i is obtained;
                Record the starting/end point of y_j' in x_i;
        $k=k+1;$
        $x_i=x_i$- {the first k line segments};
    Until $x_i = \Phi$;

The distance functions are defined as in Eq. (14)~(16).

$$\mathrm{R}(x_{i,m}, y_{j,n}) = \begin{cases} 0 & ,if\ x_{i,m} = y_{j,n} \\ \left| dir(x_{i,m}) - dir(y_{j,n}) \right| \bmod 6, & otherwise \end{cases} \tag{14}$$

$$\mathrm{D}(x_{i,m}, y_{j,n}) = 1 \tag{15}$$

$$\mathrm{I}(x_{i,m}, y_{j,n}) = 1 \tag{16}$$

where *dir* is the direction code as shown in Fig. 9(a).

6. Character Recognition

6.1 On-line Model for Character Representation

For the purpose of character recognition, each character is first represented by the on-line model (Hsieh & Lee, 1992) which is actually a 1-D stroke sequence according to the temporal information. Not only stroke types but also stroke relationships are used for character description. For example, the stroke sequence of '4' starts from '/', '—', and ends at '□'. If the stroke relationships between two consecutive strokes are not utilized, then the character '7' could also have the same stroke sequence as '4'. With the relationships introduced into the on-line model, we can not only describe characters but also recognize them. The relationships between any two consecutive strokes can be divided into six classes as shown in Fig. 11.

- Case a: The tail of the first stroke connects to the head of the next stroke as shown in Fig. 11(a).
- Case b: Two consecutive strokes connect at their head positions as shown in Fig. 11(b).
- Case c: The head of the second stroke touches the middle part of the first stroke as shown in Fig. 11(c).
- Case d: The tail of the first stroke touches the side of the second stroke as shown in Fig. 11(d).
- Case e: Two strokes intersect with each other as shown in Fig. 11(e).
- Others: This kind of relationship is used when none of the above cases could be applied. It is simply represented by the direction code as shown in Fig. 9(a).

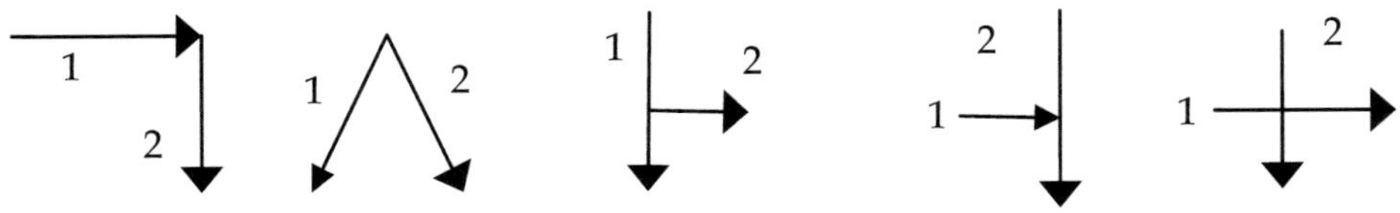

(a) R_a: tail-head (b) R_b: head-head (c) R_c: side-head (d) R_d: tail-side (e) R_e: intersection
Fig. 11. Stroke relationships between two consecutive strokes.

By the defined stroke types and stroke relationships, on-line models for characters recognition could be built manually. Some examples are given in Fig. 12. The on-line models for the same character may be created differently for the different writing sequences. Usually, we would like to choose the most discriminative one. On the other hand, the on-line model could be used for character recognition if there are no more than two characters share the same model.

A: ↙R_b↘R_3→ B:↓R_b⮌R_a⮌ H:↓ R_c→R_d↓ W:ƱR_aƱ

Fig. 12. On-line models for alphanumeric characters 'A', 'B', 'H', and 'W'.

6.2 Character Recognition

After strokes extraction, the input character can be represented as many 1-D sequences of extracted pen-down strokes interleaved by pen-up stroke relationships. In Section 5.2, the detected pen-up strokes could be further used to aid the classification of the stroke relationship defined in Fig. 11. These 1-D sequences are then matched with each on-line model in the character set. In this chapter, character recognition is conducted again by the Dynamic Time Warp matching algorithm which could tolerate stroke insertion, replacement, and deletion.

In general, DTW is a method to find an optimal match between two given sequences. It determines the measurement of their similarity in the time domain. We could apply DTW to do matching directly on the written trail which was represented by a sequence of straight line segments. Assume the input sequence is $w(1{:}m)$ and the reference sequence is $t(1{:}n)$. The time complexity is $O(mn)$ for DTW at line segment level. However, the detected pen-up strokes could be used to segment the input sequence into $w_1(1{:}m_1)$, $w_2(1{:}m_2)$, …, and $w_s(1{:}m_s)$, where $m>=m_1+ m_2+\ldots m_s$ and s is the number of pen-down strokes. Note that the reference sequence t could also be defined as $t_1(1{:}n_1)$, $t_2(1{:}n_2)$, …, and $t_s(1{:}n_r)$, where $n>=n_1+ n_2+\ldots n_r$

and r is the number of pen-down strokes. Take the fault tolerance of pen-up strokes into consideration, the time complexity would be $O(\sum_{j=1}^{r}\sum_{i=1}^{s} m_i * n_j)$.

To be more robust and save computation time for character recognition, we apply DTW at stroke level instead of straight line segment level. The algorithm is stated as follows.

Algorithm: Character recognition
Input: All possible strokes for each stroke type are stored in linked lists.
Output: The character on-line model with the highest similarity.

1. *max=0;*
2. **For** each character on-line model y_i
    - Build the multi-stage graph according to the strokes in y_i;
    - **For** each combination x_j of extracted strokes according to y_i;
        - Check validity of x_j by the pen-up strokes in y_i;
        - Discard invalid x_j;
        - Do DTW matching on pen-down strokes in x_j and y_i ;
        - Calculate all the partial sum
            - $S_{m,,n} = min\{ S_{m-1,n-1}+R(x_{i,m}, y_{j,n}), S_{m-1,n},+D(x_{i,m}), S_{m,n-1}+I(y_{j,n})\}$
            - between x_i and y_j by dynamic programming;
        - **If** the final score is greater than *max*
            - Update *max* and set y_i is the recognized character;

By extracting all the possible strokes from the 1-D straight line segment sequence, the computational cost would become $O(m'_1 \times m'_2 \times ... \times m'_s)$, where m'_i ($<m_i$) is the number of strokes of type n'_i, $i=1, 2, ..., s$. In our case, $O(m'_1 \times m'_2 \times ... \times m'_s \times s^2)$ would become $O(C \times m'_1 \times m'_2 \times ... \times m'_s)$ with small s. For a typical example, if $m=n=10$, $(m_1, m_2, m_3)= (n_1, n_2, n_3) =(3, 3, 4)$, and $(m'_1, m'_2, m'_3)=(2, 2, 1)$, we would have $mn=100$, $\sum_{j=1}^{r}\sum_{i=1}^{s} m_i \times n_j =100$, and $m'_1 \times m'_2 \times m'_s \times s^2 = 36$. The time complexity of stroke level DTW would be the best.

7. Experimental Results

The video camera deployed is Logitech QuickCam®Pro for Notebooks with technical specification including auto focus, 2M pixel sensors, 24-bit true colors, and capture speed up to 30 frames per second. No restriction was made on the used camera but the image resolution should be set to 320×240 at least. Note that this is the minimum requirement. The system software is implemented in C language and runs on a Pentium 4 PC.

7.1 Fingertip Tracking Results

Accuracy is more important than execution speed in this system. If the extraction of fingertip is not precise, the application will not work effectively. Fig. 13 shows the different writing factors including camera distance, hand rotation, and view angle are all taken into considerations, and the experimental results proved that our system is robust. In addition, if the moving speed is stable, the fingertip could still be extracted in spite of overlapping with face.

A video sequence consisting of 847 frames is used for testing and the fingertip extraction accuracy achieves 98.58%. Among the fault situations, the first case was due to abrupt changes of luminance. The bright light affected the skin color seriously as shown in Fig. 14(a). In the second case, the moving hand as shown in Fig. 14(b) passed the face. It would be very challenging to extract fingers when fingers were overlapped with face. Both finger and face were of similar skin color and moving regions.

Fig. 13. The extracted fingertips from variety of conditions in a real video sequence.

(a) (b)

Fig. 14. The fault scenarios. (a) The bright light affected the skin color of fingertip. (b) The face affected the fingertip verification.

7.2 Alphanumeric Character Recognition Results

To prove the robustness of proposed video based character recognition system, thirty-six characters including English letters from A to Z and numbers from zero to nine were tested. In order to facilitate the user to write with the proposed system, the input method from Palm Graffiti[3] was adopted. It is released from Palm and in widespread use on PDA. Fig. 15

[3] http://en.wikipedia.org/wiki/Graffiti_(Palm_OS)

gives all the alphanumerical characters. Note that some characters are written different from traditional writing habit.

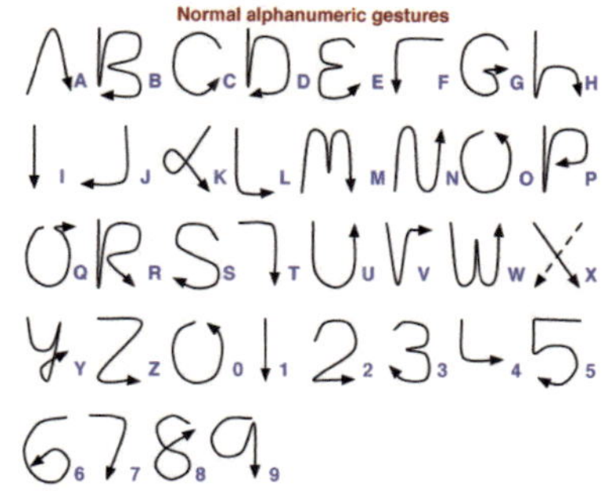

Fig. 15. Palm Graffiti designed for easy writing and easy character recognition.

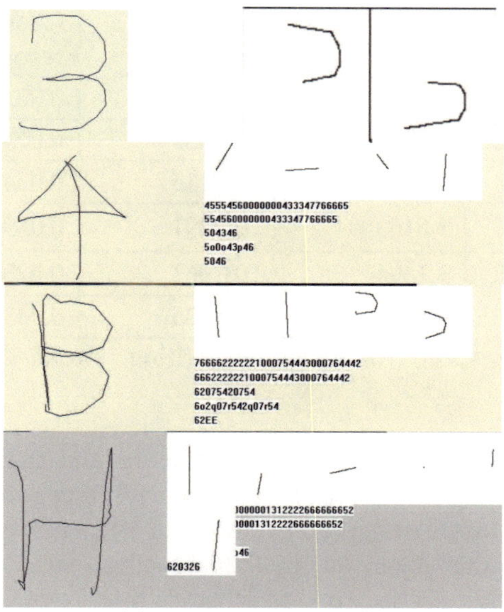

(a) (b)

Fig. 16. Screenshots of the two stage DTW matching on some input characters. The intermediate process demonstrates the system capability of stroke extraction and character recognition. (a) Written characters. (b) Extracted strokes and the correct on-line model.

Fig. 16(a) shows several characters that were written by fingertip. After pen-up strokes detection, the written 1-D straight line sequence could be segmented for stroke extraction. It was conducted by matching segmented line sequence with each defined stroke types. All possible strokes could be extracted and then arranged as a multi-stage graph according to the character on-line model. Finally, valid combinations of the extracted strokes are matched with the on-line model. Here, the matching was done by two stage DTW matching algorithm. The first one was for stroke extraction and the second one was for character matching. Fig. 16(b) shows the extracted strokes and the recognition results. For example, character 'B' was recognized as the on-line model "62EE"=pen-down '' + pen-up '' + pen-down '' + pen-down ''.

Five persons were invited to write 36 alphanumeric characters five times and we have 900 character test videos. The recognition rate is 82.77% because we can not differentiate '0', '1', and '7' from 'O', 'I', and 'T', respectively, for they have the same written strokes sequences. If these ambiguous characters were counted as correct, the system performance could reach 91.11%. Table 1 shows the time spent for character writing, stroke extraction, and character recognition. The finger writing speed is 3.4543 seconds per character on average, and the character recognition speed is 0.05437second/char including strokes extraction 0.02125 second/char and character recognition 0.03312 second/char. The recognition result comes out immediately after the character was written completely.

	Character writing	Strokes extraction	Character recognition
People 1	2.7965	0.01768	0.02168
People 2	3.9722	0.02387	0.04399
People 3	3.5166	0.02115	0.03465
People 4	3.8168	0.02391	0.03966
People 5	3.1694	0.01963	0.02566
Average	3.4543	0.02125	0.03312

Table 1. The processing speed for character writing, stroke extraction, and character recognition.

Table 2 summaries the accuracies for fingertip extraction and character recognition among different methodologies. The time spent for character recognition was also indicated. Although DTW could achieve recognition rate up to 94%, it spent too much time doing DTW matching. On the other hand, our method based on stroke matching could achieve much higher speed with little sacrifice on the accuracy rate. To improve the recognition rate, we can create more than one on-line models tailed for the mis-recognized characters.

	Fingertip Extraction	Character Recognition	
	Accuracy	Accuracy	Time
HMM2 (Chen et al., 2006)	97.74%	88.1%*	1.08s
DTW (Chen et al., 2006)	97.74%	94%	21.14s
Ours	98.58%	91.11%	0.033s

*with one training sample per character.

Table 2. Comparisons among different methodologies.

8. Conclusions

In this chapter, we firstly designed an adaptive skin color model for fingertip extraction and its application to handwritten character recognition. A cheap webcam is used to serve as the input device and the forefinger tip is extracted by integrating skin-color, motion, curvature, and its relatively higher position. The fingertip position is recorded and tracked for each frame. Thus, a video based pointing method was developed as a choice for information input or computer system operation. Compared with currently available technologies, our system has been a non-contact, comfortable, reliable, and inexpensive communication device that could be easily adaptable to serve special needs like character input. Furthermore, this input device was also integrated with the MS-Windows just like mouse. Here, the fingertip acting as pen tip can be used to write characters. We defined some stroke types including primitive directional strokes, semi-circle strokes, and compound loop strokes for alphanumeric characters. Dynamic time warp matching algorithm was used to extract possible strokes. On-line model was also utilized to formulate the character recognition as a multi-stage searching problem. At each stage, we have extracted stroke candidates for that stroke as defined in the on-line model. The optimal path represents the stroke sequence which complies with the on-line model most. It was found again by the DTW matching algorithm. Among all the found stroke sequences, the one with the highest similarity was picked and the written stroke sequence was recognized as the corresponding on-line model. The system we implemented can be inexpensive, convenient, and intuitive. Experimental results proved that the proposed system is feasible for applications.

Up to now, users of IT products such as computer, notebook, and PDA, all need a convenient character input tool. The video-based handwritten character recognition system provides such an input method without the burden caused by holding tiny stylus pen, writing on a size quite limited touchpad, or inputting through an on-screen virtual keyboard. For future works, the character on-line model base can be extended to cover Chinese characters. For robustness improvement, the fingertip overlapped with moving skin color regions like faces would be difficult to extract. It is a challenge to achieve better recognition accuracy without increasing too much stroke extraction time.

9. References

Betke, M.; Gips, J. & Fleming, P. (2002). The camera mouse: visual tracking of body features to provide computer access for people with severe disabilities, *IEEE Trans. on Neural Systems and Rehabilitation Engineering*, Vol. 10, March 2002, pp. 1-10.

Cantzler, H. & Hoile, C. (2003). A novel form of a pointing device, *Vision, Video, and Graphics*, 2003, pp. 1-6.

Chen, Z. W.; Lin, Y. C. & Chiang, C. C. (2006). Design and implementation of a vision-based fingertip writing interface, *Proceeding of the 18th International Conference on Pattern Recognition (ICPR'06)*, pp. 104-107, 2006.

Davis, J. & Shan, M. (1994). Visual gesture recognition, *Proceedings of IEE on Vision, Image and Signal Processing*, Vol. 141, pp. 101-106, April 1994.

Hsieh, C. C. & Lee, H. J. (1992). Off-line recognition of handwritten Chinese characters by on-line model-guided matching, *Pattern Recognition*, Vol. 25, No. 11, pp. 1337-1352, 1992.

Hsieh, C. C.; Liou, D. H. & Jiang, M. K. (2010). Fast enhanced face-based adaptive skin color model, to be published in the Proceeding of the 2010 International Conference on Image Processing and Pattern Recognition in Industrial Engineering (IPPRIE 2010), Xi'an, China, Aug., 2010.

Iannizzotto, G.; Villari, M. & Vita, L. (2001). Hand tracking for human-computer interaction with graylevel visualglove: turning back to the simple way, *Proceedings of the 2001 workshop on Perceptive user interfaces*, pp 1-7, Orlando, Florida, 2001.

Lin, F. & Tang, X. (2003). Dynamic stroke information analysis for video-based handwritten Chinese character recognition, *Proceedings of the 9th IEEE International Conference on Computer Vision*, pp. 695-700, 2003.

Lienhart, R. & Maydt, J. (2002). An extended set of haar-like features for rapid object detection, *Proceedings of 2002 International Conference on Image Processing*, vol.1, pp. 900-903, 2002.

Mahmoudi, F & Parviz, M. (2006). Visual hand tracking algorithms, *Proc. of the Geometric Modeling and Imaging-New Trends*, London, UK, pp. 228-232, 2006.

Mann, S. (1996). Wearable tetherless computer mediated reality: WearCam as a wearable face recognizer, and other applications for the disabled, *AAAI Fall Symposium on Developing Assistive Technology for People with Disabilities*, pp. 9-11, November 1996.

Min, B. W. & Yoo, H. S. (1997). Hand gesture recognition using hidden Markov modes systems, *Proceedings of the IEEE Int. Conf. on Computational Cybernetics and Simulation*, Vol. 5, pp. 4232-4235, 1997.

Munich, M. E. & Perona, P. (2003). Visual identification by signature tracking. *IEEE Trans. PAMI*, Vol. 25, No. 2, pp. 200-217, Feb. 2003.

Soriano, M.; Huovinen, S.; Martinkauppi, B. & Laaksonen, M. (2000). Using the skin locus to cope with changing illumination conditions in color-based face tracking, *Proc. IEEE Nordic Signal Processing Symposium (NORSIG 2000)*, Kolmarden, Sweden, June 13-15, pp. 383-386, 2000.

Tang, X.; Yung, C. & Liu, J. (2000). Handwritten Chinese character recognition through a video camera, *Proceedings of Int'l Conf. Image Processing*, pp. 692-695, 2000.

Tang, X. & Lin, F. (2002). Video-based handwritten character recognition, *Proc. Int'l Conf. Acoustics, Speech, and Signal Processing*, pp. 3748-3751, 2002.

Viola, P. & Jones, M. (2001). Rapid object detection using a boosted cascade of simple features, *Proceedings of the 2001 IEEE Computer Society Conference on Computer Vision and Pattern Recognition CVPR 2001*, vol. 1, pp. 511-518, 2001.

Weste, N.; Burr, D. J. & Ackland, B. D. (1983). Dynamic time warp pattern matching using an integrated multiprocessing array, *IEEE Trnas. on Computers*, Vol. C-32. No. 8, pp. 731-744, August 1983.

Zhou, H.; Xie, L. & Fang, X. (2007). Visual mouse: SIFT detection and PCA recognition, *Proceedings of the 2007 International Conference on Computational Intelligence and Security Workshops*, pp. 263-266, 2007.

8

Communication assistive method using sympathetic skin response

Fumihiko Masuda and Chikamune Wada
Graduate School of Life Science and Systems Engineering, Kyushu Institute of Technology
Japan

1. Introduction

Persons with seriously disabled speech organs and motor function have difficulty in speaking and communicating through hand gestures. Communication aids have been developed based on AAC (Augmentative and Alternative Communication) concept, and are being used to assist in the transmission of the user's intention. However, the disabled person must have residual motor function to operate most of these aids. If the disabled person has few motor functions, such communication aids can hardly be used; also, if the disabled person has a progressive disease, it is necessary to constantly adjust the communication aid to the level of residual motor function. To overcome this problem, a device that does not depend on residual motor function must be developed.
Recently, a study on BCI (Brain Computer Interface) was carried out, which used electroencephalograms as a communication aid that does not depend on residual motor function (Friedrich et al., 2009). The electroencephalogram switch MCTOS (Technos Japan Co., Ltd.) has already been put to practical use. However, MCTOS must recall exciting and frustrating when the user switches it on. Therefore, MCTOS is hard to operate and to have the feeling that it was switched on purposefully (Nakabayashi et al., 2003).
A possible solution to this problem is to use SSR (Sympathetic Skin Response), which can be measured non-invasively and is independent of residual motor function. SSR, which is a biomedical signal that reflects the activity of the sympathetic nervous system, is affected by both cognitive thinking and decision-making (Ito et al., 1996). We hypothesized that the SSR response could be used as a switch in a communication aid which can convey the user's wish to see a character or a picture displayed on a personal computer. In addition, the advantage of SSR is that measurements can be made easily, unlike with the electroencephalogram, and it is not necessary to think about something else (mental arithmetic, exciting and frustrating) irrelevant to the operation of switching on the communication aid; thus, intuitive operation is possible (Fig.1). It has been reported that disabled persons with SCI (Spinal Cord Injury) and ALS (Amyotrophic Lateral Sclerosis) show amplitude reduction and extension of the SSR latency period. In addition, the absence of SSR response has been confirmed in several patients. However, there are few reports on completely absent SSR (Masur et al., 1995, Oey et al., 2002, Nicotra et al., 2002). On the other

hand, differences in SSR response by measurement site have been found and investigated (Masur et al., 1995, Nicotra et al., 2002).

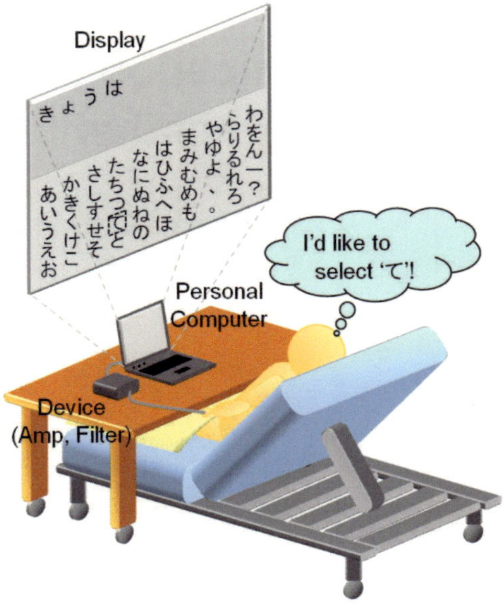

Fig. 1. Image of communication assistive method with sympathetic skin response

In our previous study (Masuda & Wada, 2005), we performed an experiment in which a character was selected on a display by mental intention based on the subject's SSR; we demonstrated the possibility of using SSR as a substitute for the on/off switching of the communication aid. However, this is not to say that SSR was invariably evoked precisely when the user intended; the rate at which the user was able to select a character definitely was 50 to 80%. Tsukahara and Aoki brought up that the SSR appearance ratio was low (Tsukahara & Aoki, 2002).

As one of the causes that SSR was evoked irrespective of the user intention, we thought the psychological change of the user. We hypothesized that the psychological change of the user was evoked the endogenous and the exogenous stimulus. The endogenous stimulus evoke the user's other thought that irrespective of the original task. At the same time, the exogenous stimulus is caused by the environmental sounds and the display method etc. The environmental sounds is stimuli from auditory sense, the display method is stimuli from visual sense. There are sound (Hilz et al., 1999) and visual (Yamashiro et al., 2004) stimuli as factor which SSR evokes. It was reported that these stimuli evoke SSR because of the psychological change (Damasio et al., 1990, Khalfa et al., 2002). It is difficult to control the endogenous stimulus. However, it is possible to control the some exogenous. Therefore, we thought that if the influence of the exogenous stimuli is clear, it is possible to clarify whether a condition exists under which the SSR appears readily or not readily.

In previous our study, we explained the influence of sound stimuli on SSR (Masuda & Wada, 2007). In this study, we first indicated the possibility of using SSR as a substitute for the on/off switching of the communication aid in ALS based on our previous study (Masuda & Wada, 2005). Additionally, we had an interest in the visual stimuli, investigated the optimal visual scanning speed (kana display time) in order to development of communication assistive device using SSR. We constructed a communication aid based on SSR experimentally using a visual scanning system. However, there is a time lag between the imagining of the kana and observable skin potential change in SSR. This time lag (latency) is approximately 1.3 seconds when the SSR was measured on the hand (Yokota et al., 1991). Thus, we expected the kana selection accuracy with SSR to show a change if the optimal visual scanning speed (kana display time) was used.

2. Sympathetic skin response

2.1 Fundamentals

The emotional state, cognitive activity, and information processing ability of an individual can be evaluated by mental sweating using electricity to measure mental activity through the galvanic skin response (GSR) (Fujisawa et al., 1998). The GSR was first reported in 1888 by Féré, and has been widely used in fields such as psychology (Féré, 1888).

Sympathetic skin response (SSR), proposed by Shahani et al. in 1984, is a test performed to measure a change in the electrical potential by applying a spiritual or emotional impulse, which can be measured in the palm or sole (Shahani et al., 1984). Because the detection potentials of SSR widely range from several millivolts to several hundred volts, we can obtain by the electroencephalograph or electromyograph more easily than the GSR. SSR has recently become more widely used as an objective evaluation test for assessing autonomous nervous system functions (Mitani & Ishiyama, 2008, Uozumi & Matsunaga, 2005).

2.2 Characteristics

SSR generation source is thought that 2 of an electric potential change by the sweat gland activity (the depolarization of the secreting cell, the fullness of duct in sweat gland, Na^+ and Cl^- reabsorption etc.) and the epidermal membrane potential change were complicatedly composed as for the generation source of electric potential change in SSR (Uozumi & Matsunaga, 2005).

The mechanism of development in SSR is not completely found out. However, the reflex path is similar the reflex path of GSR (Watahiki, 1987).

It is often used that the electric stimuli, magnetic stimuli, inspiratory gasp and sound stimuli for stimulation to evoke SSR. Generally, the wave pattern of an SSR consists of two or three phases: in most patterns, the skin potential varies from negative to positive (Fig. 2).

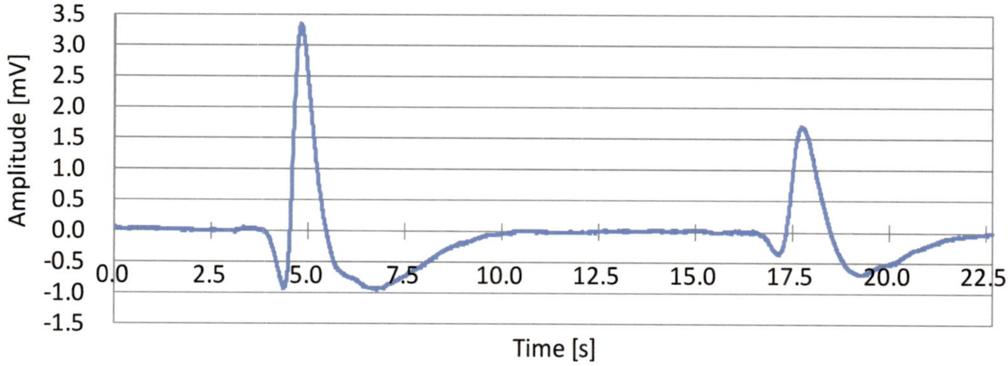

Fig. 2. A typical SSR pattern

However, some potential changes are seen only in the positive phase, while some are seen only in the negative phase and some in other changes including positive–negative patterns (Uozumi & Matsunaga, 2005). The changes in amplitude differ for every trial and subject. In addition, many studies have reported latency (a time lag between imagining the kana and observable skin potential changes) as 1.27 to 1.51 s as the mean for the palm (Uozumi & Matsunaga, 2005). Latency is less apt to change with changes in the type and strength of the stimulus.
Tables 1 and 2 show typical data for the latency and amplitude of an SSR (Iwase & Mano, 1996).

Author	Palmar Response	
	Latency (s)	Amplitude (mV)
Baba (Baba et al., 1988)	1.34 ± 0.11	1.79 ± 0.83
Elie (Elie & Guiheneuc, 1990)	1.49 ± 0.07	2.90 ± 1.70
Knezevic (Knezevic & Bajada, 1985)	1.52 ± 0.13	0.48 ± 0.10
Schondolf (Shondorf & Gendron, 1990)	1.48 ± 0.24	2.54 ± 1.27
Shahani (Shahani et al., 1984)	1.39 ± 0.07	0.81 ± 0.32
Soliven (Soliven et al., 1987)	1.31 ± 0.18	0.79 ± 0.35
Valls-Sole (Valls-Sole et al., 1991)	1.53 ± 0.24	0.47 ± 0.18
Van den Bergh (Van den Bergh & Kelly, 1986)	1.40 ± 0.10	0.18 ± 0.09
Yokota (Yokota et al., 1991)	1.34 ± 0.10	5.53 ± 3.24

Table 1. The characteristic latency and amplitude of palmar SSRs (Iwase & Mano, 1996)

Author	Plantar Response	
	Latency (s)	Amplitude (mV)
Elie (Elie & Guiheneuc, 1990)	2.70 ± 0.12	1.40 ± 0.80
Knezevic (Knezevic & Bajada, 1985)	2.07 ± 0.16	0.10 ± 0.04
Schondolf (Shondorf & Gendron, 1990)	2.04 ± 0.31	2.17 ± 1.62
Shahani (Shahani et al., 1984)	1.88 ± 0.11	0.64 ± 0.28
Soliven (Soliven et al., 1987)	1.93 ± 0.17	0.39 ± 0.23
Valls-Sole (Valls-Sole et al., 1991)	2.10 ± 0.25	0.16 ± 0.09
Van den Bergh (Van den Bergh & Kelly, 1986)	1.80 ± 0.10	0.08 ± 0.05
Yokota (Yokota et al., 1991)	1.84 ± 0.28	1.64 ± 1.08

Table 2. The characteristic latency and amplitude of plantar SSRs (Iwase & Mano, 1996)

2.3 Previous studies

From the many published reports on the SSR of severely disabled individuals, we hypothesized that SSR could be used as a switch in a communication-assistive device for individuals with severely disabled speech organs and motor functions.
Thus far, the autonomic nervous symptoms observed in ALS. However, Masur et al. systematically investigated the autonomic functions in ALS patients by SSR (Masur et al., 1995); the absence of SSR was seen in 4 of 15 patients in one or in all measurement sites. Assessing the involvement of the autonomic nervous system other than the cardiovascular system in ALS, Oey et al. found that palmar SSR was present in all ALS patients, whereas plantar SSR could not be measured in 3 of 15 patients (Oey et al., 2002). Dettmers et al.

assessed the involvement of the autonomic nervous system in 25 ALS patients; SSR was absent in 40% patients and the latency of SSR was prolonged (Dettmers et al., 1993).
When the sympathetic sudomotor function was evaluated in disabled individuals with SCI, the presence or absence of SSR was observed in chronic SCI patients (Nicotra et al., 2002). In patients with SCI, Kumru et al. aimed to characterize the expected dysfunction of the circuits responsible for SSR; SSR to any stimulus were absent in hand and foot (Kumru et al., 2009). Wang et al. reported that abnormal SSR was seen in 9 of 62 patients with Parkinson disease (Wang et al., 1993).
Although these studies investigated the absence of SSR, prolonged SSR latency, and abnormal SSR amplitude, there are few reports on completely absent SSR. Thus, we studied the effective use of SSR by including ALS patients.

3. Character selection with SSR in ALS patients

3.1 Purpose of the experiment

In our previous study (Masuda & Wada, 2005), the effectiveness of determining SSR by including healthy individuals led us to investigate the effectiveness of determining SSR as an input switch for ALS patients.

3.2 Methods

The subjects comprised four healthy males (mean age 23.0 ± 1.4 years) without any abnormality and five ALS patients (mean age 63.6 ± 6.5 years, mean disease duration 124.8 ± 57.9 months, four males and one female) (Table 3). They understood the nature of the experiment and provided prior consent for inclusion in the study.

Patient No.	Sex	Age Years	Duration of the disease Months
1	Male	65	192
2	Male	67	168
3	Male	70	72
4	Male	63	132
5	Female	53	60
Mean value		63.6	124.8
Standard deviation		6.5	57.9

Table 3. The characteristics of the patients with ALS.

Figures 3 and 4 depict the experimental setup. The experiment was performed in a quiet room in which the temperature was maintained between 25–28°C. A laptop computer was placed in front of each subject. The computer was used to show kana (Japanese written characters) for character selection.
Three Ag/AgCl electrodes were used to detect skin potential activity. The detection electrode was placed on the palm, and the reference and earth electrodes were placed on the back of the hand. Biomedical amplifier (LEG-1000, Nihon Kohden) was used for recording at a sampling frequency of 200 Hz.

The corresponding kana were displayed sequentially on the screen. The subject was asked to imagine selecting a predetermined kana (target kana) as it was displayed at an interval of 3.0 s. The other characters were assumed to be nontarget kana. The SSR signals were detected with templates from previously recorded skin potential activity.
The kana selection accuracy was calculated by dividing the total number of times the SSR signals were detected by the total number of times the kana were displayed. The kana selection accuracy is then calculated for the target and nontarget kana.

Fig. 3. Experimental setup involving a healthy subject

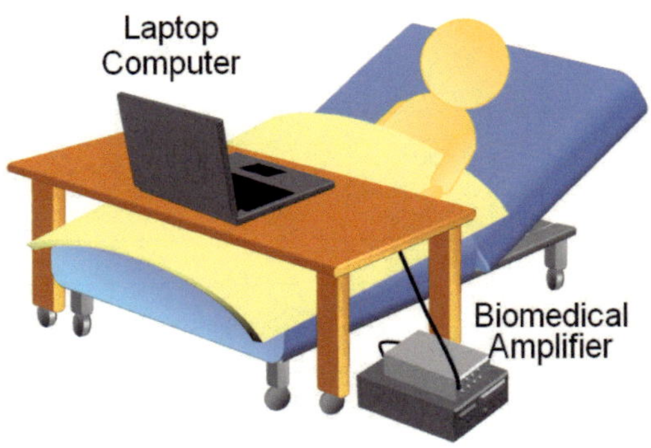

Fig. 4. Experimental setup for an ALS patient

3.3 Results and discussion

For the target and nontarget kana, the kana selection accuracy by SSR is shown in Fig. 5, amplitude of SSR in Fig. 6, and latency of SSR in Fig. 7. The left bar indicates the healthy group and the right bar indicates the ALS group. The graph shows average values ± standard deviation [%].
In Fig. 5, an SSR appeared in all subjects for the nontarget kana. However, it did not appear in two subjects with ALS for the target kana. We assumed that this absent SSR is not a clinical sign for ALS, because SSR appeared in all ALS subjects for the nontarget kana. Regarding kana selection accuracy, no difference was confirmed between the healthy and ALS groups.

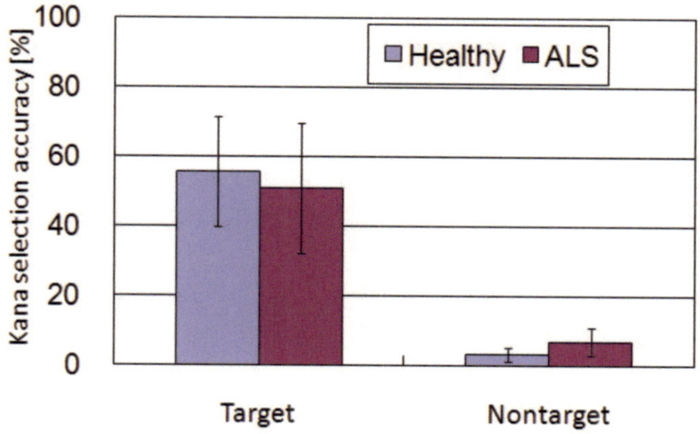

Fig. 5. Kana selection accuracy in healthy individuals and those with ALS

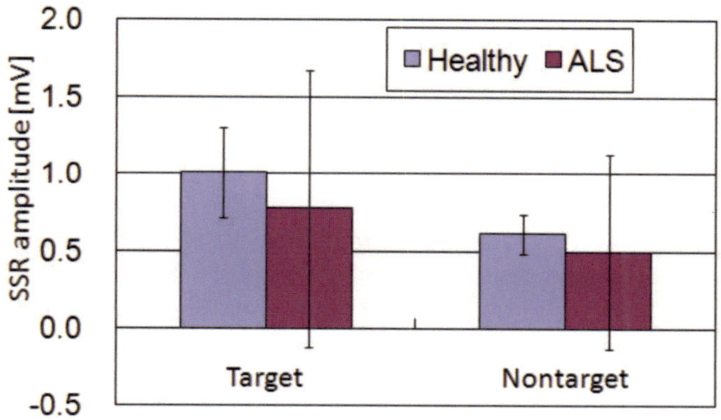

Fig. 6. The amplitude in healthy individuals and those with ALS

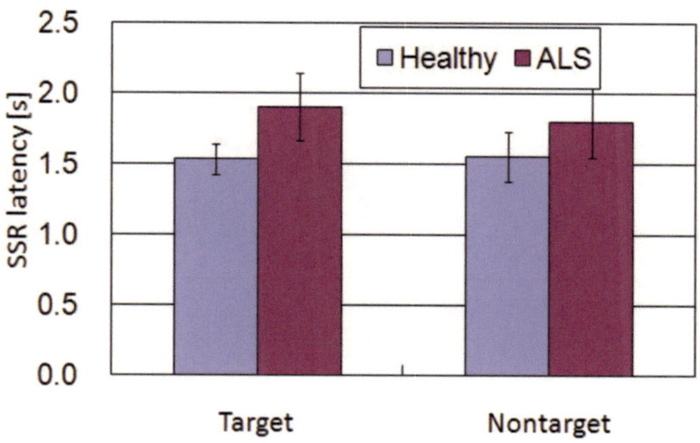

Fig. 7. SSR latency in healthy individuals and those with ALS

Regarding the amplitude, a large SSR evoked in one ALS patient resulted in a large standard deviation in the ALS group. The amplitude in the ALS group was slightly smaller than in the healthy group. The latency in the ALS group was slightly longer than in the healthy group. The decrease in the amplitude and extension of latency are in agreement with those reported in a previous study (Dettmers et al., 1993, Masur et al., 1995, Oey et al., 2002). However, SSR was not completely absent in ALS patients. Therefore, we hypothesized that even severely disabled individuals such as those with ALS might use a communication-assistive device based on SSR.

4. Visual scanning speed

4.1 Purpose of the experiment

We constructed an experimental communication device based on SSR using a visual scanning system. Because there is latency in SSR, we must compensate for latency in the design for the visual scanning speed of the system because there is a possibility that the user cannot discern how to properly choose a kana. In addition, we believed that the selection accuracy of a kana with SSR might change with a change in the visual scanning speed. Therefore, we also examined the effect of the visual scanning speed on SSR.

4.2 Methods

The subjects were healthy males without any abnormality. He understood the nature of the experiment and provided their consent prior to their inclusion in the study.
Fig. 8 depicts the experimental setup. It was similar to that shown in Fig. 3. The experiment was performed in a quiet room in which the temperature was maintained between 24-26°C. A display was placed in front of the subject at a distance of 50 cm from him.

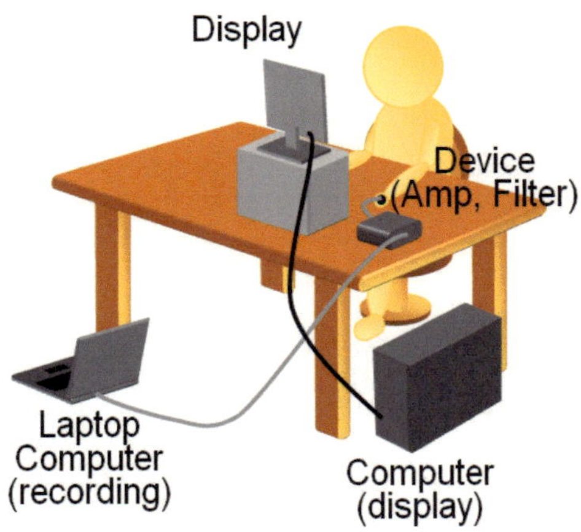

Fig. 8. Experimental setup

In Fig. 3, LEG-100 was used to measure the skin potential activity. In this experiment, the skin potential activity was measured by a prototype communication-assistive device that detects SSR. Fig. 9 shows a block diagram of a communication-assistive device using SSR. The device comprised an amplifier, filter, and A/D converter. Recordings were amplified

1000 times, filtered using a band pass filter between 0.05 and 30 Hz, converted at a sampling rate of 200 Hz using the A/D converter, and recorded using a computer. Recorded data were analyzed using self-produced software in real-time; the execution screen of software is shown in Fig. 10.

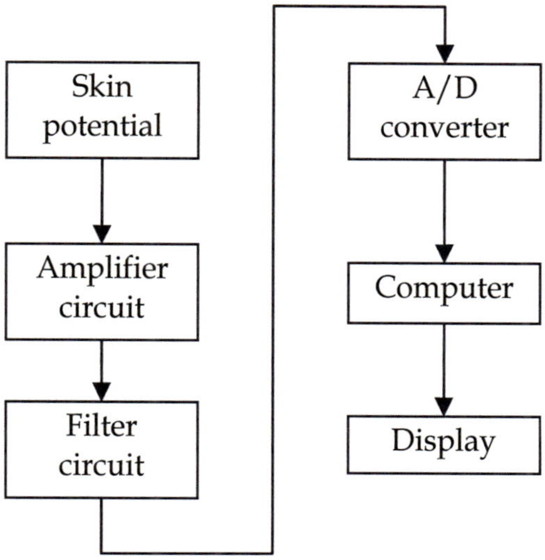

Fig. 9. Block diagram of a communication-assistive device using SSR

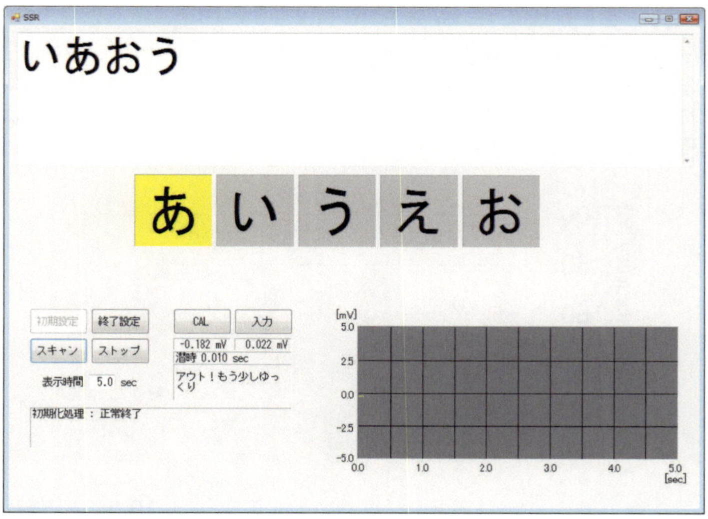

Fig. 10. The execution screen of the software

The threshold of the SSR amplitude was determined to assess whether or not an SSR appeared due to a change in skin potential. The threshold of each subject was determined based on the amplitude of SSR evoked by an inspiratory gasp before the experiment; any change in the skin potential with two or three phases beyond this threshold was considered an SSR. Usually, SSR latency is defined as the time between the stimulus and the change in skin potential. However, in this experiment, it was difficult to precisely identify the moment when the subjects began to imagine selecting the kana. Therefore, we defined SSR latency as the time between the time when the kana was displayed on the screen and the change in skin potential. The kana selection accuracy was calculated by dividing the total number of times SSR signals were detected by the total number of times kana were displayed. The kana selection accuracies were calculated for the target and nontarget kana.

Three Ag/AgCl electrodes were used to detect skin potential activity. The detection electrode was placed on the palm of one hand, and the reference and earth electrodes were placed on the back of the same hand.

During the experiment, the subject was asked to imagine selecting a predetermined kana (the target kana) as soon as it was displayed. Although the Japanese syllabary is commonly used with the help of a visual scanning system, in order to investigate the relationship between the display time for the kana in this experiment, the latency period and the appearance ratio of SSR, five characters ('あ', 'い', 'う', 'え' and 'お') were individually displayed 10 times each. The target kana was 'う'. The display times were 2.5, 5.0, 7.5, and 10.0 s. This set of display times was based on the results of our past experiments, and 2.5 s was set as the standard display time. These four display times were randomly deployed and the experiment was repeated five times.

4.3 Results

Figure 11 shows the relationship between kana selection accuracy and display time. The graph shows average values ± standard error [%]. The purposeful selection accuracy, when an SSR appeared for the target kana, was 52.0 ± 5.8% (display time: 2.5 s), 76.0 ± 4.0% (display time: 5.0 s), 80.0 ± 6.3% (display time: 7.5 s), and 80.0 ± 5.5% (display time: 10.0 s). The accidental selection accuracy, i.e., when an SSR appeared for the nontarget kana, was 2.0 ± 0.9% (display time: 2.5 s), 14.0 ± 3.5% (display time: 5.0 s), 20.5 ± 3.5% (display time: 7.5 s), and 21.5 ± 3.8% (display time: 10.0 s).

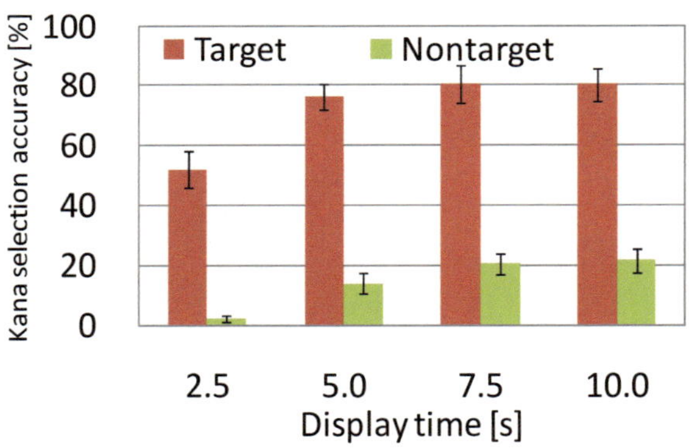

Fig. 11. Kana selection accuracy

One-way ANOVA analysis showed that the display time was significant for both target and nontarget kana (target kana: $F = 0.006$, $p < 0.01$; nontarget kana: $F = 0.001$, $p < 0.01$). The results of multiple comparisons using the Tukey test revealed that the display time of 2.5 s was significantly lower than that of the other display times for both the target and nontarget kana.

Figure 12 shows the relationship between SSR latency and display time. The SSR latency values in Fig. 12 are averages ± standard error [s] when an SSR appeared for the target kana. SSR was also detected when nontarget kana were displayed: this SSR was a response not intended by the subjects. It was difficult to precisely identify the moment of stimulus onset; therefore, SSR latency was analyzed only for the target kana.

SSR latency was 2.04 ± 0.04 s (display time: 2.5 s), 2.60 ± 0.10 s (display time: 5.0 s), 3.79 ± 0.18 s (display time: 7.5 s), and 4.21 ± 0.37 s (display time: 10.0 s). The graph shows that SSR latency increases with the kana display time. In addition, the standard error increases with display time.

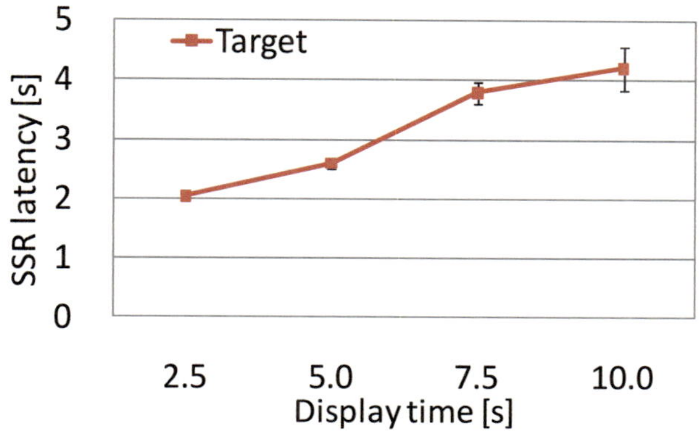

Fig. 12. SSR latency

4.4 Discussion

Figure 11 indicates that the kana selection accuracy for the display time of 2.5 s was significantly lower than that for the other display times. In other words, the selection accuracy was not significantly different for the display times of 5.0, 7.5, and 10.0 s. For the target kana, the selection accuracy was approximately 50% for the display time of 2.5 s. We assumed that the selection accuracy decreased in this case compared with the other display times because the display time was short. SSR latency was approximately 2.0 s for the display time of 2.5 s (Fig. 12), indicating that it took 2.0 s to recognize the displayed kana and hence we can acknowledge the difficulty in selecting it before the skin potential changed. Therefore, even if there is no change in skin potential, and the subject understands that he was not able to choose a kana 2.0 s later without the appearance of an SSR for the same kana, it is difficult for the subject to imagine selecting a kana again. Thus, when the subject intends to imagine selecting a kana again, the next kana has already been displayed. At the same time, SSR latency was approximately 2.6–4.2 s for the display times of 5.0, 7.5, and 10.0 s (Fig. 12). Therefore, even if the subject understands that he was not able to select a kana without the appearance of an SSR for the same kana, this is a situation in which the subject can imagine selecting a kana again. As a result, for the display times of 5.0, 7.5, and 10.0 s, we assumed that the selection accuracy increased compared with the display time of 2.5 s. At the same time, for the nontarget kana, the subject's attention would wander while the kana was displayed. Therefore, that time becomes longer so that the display time for a kana increases. This is probably the reason why unintended responses appeared so easily.

Based on these findings, we conclude that kana selection accuracy increases if the display time for the target kana is prolonged. However, at the same time, the selection accuracy also increases for the nontarget kana. Also, according to the feedback from the subjects after the experiment, the display times of 7.5 and 10.0 s were considered to be very long. When the visual scanning system is used, it is best if the user can accurately select the kana within a short visual scanning time. In Fig. 10, it can be seen that the selection accuracy was not significantly different above the display time of 5.0 s. We believe that the optimal display time is 2.5–5.0 s based on the selection accuracy graph (Fig. 11). In fact, the average latency of all SSRs for the target kana was 3.29 ± 1.63 s. This result of the optimal display time is in accordance with the one discussed previously.

5. Optimal visual scanning speed

5.1 Outline of the experiment

In Chapter 4, we found that the optimal display time is 2.5–5.0 s. Thus, we investigated the display time to choose the optimal visual scanning speed. The experimental setup was the same as that in Chapter 4. However, the display times were 2.5, 3.0, 3.5, 4.0, 4.5, and 5.0 s, and randomly deployed. The experiment was repeated five times.

5.2 Results

Figure 13 shows the relationship between kana selection accuracy and display time. The graph shows average values ± standard error [%]. The purposeful selection accuracy, when an SSR appeared for the target kana, was 46.0 ± 5.1% (display time: 2.5 s), 56.0 ± 5.1% (display time: 3.0 s), 50.0 ± 5.5% (display time: 4.5 s), 76.0 ± 5.1% (display time: 4.0 s), 80.0 ± 7.1% (display time: 4.5 s), and 82.0 ± 3.7% (display time: 5.0 s). The accidental selection accuracy, when SSR appeared for the nontarget kana, was 2.5 ± 0.8% (display time: 2.5 s), 2.0 ± 0.9% (display time: 3.0 s), 3.0 ± 1.5% (display time: 4.5 s), 10.5 ± 2.8% (display time: 4.0 s), 8.0 ± 2.2% (display time: 4.5 s), and 8.0 ± 2.0% (display time: 5.0 s).

For both the target and nontarget kana, the selection accuracy in the display times of 2.5, 3.0, and 3.5 s was lower than that for the other display times.

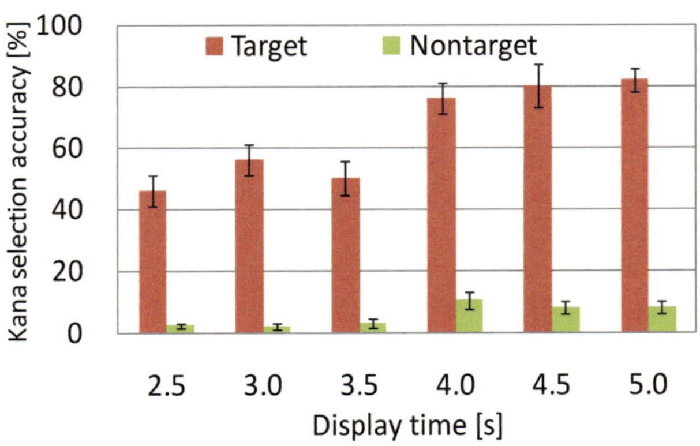

Fig. 13. Kana selection accuracy

Figure 14 shows the relationship between SSR latency and display time. The SSR latency values in Fig. 14 are averages ± standard error [s] when an SSR appeared for the target kana. An SSR was also detected when nontarget kana were displayed: this SSR was a response not

intended by the subjects. It was difficult to precisely identify the moment of stimulus onset; therefore, SSR latency was analyzed only for the target kana.
SSR latency was 2.03 ± 0.04 s (display time: 2.5 s), 2.14 ± 0.06 s (display time: 3.0 s), 2.36 ± 0.07 s (display time: 3.5 s), 2.69 ± 0.10 s (display time: 4.0 s), 3.07 ± 0.11 s (display time: 4.5 s), and 3.03 ± 0.12 s (display time: 5.0 s). The graph shows that SSR latency increases with the kana display time and that the standard error increases with the display time.

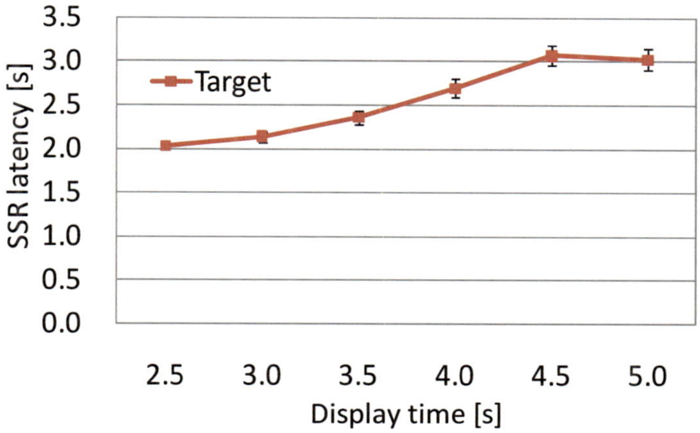

Fig. 14. Latency of SSR

5.3 Discussion

The kana selection accuracy for the display times of 2.5, 3.0, and 3.5 s was lower than that for the other display times. Similar to the results mentioned in Chapter 4, when the display time is short, even if there is no change in skin potential, and the subject understands that he is not able to choose a kana approximately 2.0–2.3 s later without the appearance of an SSR for the same kana, it is difficult for the subject to imagine selecting a kana again. For the display times of 4.0, 4.5, and 5.0 s, it is possible that even if the subject understands that he was not able to select a kana without an SSR appearing for the same kana, this is a situation in which the subject can imagine selecting a kana again.
Based on these findings, we concluded that the optimal display time is 4.0–5.0 s. For the display times of 4.0, 4.5, and 5.0 s, the kana selection accuracy was high and the latency of SSR was not very long. We can expect that kana selection will be accurate if we make a communication-assistive devise using SSR with these display times.

6. Conclusion

In this study, we indicated the possibility of using SSR as the switching of the communication aid in ALS. Additionally, we investigated the influence of the visual scanning speed on the kana selection accuracy and latency of SSR. The following results were obtained:

1. In ALS patients, we believe that it is possible to using SSR as a switching of communication assistive method.

2. Kana selection accuracy was more and SSR latency was long when the display time was long.
3. The optimal visual scanning speed is 4.0 - 5.0 seconds

If the optimal display time is set, we believe that the selection accuracy increases. In the future, we aim to investigate the optimal display time and develop a communication device based on SSR.

7. References

Baba, M.; Watahiki, Y., Matsunaga, M., Takebe, K. (1988). Sympathetic skin response in healthy man, *Electromyography and clinical neurophysiology*, Vol. 28, No.5, pp. 277-283

Damasio, AR.; Tranel, D., Damasio, H. (1990). Individuals with sociopathic behavior caused by frontal damage fail to respond autonomically to social stimuli, *Behavioural Brain Research*, Vol. 41, No. 2, pp. 81-94

Dettmers, C.; Fatepour, D., Faust, H., Jerusalem, F. (1993). SYMPATHETIC SKIN RESPONSE ABNORMALITIES IN AMYOTROPHIC LATERAL SCLEROSIS, *Muscle & nerve*, Vol. 16, pp. 930-934

Féré, C. (1888). Note sur des modifications de la résistance électrique sous l'influence des excitations sensorielles et des émotions, *Compte Rendus des Séances de la Société de Biologie et de ses Filiales*, Paris 40, pp. 217-219

Fujisawa, K.; Kakigi, S., Yamazaki, K. (1998). Electrodermal activity, In: *New physiological psychology Vol.1 Basic of physiological psychology*, pp.210-221, Kitaohji Shobou Co., Ltd., ISBN4-7628-2114-4 (Written in Japanese)

Friedrich, E.V.C.; McFarland, D.J., Neuper, C., Vaughan, T.M., Brunner, P. & Wolpaw, J.R. (2009). A scanning protocol for a sensorimotor rhythm-based brain-computer interface, *Biological Psychology*, Vol. 80, pp. 169-175

Hilz, MJ.; Axelrod, FB., Schweibold, G., Kolodny, EH. (1999). Sympathetic skin response following thermal, electrical, acoustic, and inspiratory gasp stimulation in familial dysautonomia patients and healthy persons, *Clinical autonomic research*, Vol.9, No.4, pp. 165-177

Ito, H.; Sugiyama, Y., Mano, T., Okada, H., Matsukawa, T. & Iwase, S. (1996). Skin sympathetic nerve activity and event-related potentials during auditory oddball paradigms, *Journal of the Autonomic Nervous System*, Vol. 60, pp. 129-135

Iwase, S.; Mano, T. (1996). Sympathetic skin response (SSR); 2. Clinical aspects, *Clinical electroencephalography*, Vol. 38, No. 9, pp. 643-652

Khalfa, S.; Isabelle, P., Jean-Pierre, B., Manon, R. (2002). Event-related skin conductance responses to musical emotions in humans, *Neuroscience Letters*, Vol. 328, No. 2, pp. 145-149

Knezevic, W.; Bajada, S. (1985). Peripheral autonomic surface potential. A quantitative technique for recording sympathetic conduction in man, *Journal of the neurological sciences*, Vol. 67, No. 2, pp. 239-251

Kumru, H.; Vidal, J., Perez, M., Schestatsky, P., Valls-Solé, J. (2009). Sympathetic skin responses evoked by different stimuli modalities in spinal cord injury patients, *Neurorehabilitation and Neural Repair*, Vol. 23, No. 6, pp. 553-558

Masuda, F. & Wada, C. (2005). Basic research into the environmental conditions necessary to develop a sympathetic skin response input supporting device, *Proceedings of the Society of Instrument and Control Engineers Annual conference 2005*, pp. 820-824

Masuda, F. & Wada, C. (2007). Character selection with sympathetic skin response when listening to sounds, *Proceedings of Second International Conference on Innovating Computing, Information and Control*, A01-03 (CD-ROM)

Masur, H.; Oversohl, U.S., Papke, K., Oberwittler, C. & Vollmer, J. (1995). SYMPATHETIC SKIN RESPONSE IN PATIENTS WITH AMYOTROPHIC LATERAL SCLEROSIS, *FUNCTIONAL NEUROLOGY*, Vol. 10, No. 3, pp. 131-135

Mitani, H. & Ishiyama, Y. (2008). Sweating and sympathetic skin response (1), *Clinical electroencephalography*, Vol. 50, No. 3, pp. 165-172 (Written in Japanese)

Nakabayashi, T. & Igarashi, M. (2003). The Effectiveness of Somato-switches to improbe upon the Ability of Communication for Sever multiple Handicapped - The Application of a Brain wave Switch and an Electromyographical Switch, *Human Sciences Research*, Vol. 11, No. 1, pp. 63-74 (in Japanese)

Nicotra, A.; Catley, M., Ellaway, P.H. & Mathias, C.J. (2005). The ability of physiological stimuli to generate the sympathetic skin response in human chronic spinal cord injury, *Restorative Neurology and Neuroscience*, Vol. 23, pp. 331-339

Oey, P.L.; Vos, P.E., Wieneke, G.H., Wokke, J.H.J., Blankestijn, P.J. & Karemaker, J.M. (2002). SUBTLE INVOLVEMENT OF THE SYMPATHETIC NERVOUS SYSTEM IN AMYOTROPHIC LATERAL SCLEROSIS, *MUSCLE & NERVE*, Vol. 25, pp. 402-408

Schondorf, R.; Gendron, D. (1990). Properties of electrodermal activity recorded from non palmar/plantar skin sites, *Neurology*, Vol. 40, pp. 128

Shahani, B.T.; Halperin, J.J., Boulu, P. & Cohen, J. (1984). Sympathetic skin response - a method of assessing unmyelinated axon dysfunction in peripheral neuropathies, *Journal of neurology, neurosurgery, and psychiatry*, Vol. 47, No. 5, pp. 536-542

Soliven, B.; Maselli, R., Jaspan, J., Green, A., Graziano, H., Pertersen, M. & Spire, JP. (1987). Sympathetic skin response in diabetic neuropathy, *Muscle & nerve*, Vol. 10, pp. 711-716

Tsukahara, R. & Aoki, H. (2002). Skin potential response in letter recognition task as as alternative communication channel for individuals with severe motor disability, *Clinical neurophysiology*, Vol. 113, pp. 1723-1733

Uozumi, T. & Matsunaga, K. (2000). Sympathetic skin response, In: *Autonomic nerve function test third edition*, Japan Society of Neurovegetative Research, pp. 223-226, BUNKODO Co., Ltd., ISBN4-8306-1527-3 (Written in Japanese)

Valls-Sole, J.; Monforte, R. & Estruch, R. (1991). Abnormal sympathetic skin response in alcoholic subjects, *Journal of the neurological sciences*, Vol. 102, pp. 233-237

Van den Bergh, P. & Kelly, JJ. (1986). The evoked electrodermal response in peripheral neuropathies, *Muscle & nerve*, Vol. 9, pp. 656-657

Wang, SJ.; Fuh, JL., Shan, DE., Liao, KK., Lin, KP., Tsai, CP. & Wu, ZA. (1993). Sympathetic skin response and R-R interval variation in Parkinson's disease, *Movement disorders*, Vol.8, pp.151-157

Watahiki, Y. (1987). Sympathetic skin response (SSR) - a simple quantitative method for assessing sympathetic dysfunction (1) SSR in normal man, *Clinical Neurology*, Vol.27, pp. 442-448 (Written in Japanese)

Yamashiro, D.; Aihara, M., Ono, C., Kanemura, H., Aoyagi, K., Goto, Y., Iwadare, Y. & Nakazawa, S. (2004). Sympathetic Skin Response and Emotional Changes of Visual Stimuli, *No To Hattatsu,* Vol. 36, No. 5, pp. 372-377 (Written in Japanese)

Yokota, T.; Matsunaga, T., Okiyama, R., Hirose, K., Tanabe, H., Furukawa, T. & Tsukagoshi, H. (1991). Sympathetic skin response in patients with multiple sclerosis compared with patients with spinal cord transection and normal controls, *Brain,* Vol. 114, pp. 1381-1394

9

Finger Braille Teaching System

Yasuhiro Matsuda and Tsuneshi Isomura
Kanagawa Institute of Technology
Japan

1. Introduction

Deafblindness is a condition that combines varying degrees of both hearing and visual impairment. All deafblind people experience problems with communication, access to information, and mobility. Deafblind people use many different communication media, depending on the age of onset of deafness and blindness and the available resources. For example, "deafblind manual alphabet" is a method of spelling out words onto a deafblind person's hand. Each letter is denoted by a particular sign or place on the hand. "Block" is a manual form of communication where words are spelled out on the palm of the deafblind person's hand. "Hands on signing" is based on sign language. With this system, the deafblind person follows the signs by placing his hands over those of the signer and feeling the signs formed. "*Yubi-Tenji*" (Finger Braille) is one of the tactual communication media developed by Satoshi Fukushima in Japan (see Fig. 1). In Finger Braille, the index finger, middle finger and ring finger of both hands function like the keys of a Braille typewriter. A sender dots Braille code on the fingers of a receiver as if typing on a Braille typewriter. The receiver is assumed to be able to recognize the Braille code. Deafblind people who are skilled in Finger Braille can understand speech conversation and express various emotions because of the prosody (intonation) of Finger Braille (Fukushima, 1997). Because there is such a small number of non-disabled people who are skilled in Finger Braille, deafblind people communicate only through an interpreter.

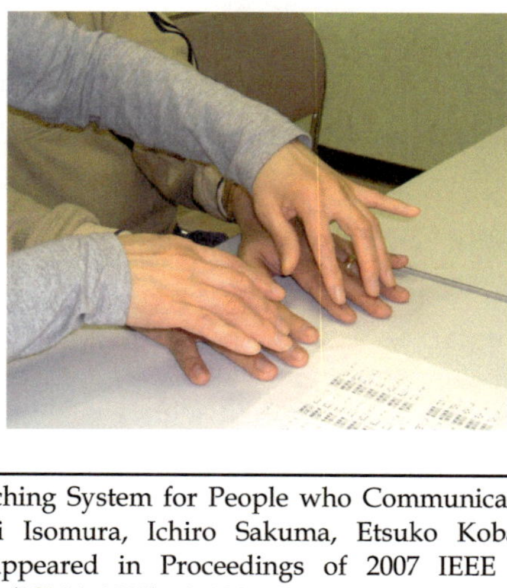

Fig. 1. Finger Braille

Based on "Finger Braille Teaching System for People who Communicate with Deafblind People", by Yasuhiro Matsuda, Tsuneshi Isomura, Ichiro Sakuma, Etsuko Kobayashi, Yasuhiko Jimbo and Tatsuhiko Arafune which appeared in Proceedings of 2007 IEEE International Conference on Mechatronics and Automation (ICMA 2007).

Various Braille input devices have recently been developed (Amemiya et al., 2004; An et al., 2004), but they require deafblind people to wear gloves or type on a keyboard to input the Finger Braille, or to use actuators to output and convert the speech of non-disabled people to Finger Braille. With these devices, deafblind people are burdened with wearing sensors and actuators, and they must master a new communication system with these support devices.

The objective of this study is the development of a Finger Braille support device which employs the skin-contact communication of deafblind people, because skin contact is the only form of nonverbal communication for deafblind people. The concept of the Finger Braille support device is shown in Fig. 2. The advantages of this device are as follows: both deafblind people and non-disabled people unskilled in Finger Braille can communicate using conventional Finger Braille, and deafblind people are not encumbered by a support device because the non-disabled people operate the support device and wear all of the sensors. Our support device consists of a Finger Braille teaching system and a Finger Braille recognition system. The teaching system recognizes the speech of a non-disabled person and displays the associated dot pattern of Finger Braille. The non-disabled person can then dot Finger Braille on the fingers of the deafblind person by observing the displayed dot pattern (Matsuda et al., 2007). The recognition system recognizes the dotting of Finger Braille by the deafblind person and synthesizes this tactile communication into speech for the non-disabled person (Matsuda et al., 2010a).

In this chapter, we describe the Finger Braille teaching system and present experimental results. We first developed the Finger Braille teaching system and designed the teaching interface, which taught clauses explicitly. Then, an evaluation experiment between a blind person who was skilled in Finger Braille and two non-disabled people who were unskilled in Finger Braille was conducted.

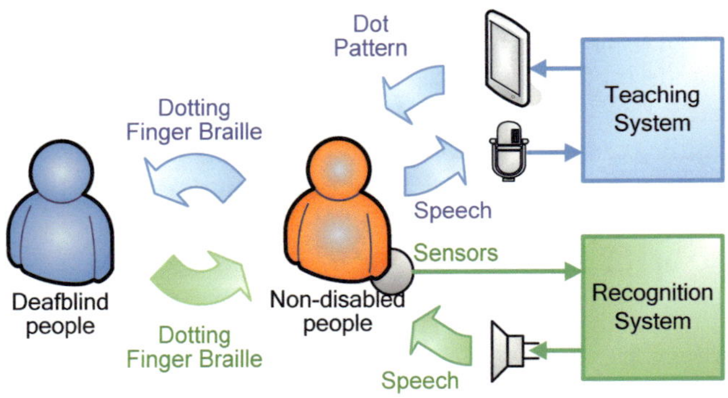

Fig. 2. Concept of Finger Braille support device

2. Japanese Braille system and Finger Braille

In Japanese script, Kanji (the Chinese ideographic script), Hiragana and Katakana (syllabic script) are the three kinds of Japanese writing symbols used (The Association for Overseas Technical Scholarship, 1975). Hiragana and Katakana are collectively called Kana characters because Japanese sentences are usually written with a combination of these two scripts. Foreign names and words of foreign derivation are usually written in Katakana. In addition to the abovementioned scripts, Romaji (Roman letters) is used. The Japanese sentence does not include spaces between words.

The Japanese Braille system was created by Kuraji Ishikura in 1890 (see Fig. 3). The Japanese Braille system is different from Japanese script in the following ways: (1) Japanese Braille consists only of Kana; (2) particles [ha] and [he] are described with their pronunciations [wa] and [e]; (3) long vowels [ū] and [ō] are described with their pronunciations [-]; (4) the symbols marked voiced sound, semivoiced sound and diphthong are used as prefixes to modify the consonants; (5) the Japanese Braille sentence has a space between clauses (Bunsetsu unit).

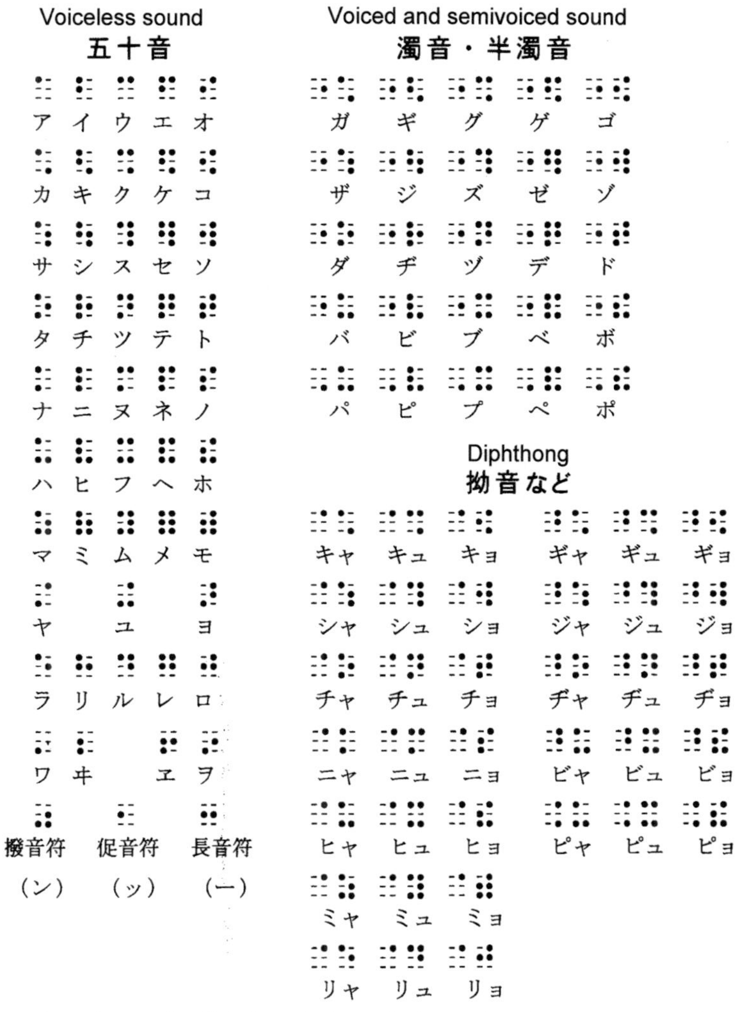

Fig. 3. Japanese Braille code (National Association of Information Service for Visually Impaired Persons, 2002)

In Finger Braille, the sender dots the Braille codes directly on the fingers of the receiver as if typing on a Braille typewriter. The receiver is assumed to be able to recognize the Braille code. A rule of Finger Braille is that the sender keeps touching the fingers of the receiver even when not dotting, because receivers feel uneasy in the absence of touching or tactile cues. Prosody (intonation) of Finger Braille helps the receiver recognize the dotted Braille code. The features of prosody of Finger Braille are as follows: (1) the sender dots long at the end of clauses; (2) the sender dots long and strongly at the end of sentences; (3) the sender dots short and strongly at the double consonants; (4) the sender dots short and strongly at the symbols of voiced sound, semivoiced sound and diphthong; (5) the sender pauses between clauses; (6) the sender must not pause during a clause (Miyagi et al., 2007; Matsuda et al., 2010b).

3. Development of the teaching system

3.1 Configuration of the teaching system

Fig. 4 shows the configuration of the Finger Braille teaching system. First, a speech recognition (SR) engine recognizes the speech by the sender. Second, by using the results of the speech recognition, the teaching system converts the Kana to the Braille code. Third, by parsing the Braille code, the teaching system retrieves the clause information and segments the Braille code into clauses. Finally, the teaching system displays the associated dot pattern of the Braille code. The teaching system was developed on a tablet PC (HP TC1100, CPU Pentium M 1.1 GHz, RAM 1024 MB, 10.4 inches XGA LCD). The operating system was Microsoft Windows XP. The programming languages were Microsoft Visual Basic 6 and LPA WIN-PROLOG 4.500. The speech recognition engine was Microsoft Speech SDK (SAPI5.1).

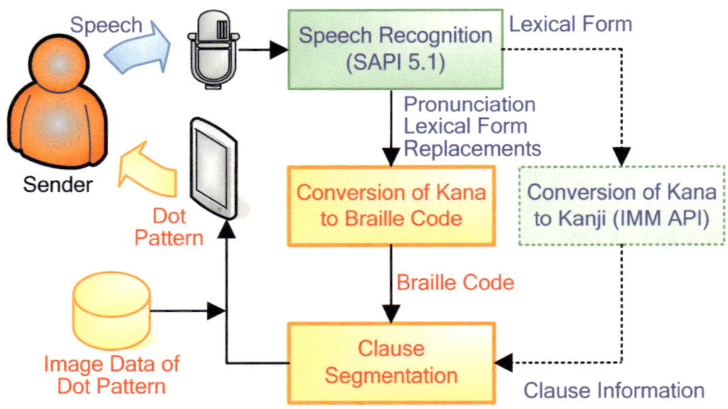

Fig. 4. Configuration of the teaching system

3.2 Speech recognition

Because the sender must keep touching the fingers of the receiver, speech recognition is suitable for the input interface of the teaching system. First, the teaching system was created and the dictation grammar of SAPI5.1 was loaded, and then SAPI5.1 was ready for recognition. When the sender spoke into a microphone, SAPI5.1 attempted to recognize it. Following successful speech recognition, the teaching system retrieved the results of the speech recognition.

The sender could train SAPI5.1 by a speech training wizard. After speech training, the SR engine could perform better and improve SAPI's personalization experience.

3.3 Conversion of Kana to Braille code

Table 1 shows an example of the Braille code and the results of the speech recognition. Because the Japanese Braille system consists only of Kana, the pronunciation and lexical form of the phrase elements are suitable for converting to the Braille code. The teaching system checked each character of the pronunciation and lexical form of the phrase elements and adopted the suitable character for the Japanese Braille code. Fig. 5 shows the flow chart of the conversion of Kana to Braille code. The following were the rules for conversion: (1) generally, the lexical forms of the phrase elements were adopted; (2) in the particles [ha] and [he], the pronunciations of the phrase elements were adopted; (3) in the long vowels [ū] and [ō], the pronunciations of the phrase elements were adopted.

Input Speech	お姉さんは学校へ行きました (My sister went to school.)
Braille Code	おねえさんわ　がっこーえ　いきました ⠊⠏⠋⠱⠴⠄ ⠐⠡⠂⠪⠒⠋ ⠃⠣⠵⠳⠕ O ne e san wa / ga k ko - e / i ki ma shi ta.
Results of speech recognition	
Get Text	お姉さんは学校へ行きました
Pronunciation	お　ねーさん　わ　がっこー　え　い　き　ました O / ne – sa n / wa / ga k ko - / e / i / ki / ma shi ta
Lexical Form	お　ねえさん　は　がっこう　へ　い　き　ました O / ne e sa n / ha / ga k ko u / he / i / ki / ma shi ta
Display Text	お　姉さん　は　学校　へ　行　き　ました

Table 1. Example of the Braille code and results of speech recognition

3.4 Clause (Bunsetsu) segmentation

To realize the non-disabled sender's prosodic dotting, the dot pattern of clauses was displayed explicitly. SAPI5.1 cannot retrieve the clause information of the result of speech recognition. Thus, we developed a Braille code parser that applies natural language processing (BUP system) (Matsumoto et al., 1983). The Braille code parser parsed the Braille code and segmented it into clauses by inserting a space between the clauses. The Braille code parser consisted of a dictionary, grammar, BUP translator and control program. The dictionary and the grammar were described in the definite clause grammars (DCG). The BUP translator translated the dictionary and grammar into a Prolog program. The control program controlled the execution of parsing.

If the Braille code was not grammatically because of misrecognition of SR, the Braille code parser could not parse it. As a backup of the Braille code parser, we used Microsoft Global IME (Japanese) (IMM API). The teaching system set the lexical form of the phrase elements as the reading string of the composition string of IMM API and directed IMM API to convert the composition string. Then the teaching system retrieved the clause information of the lexical form of the phrase elements and inserted a space between the clauses of the Braille code.

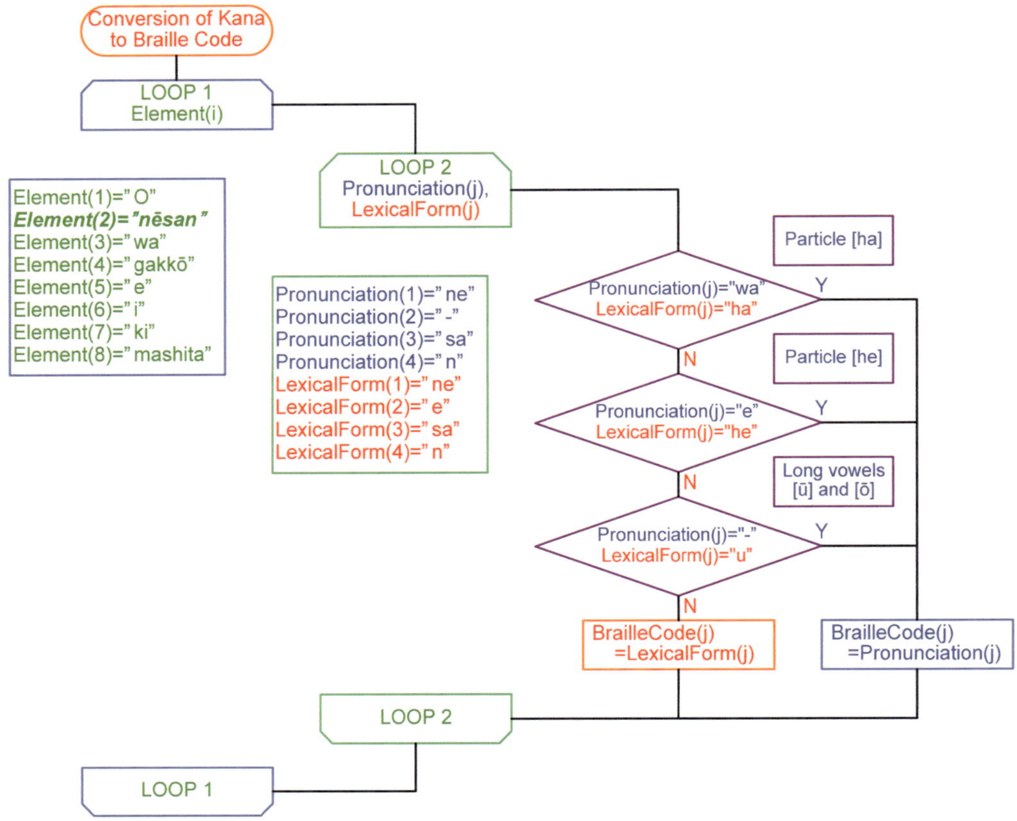

Fig. 5. Flow chart of conversion of Kana to Braille code using "ne - sa n" as an example

3.5 Design of the teaching interface

Finally, the teaching system displayed the dot pattern of the Braille code by reading from the image database of dot patterns. Fig. 6 shows the teaching interfaces that we designed. The Braille code was displayed in an upper text box. The dot pattern was displayed in fourteen picture boxes (two columns and seven rows). The first clause was displayed in the left column (from the upper left to the lower left) and the second clause was displayed in the right column (from the upper right to the lower right). The third clause was displayed on the next page. The clause that did not consist of more than seven characters was displayed in one column and the clause that consisted of more than seven characters was displayed in two columns. After one clause was displayed in the left column, the next clause was displayed in the right column or the next page. Thus, the dot pattern of the clauses was displayed explicitly in the columns.

The red pattern indicated the left hand and the blue pattern indicated the right hand. We designed two kinds of presentation methods for the sender. Presentation method A only displayed the dot pattern and presentation method B displayed the dot pattern on the illustration of the fingers. Presentation method B was more symbolic and easier for beginners to recognize the dotting fingers. Presentation method A had the most simplified signing and was suitable for the experienced senders (Matsuda et al., 2005).

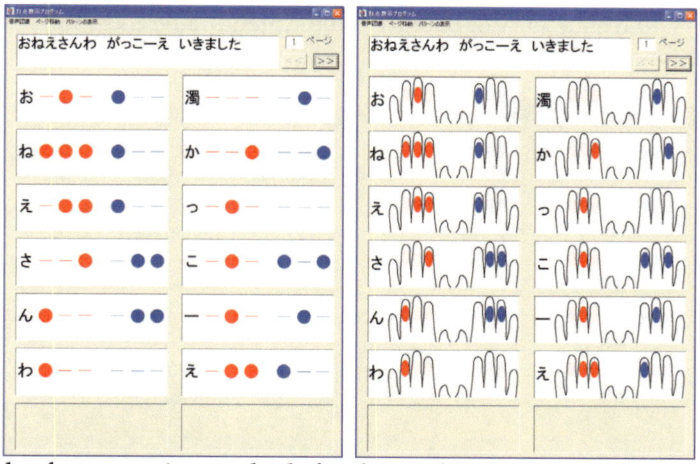

Fig. 6. Two kinds of presentation methods for the teaching interface, presentation method A (left) and B (right). The displayed dot pattern is "Oneesanwa / gakko-e {My sister / to school.}"

3.6 Editing Braille code

Because the sender keeps touching the fingers of the receiver with at least one hand, we installed a trackball (Kensington Expert Mouse USB/PS2) to operate the teaching system by the left hand of the sender. We allocated six functions to the keys of the trackball (see Fig. 7). If the Braille code included any mistakes because of misrecognition of SR, the sender could edit the Braille code by using the track ball and a software keyboard (see Fig. 8).

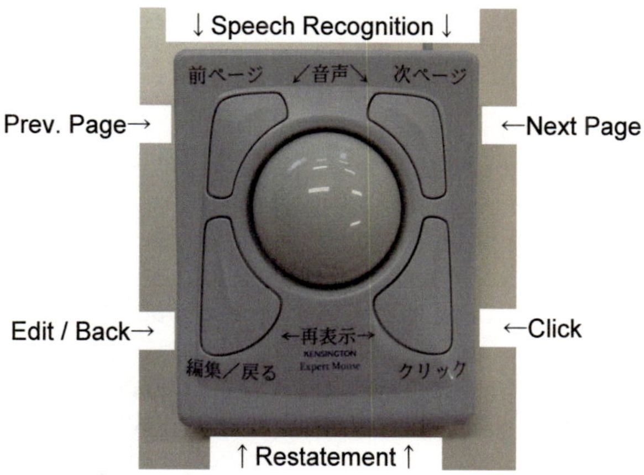

Fig. 7. Trackball to operate the teaching system

To start speech recognition, the sender pushed the upper two keys at the same time. To display the next page of the dot pattern, the sender pushed the upper right key. To display the previous page of the dot pattern, the sender pushed the upper left key. To start editing the Braille code, the sender pushed the lower left key. To select the character of the software keyboard, the sender pointed to the character with the trackball and pushed the lower right key. After editing, to restate the dot pattern of the edited Braille code, the sender pushed the lower two keys at the same time.

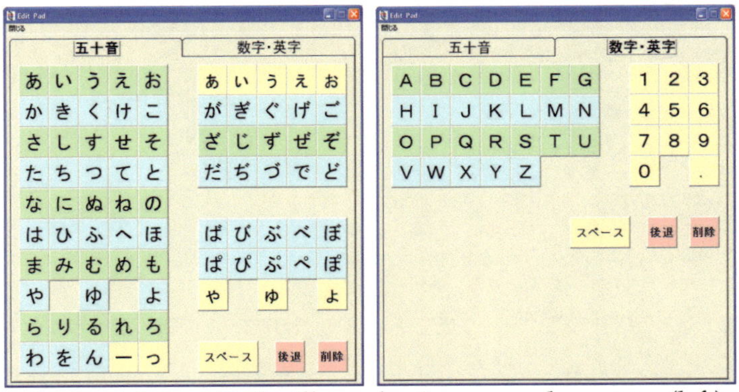

Fig. 8. Software keyboard to edit Braille code. Japanese characters (left), alphabets and numerals (right)

4. Evaluation experiment

4.1 Method

The objectives of the evaluation experiment were as follows: (1) evaluate the accuracies of the fundamental functions (speech recognition, conversion to Braille code and clause segmentation); (2) evaluate the accuracies of the dotting and recognition; (3) evaluate the communication speed.

The receiver was a blind person who was skilled in Finger Braille with 20 years of sending experience and 8 years of receiving experience. The senders were two college students who were unskilled in Finger Braille (one male and one female). Both senders reported normal hearing and vision abilities and were native Japanese speakers. All subjects gave informed consent after hearing a description of the study.

The dialogues (total: 51 sentences, 143 clauses, 288 words, 686 characters) comprised four daily conversations in a Japanese textbook for foreign beginners (3A Corporation, 1998).

The senders were instructed to operate the teaching system, and trained SAPI5.1 by the speech training wizards "Introduction" and "Introduction of Speech Technology." To simulate deafness, the receiver wore earplugs and headphones that played white noise.

The experimental flow is shown in Fig. 9. In the experiment, one sender and the receiver sat side by side (see Fig. 10). The sender pushed the key to begin the speech recognition and spoke one sentence of the dialogues. If the result of the speech recognition was correct, the sender dotted Finger Braille on the fingers of the receiver by observing the teaching interface. If the result of the speech recognition was not correct, the sender spoke the same sentence again or edited the Braille code and pushed the restatement key. Then the sender dotted Finger Braille on the fingers of the receiver. The receiver responded to the recognized sentence. If the receiver misrecognized the sentence, the sender dotted the same sentence again. In the experiments, the sender repeated almost all of the sentences of the dialogues.

The experiment included four experimental sessions. In session 1, sender 1 (female) dotted conversation 1; the dot patterns were displayed by presentation method B. In session 2, sender 1 dotted conversation 2; the dot patterns were displayed by presentation method A.

In session 3, sender 2 (male) dotted conversation 3; the dot patterns were displayed by presentation method B. In session 4, sender 2 dotted conversation 4; the dot patterns were displayed by presentation method A. The senders were instructed as follows: to dot as accurately as possible; to dot long in the characters at the end of the clauses and sentences; to keep touching the fingers of the receiver, at least with their right hand, even when not dotting.

All of the sessions were recorded by a digital video camera. The log of operations by the senders and the recognized speech were recorded in the hard disk drive of the teaching system. The receiver put his fingers on the pressure sensor sheets (Nitta Tactile Sensor System), which measured the change of pressure as a result of dotting, during the experiment.

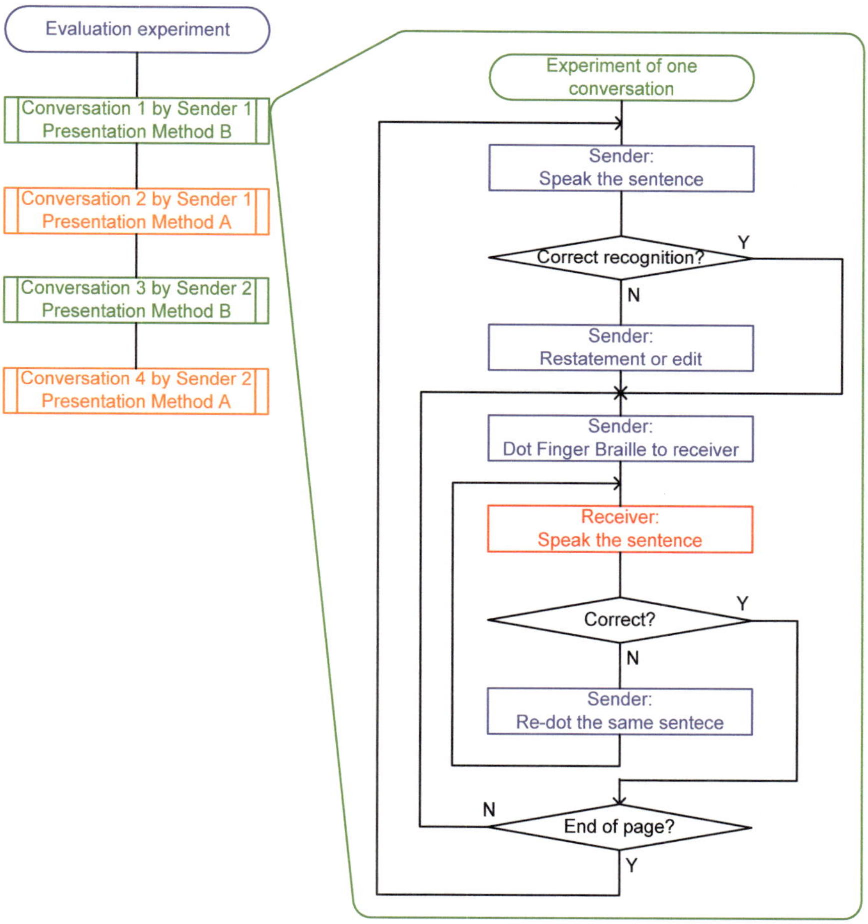

Fig. 9. Experimental flow

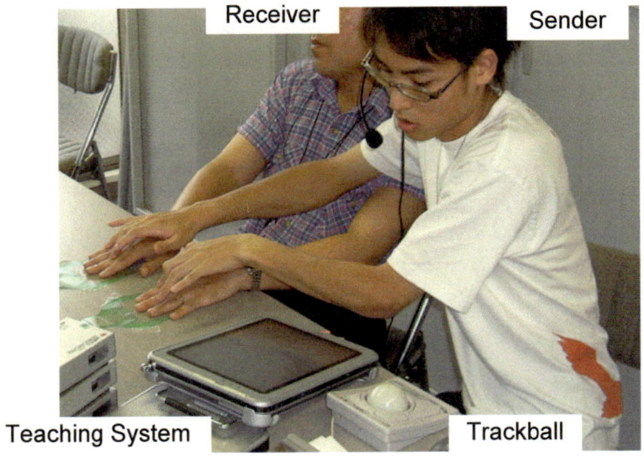

Fig. 10. Experiment in progress

4.2 Results

4.2.1 Accuracy of fundamental functions

We classified the words of the dialogues into interjections (15 words), proper nouns (14 words) and other words (259 words). To evaluate the accuracy of the speech recognition, the error number of the substitutions in each part of speech and the error number of the deletions were counted. Fig. 11 shows the error ratios of the speech recognition. The results showed that 7% of the proper nouns (1 word) and 5% of other words (13 words) were substituted and 0.7% of the words (2 words) were deleted. Because 47% of the interjections (7 words) were substituted, SAPI5.1 had difficulty in recognizing the interjections (Matsuda et al., 2007). Then, the *Correct Ratio* of speech recognition was calculated, as follows.

$$Correct\ Ratio = \frac{N - sub - del}{N} \times 100\ (\%)$$

where N is the number of the words, *sub* is the number of substitution errors, and *del* is the number of deletion errors. *Correct Ratio* was 92.0% for all of the words and 94.4%without substitution of the interjections (see Fig. 12).

Because of misrecognition of the speech recognition, the senders re-spoke 5 sentences (8 times) and edited 15 sentences (56 characters).

The results of the speech recognition were accurately converted to the Braille codes. Because the senders edited the Braille codes incorrectly, 0.4% of the dialogues (3 characters) were not correct Braille codes. Thus, the accuracy of the conversion to the Braille code was 99.6% (see Fig. 12).

When the results of the speech recognition were correct, the grammatical Braille codes were accurately segmented into clauses by the Braille code parser. When the results of the speech recognition were not correct, 3.5% of the clauses (5 clauses) were slipped their segmentation points by the backup of the Braille code parser (IMM API). When the senders edited the Braille codes, 1.4% of the clauses (2 clauses) deleted the spaces between the clauses. Thus, the accuracy of the clause segmentation was 95.1% (see Fig. 12).

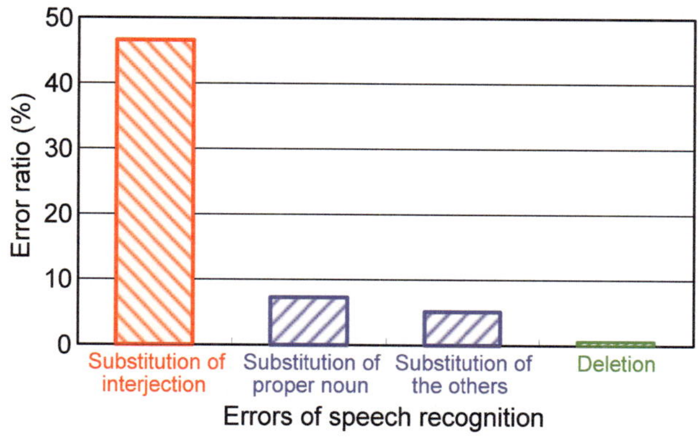

Fig. 11. Error ratios of speech recognition

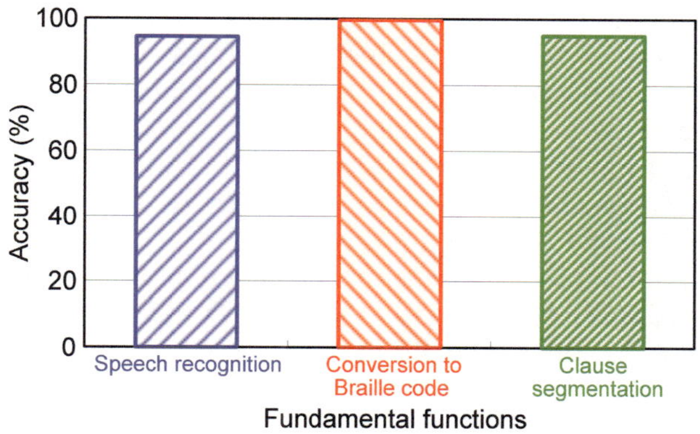

Fig. 12. Accuracy of the fundamental functions

4.2.2 Accuracy of dotting and recognition

The error ratio of dotting by the senders was only 1.2% of the characters (8 characters). The receiver could not recognize 7.8% of the dialogues (4 sentences) because of the dotting errors of the senders. As the senders re-dotted the same sentences, the receiver could recognize them. Thus, the accuracy of dotting by the senders was 98.8% and the accuracy of recognition by the receiver was 92.2% in the first dotting and 100% in the re-dotting (see Fig. 13).

4.2.3 Operation time

An operation time was divided into five sections. The operation times were calculated in the log of the operations and the video images. Fig. 14 shows the distribution of operation times. The speech recognition time was the time until the dot pattern was displayed, after the sender pushed the key for the speech recognition (including the time of re-speech). The mean of the speech recognition time was 7.4 sec (S.D.=8.2) and the mean of the speech recognition time per speech was 5.7 sec (S.D.=2.9).

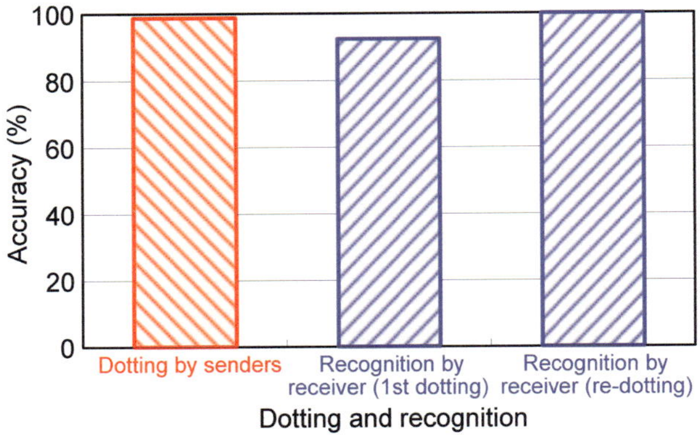

Fig. 13. Accuracy of dotting and recognition

The decision time was the time until the sender pushed the edit key, after the dot pattern was displayed. The mean of the decision time, except for 36 non-edited sentences, was 8.5 sec (S.D.=2.8). The mean of the decision time of all sentences was 2.5 sec.

The edit time was the time until the sender pushed the restatement key, after the sender pushed the edit key. The mean of the edit time except for the 36 non-edited sentences was 28.5 sec (S.D.=26.1) and the mean of the edit time per character was 8.1 sec (S.D.=4.3). The mean of the decision time of all sentences was 8.5 sec.

The response time meant the time until the sender started dotting, after the dot pattern was displayed. The mean of the response time was 5.1 sec (S.D.=2.5).

The dotting time was the time until the sender finished dotting, after dotting started (including the time of changing pages and re-dotting). The mean of the dotting time was 23.9 sec (S.D.=19.3) and the mean of the dotting speed was 48.3 characters/min (S.D.=25.3).

The total communication time was the time until the sender finished dotting, after the sender pushed the speech recognition key (including the time of re-speech, editing, changing pages and re-dotting). The mean of the total communication time was 47.7 sec (S.D.=39.8) and the mean of the total communication speed was 23.1 characters/min (S.D.= 10.3).

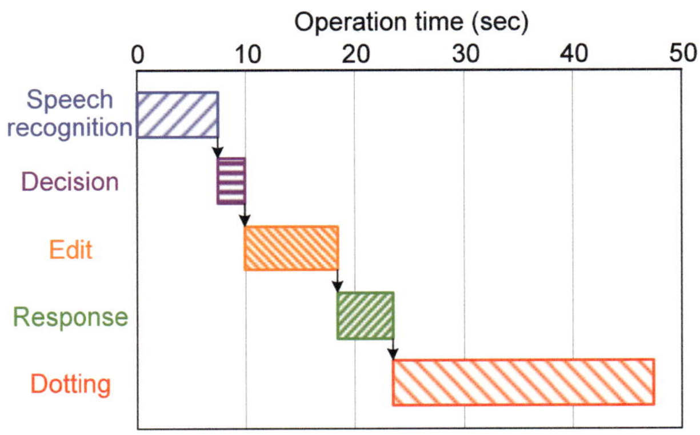

Fig. 14. Distribution of the operation times

4.3 Discussion

4.3.1 Accuracy of fundamental functions

As the accuracy of the fundamental functions, *Correct Ratio* was 94.4% except for substitution of the interjections. The accuracy of the conversion to Braille code was 99.6%. The accuracy of clause segmentation was 95.1%. It was confirmed that these results corresponded to those in our previous study (Matsuda et al., 2007), and the fundamental functions were practicable. As for editing the Braille code, the senders were puzzled the first time, but they could edit smoothly the second time.

4.3.2 Accuracy of dotting and dotting speed

In this experiment, the error ratio of dotting by the senders was only 1.2% of the characters, and the mean of the dotting speed was 48.3 characters/min (S.D.=25.3).

As previously mentioned, Amemiya et al. (2004) developed a Braille input device. In an evaluation experiment, five non-disabled people who had no experience using a Braille typewriter were given a sheet of paper with a list of Braille codes and instructed to input the codes as quickly and accurately as possible. As a result of this test, the error ratio was 8-6.76% (sessions 1-5) and the input speed was 20-35.4 characters/min (sessions 1-5).

Thus, for non-disabled people, dotting Finger Braille using the teaching system was more accurate and quicker than inputting the Braille code using a sheet of paper with the list of Braille codes.

As mentioned above, An et al. (2004) carried out an experiment in which ten visually impaired people who had just started to learn Braille codes inputted Braille code using a Braille typewriter. As a result, the error ratio was 2.8±2.3% and the input speed was 135.9±37.0 characters/min.

For the visually impaired people, dotting Finger Braille using the teaching system was more accurate than inputting Braille code using the Braille keyboard. The dotting speed by the non-disabled senders in our experiment was one-third of the input speed by the visually impaired subjects.

The non-disabled senders who were unskilled in Finger Braille could communicate with the blind receiver in Finger Braille directly, but the total communication speed was limited to 23.1 characters/min. Therefore, it was considered that the teaching system was effective.

4.3.3 Rule of communication with deafblind people

In this experiment, we found that both senders could not understand and execute the rule of communication with deafblind people. The senders were directed to keep touching the fingers of the receiver with at least their right hand. But the senders removed both hands at the beginning of the experiment, because they were preoccupied with the operation of the teaching system, especially when they were editing. Then, the receiver felt uncomfortable in the absence of touching or tactile cues.

Therefore, the non-disabled sender must constantly touch the fingers of the deafblind receiver even when not dotting and must decide the cues to edit or re-dot (e.g., back-slapping).

5. Future plans

5.1 Improvement of interfaces

The present teaching system consists of the tablet PC, microphone and trackball. To improve the input interface for operating the teaching system, we adopted a touch panel on the LCD. To expand the teaching interface, we adopted a WXGA display. Fig. 15 shows the expanded teaching interfaces that were developed on another tablet PC (Dell Latitude XT, CPU Core 2 Duo 1.33 GHz, RAM 2 GB, 12.1 inch WXGA LCD with touch panel). The Braille code is displayed in the upper text box. The dot pattern is displayed in sixteen picture boxes (two columns and eight rows). The buttons of speech recognition, edit, restatement, previous page and next page are located on the lower part. The sender can touch the LCD directly to operate the teaching system and edit the Braille code. The teaching interface is expanded and the number of pages to display the Braille code of one sentence can be reduced. We have been evaluating the improved teaching system.

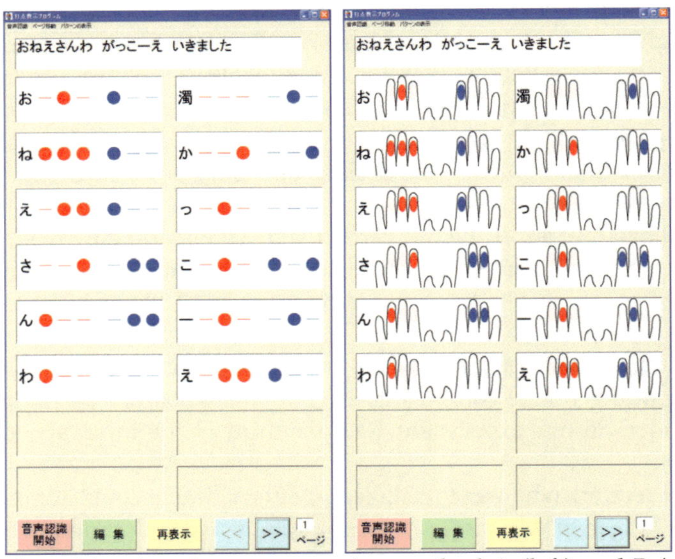

Fig. 15. Expanded teaching interface, presentation method A (left) and B (right). Displayed dot pattern is "Oneesanwa / gakko-e {My sister / to school.}"

5.2 Teaching of prosody and emotional expression

For the prosody of Finger Braille, the sender dots long at the end of clauses and sentences, and dots short at double consonants and voiced sound. To realize the non-disabled sender's prosodic dotting, the dot pattern of clauses was displayed explicitly in the present teaching system. We designed the dot pattern with long and short arrows to indicate the duration of dotting (see Fig. 16) (Matsuda et al., 2009).

In Finger Braille, the sender can express various emotions by changing the duration and strength of dotting (Fukushima, 1997; Matsuda et al., 2010b). The intent of our support device is to assist not only verbal communication but also nonverbal (emotional) communication. To assist in emotional communication, we have been developing an emotion teaching system and an emotion recognition system (Matsuda et al., 2010c).

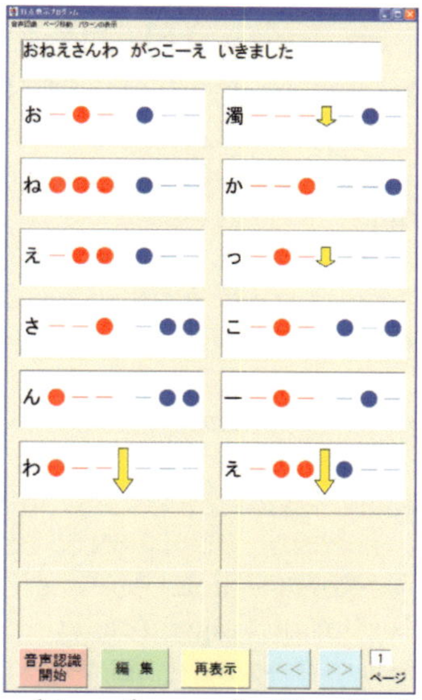

Fig. 16. Teaching interface for teaching of prosody. The displayed dot pattern is "Oneesanwa / gakko-e {My sister / to school.}"

6. Conclusion

In this chapter, we developed the Finger Braille teaching system and designed a teaching interface that teaches clauses explicitly. An evaluation experiment between a blind receiver who was skilled in Finger Braille and two non-disabled senders who were unskilled in Finger Braille was conducted. For the accuracy of fundamental functions, *Correct Ratio* was 94.4%, except for the substitution of interjections. The accuracy of the conversion to Braille code was 99.6%. The accuracy of clause segmentation was 95.1%. The error ratio of dotting by the senders was only 1.2% of all of the characters. The dotting speed was 48.3 characters/min and the total communication speed was 23.1 characters/min. The results show that the fundamental functions are practicable; the non-disabled senders could dot Finger Braille accurately and communicate with the blind receiver directly. Therefore, it was considered that the teaching system was effective.

7. Acknowledgment

We greatly thank Ms. Satoko Mishina and Mr. Shinichi Hashima (interpreters of Finger Braille) for their support.
This study was supported by the Japan Society for the Promotion of Science under a Grant-in-Aid for Scientific Research (No. 21500522) and the Ministry of Education, Culture, Sports, Science and Technology of Japan under a Grant-in-Aid for Scientific Research (No. 16700430). This study was partly supported by Kanagawa Academy of Science and Technology (KAST) under a research grant.

8. References

Amemiaya, T.; Hirota, K. & Hirose, M. (2004). OBOE: Oboe-Like Braille Interface for Outdoor Environment, *Proceedings of 9th International Conference on Computers Helping People with Special Needs*, pp. 498-505, ISBN 978-3-540-22334-4, Paris, France, July 2004, Springer, Berlin

An, S.S.; Jeon, J.W.; Lee, S.; Choi, H. & Choi, H.G. (2004). A Pair of Wireless Braille-Based Chording Gloves, *Proceedings of 9th International Conference on Computers Helping People with Special Needs*, pp. 490-497, ISBN 978-3-540-22334-4, Paris, France, July 2004, Springer, Berlin

Fukushima S. (1997). *Person with Deafblind and Normalization*, Akashi Shoten, ISBN 4-7503-0982-6, Tokyo, Japan

National Association of Information Service for Visually Impaired persons (2002). *Handbook of translation into Braille*, Daikatsuji, ISBN 4-86055-013-7, Tokyo, Japan

Matsuda, Y.; Sakuma, I.; Jimbo, Y.; Kobayashi, E.; Arafune T. & Isomura, T. (2005). Study on Teaching of the Way to Dot of Finger Braille - Teaching of dotting finger and position of monosyllable –, *Transaction of Human Interface Society*, Vol. 7, No. 3, pp. 379-390, ISSN 1344-7262

Matsuda, Y.; Sakuma, I.; Jimbo, Y.; Kobayashi, E.; Arafune T. & Isomura, T. (2007). Development of Finger Braille Teaching System - Teaching of dotting finger and position using speech recognition –, *Journal of the Society of Life Support Technology*, Vol. 19, No. 3, pp. 105-116, ISSN 1341-9455

Matsuda, Y. & Isomura, T. (2009). Finger Braille teaching system - teaching of prosody of finger Braille, *Journal of Communication and Computer*, Vol. 6, No. 2, pp. 55-64, ISSN1548-7709

Matsuda, Y.; Sakuma, I.; Jimbo, Y.; Kobayashi, E.; Arafune T. & Isomura, T. (2010a). Development of Finger Braille Recognition System, *Journal of Biomechanical Science and Engineering*, Vol. 5, No. 1, pp. 54-65, ISSN 1880-9863

Matsuda, Y.; Sakuma, I.; Jimbo, Y.; Kobayashi, E.; Arafune T. & Isomura, T. (2010b). Emotional Communication in Finger Braille, *Advances in Human-Computer Interaction*, Vol. 2010, Article ID 830759, 23 pages, ISSN 1687-5893

Matsuda, Y.; Sakuma, I.; Jimbo, Y.; Kobayashi, E.; Arafune T. & Isomura, T. (2010c). Emotion Recognition of Finger Braille, *International Journal of Innovative Computing, Information and Control*, Vol. 6, No. 3(B), pp. 1363-1377, ISSN 1349-4198

Matsumoto, Y.; Tanaka, H.; Hirakawa, H.; Miyoshi, H. & Yasukawa, H. (1983). BUP: A Bottom-Up Parser Embedded in Prolog, *New Generation Computing*, Vol. 1, No. 2, pp. 145-158, ISSN 0288-3635

Miyagi, M.; Miyazawa, K.; Ueno, A.; Nishida, M.; Horiguchi, Y.; Ichikawa, A. & Noshiro, M. (2007). Analysis of Prosody in Strength and Time Structure of Finger Braille, *IEICE Technical Report (WIT2007-1~15)*, Vol. 107, No. 61, pp. 25-28, ISSN 0913-5685

The Association for Overseas Technical Scholarship (1975). *Nihongo no Kiso I (Grammatical Note)*, 3A Corporation, ISBN 4-906224-13, Tokyo, Japan

3A Corporation (1998). *Minna no Nihongo I Honsatsu (Main Textbook)*, 3A Corporation, ISBN 4-88319-102-8, Tokyo, Japan